KARL ADAM

to Aunt Beatrice

with love,

Bob

Christmas 1992

Karl Adam:
Catholicism in German Culture

Robert Anthony Krieg, C.S.C.

University of Notre Dame Press

Notre Dame   London

Library of Congress Cataloging-in-Publication Data

Krieg, Robert Anthony, 1946–
    Karl Adam : Catholicism in German culture /
    Robert Anthony Krieg.
        p.   cm.
    Includes bibliographical references and index.
    ISBN 0-268-01230-X
    1. Adam, Karl, 1876–1966.   I. Title.
BX4705.A254K75   1992
230′.2′092—dc20   91-51116
                                              CIP

Contents

Foreword

For younger theologians today, Karl Adam is hardly more than a name. But undeservedly. This learned dogmatic theologian, who taught as a member of the Catholic theological faculty of the University of Tübingen from 1919 until 1946, was during his lifetime one of the most celebrated Catholic theologians, whose books were worldwide best-sellers and whose lectures have remained unforgettable to his hearers. He can be viewed as one of the pioneering theologians of the twentieth century. Karl Adam decisively influenced a whole generation of theologians and faithful Christians through his christology and his renewed vision of the church as the mystical body of Christ, and he made an essential contribution towards the awakening of the church in human hearts. He is one of the great forerunners of the Second Vatican Council and of the postconciliar renewal of the church.

In his learned book, Robert Krieg seeks to display the innovative power and meaning of the theology of Karl Adam. Drawing upon his thoughtful research, the author leads us through the main works of Adam, always considering their historical context. He does this in order to make clear a synthesis which is both richly dialectical and fruitful, a synthesis in which Adam knew how to mediate Scripture, tradition, scientific inquiry and the contemporary life of the church. Robert Krieg shows us too that Adam's theology is not a theology for every age, but is a theology for its time. That theology must say something different today does not diminish Karl Adam's significance. For it is precisely in this way that he teaches us to formulate a theology for our age.

I am delighted that—after Hans Kreidler had presented the first monograph on Karl Adam's theology in 1988—the name of this significant theologian will find further recognition also in the English-speaking world through Robert Krieg's outstanding study.

Bishop Dr. Walter Kasper
Diocese of Rottenburg-Stuttgart

Preface

I am grateful to many people for their help with this book and wish to name some of them.

Bishop Walter Kasper of the Diocese of Rottenburg-Stuttgart took time a few years ago to discuss the theology of Karl Adam, amid his then extensive academic responsibilities at the University of Tübingen. Auxiliary Bishop Hans Kreidler also of the Diocese of Rottenburg-Stuttgart and Josef Meyer zu Schlochtern at the University of Paderborn generously met with me on numerous occasions. Eugen Fesseler, director of the library at Tübingen's Wilhelmsstift, kindly located books and articles. Travel expenses were defrayed by grants from the Eastern Province of the Holy Cross Congregation and also from the Jesse Jones' Faculty Research Fund of the University of Notre Dame.

At the University of Notre Dame, Richard McBrien, as chairman of the Department of Theology, strongly encouraged rigorous inquiry in Catholic theology. Thomas O'Meara offered sound advice at key junctures of my research and writing. Leslie Griffin and Anne Volk gave insightful critiques of drafts of the entire text. Other colleagues in the College of Arts and Letters, who are mentioned in the appropriate chapters, made helpful suggestions on parts of the manuscript. Roger Skurski, associate dean of the College, provided invaluable computer assistance. The staffs of the College's secretarial pool and the Office of Interlibrary Loan at the Hesburgh Memorial Library went out of their way to help me.

My duties as the director of the Master of Divinity program in the Department of Theology were lightened by the hard work of my associates: Carole Coffin, secretary for the Master of Divinity program, Regina Coll, director of Field Education, John Melloh, director of the Marten Program in Homiletics and Liturgics, Mark

Poorman, at the time the associate director of Field Education (now M. Div. director), and Thomas Zurcher, the religious superior of Moreau Seminary.

James Langford, director of the University of Notre Dame Press, expressed a warm interest in this project at its various stages. David Schultenover at Creighton University provided a thorough critical reading of an earlier version of this text. The staff of the Notre Dame Press—especially its senior editor Ann Rice— extended fine assistance in preparing the text for publication.

While doing research, I often thought of my wonderful maternal grandparents, who were contemporaries of Karl Adam. I dedicate this book to them, Marie and Frank Battista.

1

The Making of a
Theologian (1876-1919)

In 1959 good news reached the university town of Tübingen, in southwest Germany. Church leaders were nominating Karl Adam to assist in the Second Vatican Council by serving on the Preparatory Commission on Seminaries and Universities. When family and friends brought this message to the eighty-three-year-old theologian, they were not sure that he grasped what they were saying. He was hard of hearing and losing his concentration. As a result, Adam may not have fully appreciated the honor of being proposed as an advisor for Vatican II. He may not have realized that ecclesiastical authorities were finally acknowledging his theological contributions to the renewal of Catholicism.[1]

Throughout his life Karl Adam (1876-1966) met with great success in his teaching and writing. He drew to his classes students, professors, and auditors from all parts of Germany and even from other countries. His lectures on ecclesiology in 1923 attracted more people than could fit into Tübingen's largest auditorium.[2] In 1934, at the height of his career, he gave his lectures in christology at 8 each evening to approximately 800 people. Since no single hall could hold this gathering, the overflow had to sit in rooms where his lecture was broadcast. In 1948, when he spoke on ecumenism at Protestant churches, people would arrive two hours early in order to find a seat.[3] Adam was successful, too, with his eighteen books and approximately sixty articles. He won international acclaim for *The Spirit of Catholicism* (1924), *Christ Our Brother* (1930), and *The Son of God* (1933). Each of these texts was available in at least eight languages and became a best-seller not only in Germany but also in Europe and North America. They were

1

translated into Japanese, and *The Spirit of Catholicism* appeared in Chinese.[4] Prior to the Second Vatican Council, Adam was one of the most widely read Catholic theologians in the world.[5]

Why then did institutional recognition of Adam's role in the Catholic *aggiornamento* occur so late in his life? There are at least two reasons. First, Adam pursued the renewal of theology long before it was acceptable to Rome. Writing in the shadow of Pope Pius X's condemnation of "modernism," he was required by the Vatican to revise each of his major texts. It was only after Pope John XXIII permitted fresh air to enter the Catholic edifice that church officials could acknowledge the value of Adam's work. Second, Adam held a strong German nationalism. In 1933, after Germany's bishops had lifted their ban against Catholics joining the National Socialist German Workers' party (Nazis), Adam gave a theological rationale for their decision. Six months later he publicly criticized the Nazis and, as a result, was harassed by Storm Troopers for his "betrayal." Nevertheless, because of his efforts to build a bridge to Adolf Hitler's movement, he disappointed many of his readers. As a result, after the Second World War Adam received only modest recognition for his theological work in the 1920s and 30s.[6]

Karl Adam was a pioneer in contemporary Catholic theology. He helped to clear the way for today's thought by means of what he said and also how he said it. In the first half of our century he presented ideas that were rare at the time: The church is primarily a community and only secondarily a juridical institution. Catholicism affirms the true values of every society and adapts to the forms of each culture into which it enters. And Jesus Christ is not only one with God, he is also a member of the human family. If these thoughts sound familiar to us today, it is because they were promoted by Adam sixty years ago and since then, have been refined by Karl Rahner, Edward Schillebeeckx, Hans Küng, Walter Kasper, and many others.

Karl Adam broke new ground, too, for Catholic theology because of the way in which he elucidated the wisdom of the Bible and Christian tradition. As Walter Kasper has observed, Adam did theology "for his time."[7] He undertook what we now speak of as a "local theology."[8] In the theological manuals of the early 1900s terms like "divine nature," "human nature," and "hypostatic union" functioned within the framework of neoscholastic thought.

By contrast, in his writings Adam used such words as "life," "community," and "heroism," and drew on the "*Lebensphilosophie*," the "philosophy of life," of such writers as Friedrich Nietzsche, Rainer Maria Rilke, and Max Scheler. Consequently, Adam's articles and books offered a "*Lebenstheologie*," a "theology of life," which engaged readers familiar with Western culture. In short, Adam anticipated the efforts of today's theologians to bring about a fruitful conversation between Christian faith and the world's cultures.

One of the lessons that emerge from our review and analysis of Adam's life and writings is that theologians must be attentive to their culture. That is, on the one hand, they must understand their society's ideas and values, and, on the other hand, they must maintain a critical distance on these. Adam possessed a good sense of his society's *Lebensphilosophie*, but he needed to be more aware of this mentality's irrational tendencies. A second lesson is that when ecclesiastical officials perceive inadequacies in a theologian's work, they must express their views in ways that can be heard. Rome's Holy Office had valid concerns about the ambiguities in Adam's writings. However, it communicated them in a manner that prohibited a genuine exchange of ideas with the Tübingen theologian. If the Vatican had followed a process that was not secretive and juridical but dialogical and scholarly, it might have helped the theologian to see where his theology needed improvement.

The four periods of Adam's life shape the design of this book. Adam's youth and seminary years (1876-1902) and his residence in Munich (1902-1918) constitute the first and second phases of his life. They are recalled in this first chapter.[9] Adam wrote his three major works during his thirty years as a professor in Tübingen (1919-1949).[10] *The Spirit of Catholicism* is treated in chapter 2, *Christ Our Brother* in chapter 3, and *The Son of God* in chapter 4. This third period included the rise of National Socialism. Therefore, the theologian's interaction with Nazism is described in chapter 5. Adam's years of retirement (1950-1966), the fourth phase of his life, provided an opportunity for friends and colleagues to acknowledge the professor's theological contributions. These assessments, along with Adam's impact on American Catholicism, are reviewed in chapter 6. Finally, chapter 7 takes stock of the strengths and shortcomings of Adam's theology of life.

This first chapter depicts the young Karl Adam as a moderate reformer of Catholic theology in the first two decades of the twentieth century.[11] In his patristic research Adam sought to reconcile the permanence of the church's doctrines with the historicity of these teachings. He did not, however, pursue this reconciliation in the categories of either the liberal Protestants or the conservative Catholics. Rather, he adopted a theological direction advocated by "Reform Catholicism" and pursued by the Catholic Tübingen School. Before reviewing this theological orientation, we must recollect its historical context.

1. TOWARD NEW FORMS OF UNITY

Karl Borromeo Adam was born into the family of Clemens and Babette Adam on October 22, 1876.[12] Along with his ten sisters, he grew up in the village of Pursruck, in Bavaria's Upper Palatinate, where his father taught school. Pursruck was not much different a century ago than it is now: A dozen homes and farm buildings are clustered around St. Ulrich's Church, high on a knoll which overlooks a stream, rolling fields, and thick stands of firs. As a teenager, Adam resided at the Gymnasium in the neighboring town of Amberg, situated on the Vils River. In 1895 he entered the seminary in Regensburg, a city founded by the Romans on the Danube. He was ordained a priest for the Diocese of Regensburg on June 10, 1900. After two years of parish work, he enrolled in theology at the University of Munich. At the age of twenty-six, the young man who had grown up playing near a rural mountain stream found himself in an international city along the Isar River.

At the turn of the century, Munich flourished as one of Europe's leading cultural centers, fulfilling the dream of King Ludwig I (d. 1868).[13] Henrik Ibsen took up residence here on and off throughout the late 1800s. Frank Wedekind, the actor and dramatist who prepared the way for the Theater of the Absurd, moved to Bavaria's capital in 1884 and stayed until his death in 1918. Richard Strauss held the senior appointment as the court conductor from 1894 through 1898. Rainer Marie Rilke resided in the city from 1895 until 1897, and then again from 1914 until 1915, during which time he wrote the "Fourth Duino Elegy." In Munich, Nikolai Lenin produced his seminal pamphlet *What Is to Be Done?* in 1902 and discussed ideas on international revolution with Rosa Luxemburg. In 1904 Leon Trotsky spent many months in Munich and later described it as "the most democratic and artistic city in Germany."[14] Here, too, the poet Stefan George crafted his *Gedenkbuch* (1906) and *Der Siebente Ring* (1907), and Paul Klee, Vasili Kandinsky, and Franz Marc founded their school of abstract painting, the *Blauer Reiter*, in 1911. Bruno Walter was Munich's general director of music from 1914 until 1922. The Catholic novelist and poet Gertrude von le Fort moved to Munich in 1922 and remained until 1939. Thomas Mann, who resided in Munich from 1900 until the early 1930s, caught the city's allure in the early 1900s when he wrote:

> Munich shimmered. Above the festive squares and white pillared temples, the antique monuments and baroque churches, the playing fountains, the palaces and gardens extended a glowing sky of blue silk; its broad and light, leafy and well-designed perspectives lay in the heat haze of the first beautiful June day. Birdsong and secret jubilation sounded in all the streets. On squares and in lanes the unhurried and amusing life of the handsome and easeful city rolled on, hummed and buzzed. . . . Art flourished, art was in power, art stretched its rose-garlanded scepter across the town and smiled. . . . Munich shimmered.[15]

While studying in Munich, Karl Adam had the opportunity to experience his society's dominant political, cultural, and religious forces—forces pushing toward new forms of unity in German life and thought. These currents included the emergence of German nationalism, the rebirth of German romanticism, and the élan of Roman Catholicism, and they are evident respectively in the lives of Otto von Bismarck and Kaiser Wilhelm II, Friedrich Nietzsche and Stefan George, and Pope Pius IX and Pope Leo XIII. Since these three forces left their mark on Adam's mature thought, they must be briefly reviewed.

Over a period of fifty years Otto von Bismarck (1815-1898) and then Kaiser Wilhelm II (1859-1941) forged the German people into a single nation.[16] The three hundred or so German states that existed in 1789 had been consolidated into thirty-eight polities by the end of the Congress of Vienna in 1815. Then, these states merged into the German Empire, as Prussia's premier, Bismarck, provoked the Danish War (1864), the Seven Weeks' War against Austria (1866), and the Franco-German War (1870-1871). As soon as King Wilhelm I of Prussia was enthroned as the emperor of Germany at Versailles, Bismarck directed his efforts to strengthening the country's industrial base. From 1870 to 1875 the railroad doubled in size and monies poured into the building of ships and factories. In 1873 Bismarck pressed for greater social control by instituting the "May Laws" against the Catholic church, thereby initiating the Kulturkampf, and in 1878 he enacted the "Exceptional Laws" against socialism.

Ascending to the throne in 1888, Kaiser Wilhelm II ushered in Germany's industrial revolution. From 1890 to 1914 the nation's exports tripled, and its population jumped from 40 million in 1871 to 65 million by 1910. In 1871 36 percent of the people resided in urban areas, but by 1910 60 percent of all Germans lived in cities and towns. By 1914 Germany was the world's second largest manufacturing country. Given his nation's need for materials and markets beyond its borders, Wilhelm extended his control into the African continent and Pacific islands. This imperialism led, however, to the Great War, Germany's defeat, and Wilhelm's abdication of the throne in November 1918.

Concurrent with the rise of German nationalism was the renaissance of German romanticism.[17] In the late 1700s romantic thought sprang up in Germany in response to the Enlightenment's rationalism, with its sharp and unyielding dichotomies between the knower and the known, intellect and feelings, the individual person and the group, and faith and reason. Hence, romanticism consisted of the attempt "to identify subject and object, to reconcile man and nature, consciousness and unconsciousness by poetry which is 'the first and last of all knowledge.'"[18] This definition by René Wellek is similar to the one given in *The Magic Mountain* by Thomas Mann: "The Romantic movement in Europe had been above all a movement of liberation, directed against French classicism, the old school of reason, whose defenders it derided as 'powdered wigs.'"[19] Representative of this movement were J. W. Goethe, J. G. Herder, F. H. Jacobi, and Friedrich Schlegel, each of whom emphasized the primacy of feelings, intuition, and experience in human life.[20]

Romanticism was eclipsed in the 1800s by neo-Kantianism and positivism, but it appeared again at the end of the nineteenth century. This neoromanticism grew from a general yearning for a fresh sense of the interconnectedness of all reality. European culture had become weary of detached analyses of life and the exclusion of human affect and intuition from the recognized sources of human knowledge. In Germany romantic stirrings generated a form of existentialist thought called the *Lebensphilosophie*, whose center point was a vague, inclusive notion of life. This outlook held that there is more to reality than can be known by empirical studies and stated in conceptual terms. The "philosophy of life" depended on the logic of the emotions as well as the logic of the intellect. It encompassed, therefore, a "metaphysics of the pre-rational, the rational, [and] the anti-rational."[21] And, it gained expression in the writings of such diverse thinkers as Henri Bergson, Wilhelm Dilthey, Rudolf Eucken, Stefan George, Ludwig Klages, Friedrich Nietzsche, Rainer Marie Rilke, Max Scheler, and Otto Spengler. The *Lebensphilosophie* can be glimpsed in the works of Nietzsche and George.

Nietzsche (1844–1900) had his greatest impact on German thought after his death, in the first decades of the twentieth century, when many Germans were also drawn to the operas of Richard Wagner.[22] Influenced in part by Arthur Schopenhauer's philosophy of the will to power, Nietzsche disdained Christianity and modernity for their leveling down of the human personality. In his view the church and bourgeois society foster a herd mentality, for they reward people for being submissive and conforming to external norms. In contrast, he held that authentic personal existence springs from self-determination, which frees human beings to realize their abilities and vision. Nietzsche portrayed the fully individuated person, the *Übermensch*, in the figure of Zarathustra, who in daring to push to the limits of human life discovered that God does not exist. This revelation yielded good news: "Behold, I teach you the superman. The superman is the meaning of the earth. Let your will say: The superman *shall be* the meaning of the earth!"[23] Therefore, "Stay loyal to the earth."[24] Nietzsche's message is a romantic one: Live not according to others' rules and expectations but according to your inner lights; choose the values by which you want to live and die; determine your own destiny.

Stefan George (1868–1933) represented another mode of the *Lebensphilosophie*.[25] A Catholic by birth and a medieval scholar by education, he criticized democracy and the individualism of the liberal worldview.[26] In his *Star of the Covenant* (1914) he described Nietzsche as the last prophet, the one who warned against society's reduction of human stature.[27] In his judgment, if people want to live according to their highest ideals—for example, ideals of truth and beauty—they must accept an oligarchy headed by a charismatic leader. (George wanted nothing to do with Adolf Hitler however.) Also, modern men and women must reject industrialization and return to nature. By means of poetry they must make new contact with their emotions, instincts, and intuition, for neglect of the affective dynamism in human life results in self-destruction. In George's *Kingdom Come* (1928) the faun tells the hunter:

> The worst, you do not know, is that your mind
> Which can do much, in the clouds may be enmeshed,
> May rend apart the bond with clod and creature.[28]

Nationalism and neoromanticism were strong forces in German society throughout the first decades of Karl Adam's life. So too for Catholics was the church's influence. In 1890 the population in Wilhelm II's Reich numbered just short of 50 million.[29] Two-thirds belonged to the Protestant churches, while approximately one-third were Catholics. And, one percent (567,884) were Jews. All of these groups felt the forces of nationalism and neoromanticism, but Catholics also experienced the Vatican's efforts to ensure ecclesiastical unity.

Pope Pius IX (1846–1878) regarded the Enlightenment and romanticism as threats to Catholicism and, therefore, took definite steps to defend the church's teachings and the authority of the Petrine office.[30] In the course of his long pontificate he increasingly promoted neoscholasticism in the Roman universities of religious orders. In 1863 he issued his encyclical *Quanta cura* with its *Syllabus errorum*, condemning "liberal" ideas. In December 1869 Pius convoked the Vatican Council, which passed two constitutions before abruptly suspending deliberations in October 1870 when the Italian army marched into Rome upon the withdrawal of the French troops. Of the two constitutions, *Dei Filius* maintained that faith and reason are compatible, and *Pastor Aeternus* asserted the doctrine of papal infallibility. When Bismarck cited *Pastor Aeternus* as one reason for his Kulturkampf, Pius issued his encyclical *Quod nunquam* (1875), declaring that Germany's May Laws were invalid and, therefore, not to be obeyed. As a result of the conflict between Pius and Bismarck, German Catholics felt torn between their duty as Catholics to Rome and their loyalty as Germans to Berlin.

Pope Leo XIII (1878-1903) was also intent on upholding the integrity of the church's doctrine and authority, yet he took a more subtle approach to modernity.[31] In 1879 he wrote *Aeterni Patris*, calling for the renewal of Christian learning by a retrieval of the teachings of Thomas Aquinas. By the mid-1880s Leo quietly resolved the conflict between the Vatican and the German government. In *Immortale Dei* (1885) he acknowledged the validity of a secular, democratic form of government. In *Rerum novarum* (1891) he denounced the destructive forces within capitalism and socialism, and urged governments to recognize workers' rights. With these two encyclicals the papacy formally accepted the political and social changes in Europe brought about by the Enlightenment and the French Revolution. Leo took another significant step toward bringing the church into dialogue with the modern age when in 1902 he established the Pontifical Biblical Commission, charged with evaluating the methods and results of higher criticism. The net effect of these policies was that Leo strengthened Catholics' sense both of their identity and their possible points of contact with their society.[32]

Each of the three movements which we have reviewed represented a drive toward some kind of unity. German nationalism stressed the solidarity of all states within a single polity. Neoromanticism, with its *Lebensphilosophie*, held an "organic" view of reality in which all parts were seen within a whole. Roman Catholicism strove for the union of all of its members in a fellowship transcending national boundaries. Amid these distinct and at times contending forces, Karl Adam reached maturity and tried to craft a fresh theological synthesis in the spirit of Reform Catholicism and the Catholic Tübingen School.

2.1 ON HISTORY AND DOCTRINE

As a doctoral student in Munich, Adam was confronted by the question of the integrity of Christian belief. In this, he faced forms of the same issue that had prompted John Henry Newman to write his *Essay on the Development of Doctrine* (1845) and Ignaz Döllinger to publish *Christentum und Kirche* (1860). How can the church's teachings be reconciled with historical consciousness?

How can continuity and permanence in doctrine be squared with change and contingency? Even if he had wanted to, the young theologian could not avoid these questions at a university where the faculty specialized in historical studies and where Ignaz Döllinger (1799-1890), Jacob Frohschammer (1821-1893), and later Joseph Schnitzer (1859-1939) were condemned by the Vatican for their attempts to unite the church's teachings and the results of modern historiography.[33] For his part, Adam set out to reconcile history and doctrine in a way that differed, on the one hand, from liberal Protestantism and, on the other, from conservative Catholicism.

One option for resolving the issue of history and doctrine was the historicism of the liberal Protestants.[34] This positivist approach, which refused to recognize any events that could not be confirmed according to the norms and methods of historical research, was prevalent in German universities as Adam embarked on his doctoral studies. From 1886 through 1890 Adolf von Harnack (1851-1930) published the first edition of his multi-volume *History of Dogma*, with its thesis that an analysis of the church's teachings within their historical settings reveals the doctrinal accretions which overlay the basic Christian message. To be sure, said the Berlin professor, there is a supernatural core in the church's proclamation, but this "essence" has been covered over by layers of doctrinal formulations. In 1900 Harnack focused his thesis further in his book *Das Wesen des Christentums* (The essence of Christianity), which in English was entitled *What Is Christianity?* According to Harnack, when historical-critical methods are applied to the gospels, they disclose Jesus' primary teaching, namely, concerning "the Fatherhood of God."[35] Jesus proclaimed an insight into the reality of God that constitutes *das Wesen* of Christianity.

Ernst Troeltsch (1865-1923) went one step beyond Harnack, for he took issue with Harnack's talk about Christianity's supernatural basis. According to Troeltsch, when the historical approach is consistently applied to the testimony of Jesus' followers and the church, it demonstrates that Christianity is simply one religion among many others. Troeltsch argued for this relativizing of Christian faith in such writings as "Historical and Dogmatic Method in Theology" (1898), *The Absoluteness of Christianity* (1902), and *Der Historismas und Seine Probleme* (1922). According to Troeltsch if we want to treat events, people, and ideas within their historical context, we must adhere to three canons of historiography. First, the principle of criticism recognizes that all historical judgments are open to revision, since new evidence can be found. Second, the principle of analogy insists that a report is credible only if it recounts an event comparable to an occurrence in the everyday world as we experience it. Third, the principle of correlation holds that each event must be capable of being linked with other occurrences, so that historical continuity is assured.[36] With these norms, Troeltsch questioned the possibility of doing dogmatic theology and laid the foundation for the unfolding of the study of the history of religions.

Neither Harnack's historicism nor Troeltsch's were convincing to Adam, who explained in his later writings that these scholars forced all of reality into the mold of modern historiography's presuppositions. In a book review of the sixth edition of *History of Dogma* Adam declared that in Harnack's work "the criterion by which all data are comprehended is not the living, streaming, historically tangible life of the church and its own dynamics, but an a priori, historically unprovable idea of the Christ of Christianity."[37] Adam pressed his point when in *The Son of God* he observed that Harnack's representation of Jesus in *What Is Christianity?* is a "pure fiction, a literary phantom."[38] Indeed, Harnack is guilty of "Jesus-ism," of trying to anchor Christian faith not in the living Christ, but in a historical depiction of Jesus. In regard to Troeltsch's work, Adam refused to allow the principles of criticism, analogy, and correlation to govern theology, for they rest upon "a tacit denial, antecedent to and prejudging all serious investigation of the supernatural character of our Lord's appearance."[39] In sum, in Adam's judgment Harnack and Troeltsch had resolved the tension between history and doctrine by forfeiting the church's claim regarding the permanence of its teachings.

A second option for resolving the apparent conflict between history and doctrine was provided by neoscholasticism.[40] In the mid–1800s Catholic theologians revived the scholastic thought of the Middle Ages as an alternative to the Enlightenment's turn to the knowing subject. By drawing on the writings of Thomas Aquinas, Cajetan, Suarez, and John of St. Thomas, these scholars intended to uphold an objective understanding of God. In an attempt to appreciate the continuity of the church's teachings, they did not locate texts within their historical context and in relation to their authors' intentions, but interpreted texts in relation to the entire constellation of the teachings of Scripture, tradition, and the church. Representatives of this rebirth of scholasticism included the Jesuit theologians Matteo Liberatore (1810-92), Joseph Kleutgen (1811-83), and Johannes Baptist Franzelin (1816-86). Their efforts were strengthened by the ecclesiastical policies of Pius IX and Leo XIII, especially the latter's encyclical *Aeterni Patris* (1879).

The neoscholastic theologians wrote their theology in the form of Latin manuals in which the truths of the Catholic faith were laid out in a stark, conceptual manner. The authors of these texts adhered to the scholastic mode of intellectual inquiry. That is, they explained their key notions according to Aristotle's metaphysics, and they posited propositions, based on ahistorical appeals to Scripture, patristic writings, medieval theologies, and papal and conciliar teachings. They employed these propositional assertions according to the deductive logic of syllogisms, as treated by Aristotle. Among the Latin manuals that were widely used in Germany were those of Christian Pesch (1853-1925) and Hermann Dieckmann (1880-1928), both of whom taught at the Jesuit house of studies in Valkenburg, Holland.[41] Pesch's primary works were *Praelectiones dogmaticae* (9 volumes: 1894-97) and its condensed version *Compendium theologiae dogmaticae* (4 volumes: 1913-14). Dieckmann's most widely read manuals were *De ecclesia* (1925) and *De revelatione christiana* (1930).

In Adam's judgment, the neoscholastic way of attaining a theological unity of history and doctrine was inadequate for the modern age. In a review of a new edition of Pesch's *De Deo uno secundum naturam, de Deo trino secundum personas* (1925), one of the tracts in *Praelectiones dogmaticae*, Adam commended the work for its clarity and breadth of sources, which include Scripture, the Fathers, medieval theologies, and such post-Tridentine authors as Robert Bellarmine. Nevertheless, he criticized the neoscholastic method for its disregard of the historical diversity of theology's sources and its reduction of the witness of Scripture and tradition to a "common denominator."

> It can be asked whether with this [method] all biblical and extra-biblical testimony runs together and yields, so to say, a common denominator, . . . and whether the purely logical-static manner of observation does not weaken an appreciation for the mysterious

energies of the truths of revelation and for [revelation's] continuing development in the consciousness of the church. This weakening occurs above all where the testimonies of the tradition are not treated in relation to their historical associations.[42]

Adam voiced his criticism of the neoscholastic method and its results in his book *Christ and the Western Mind* (1928). He pointed out that neoscholasticism failed to reach the synthesis which it was meant to achieve. In fact, it had fueled a hostility between religious thought and the sciences. Ironically, in its effort to be rational it appeared irrational, divorced from reason, as understood by the modern mind. "Theology, enticed by the Aristotelian conception of science, had ventured," said Adam, "too far on the thin ice of abstract speculation and had lost all contact with actual life." If neoscholastic thought were to be truly renewed, it would have to summon forth a "second St. Thomas" who would be capable of understanding "the new scientific picture of the world."[43]

Since Karl Adam could not accept either liberal Protestants' historicism or conservative Catholics' neoscholasticism, he chose a third option that in his judgment respected both the historicity of the church's doctrines and their abiding truth. But this approach itself entailed the risk of ecclesiastical censure, for anyone bringing historical consciousness to theology in the early 1900s was liable to be accused by the Vatican of "modernism."[44] Yves Congar has defined this tendency of thought as follows: "Modernism claimed the right to treat the documentarily supported content of the Christian religion purely as a matter of history and to draw from a critical study of it conclusions that should be valid at the level of rational knowledge, in complete independence of the dogmatic statements of the magisterium."[45] This attitude, manifested in liberal Protestant theologians, was, as we have seen, rejected by Adam. He wanted to produce a theology that incorporated the best values of both modern historiography and neoscholasticism. As Adam pursued this course, he became associated with Germany's Reform Catholicism.

2.2 REFORM CATHOLICISM

Pius X (1903-14) assumed a more confrontational stance toward modernity than his predecessor Leo XIII had taken.[46] In an effort to steer the church away from contemporary philosophy and historiography, Pius issued in 1907 the decree *Lamentabili sane exitu* and the encyclical *Pascendi Dominici gregis*. Then, in 1910, he enforced these documents through a *motu proprio*, *Sacrorum antistitum*, with its "Oath against Modernism." In these writings, the pope condemned modernism and, in particular, "immanentism," that is, the tendency to conceive of God's being and activity solely within the limits of time and space, thereby disavowing God's transcendence. He insisted that ecclesiastical censure be imposed on Catholic scholars whose writings were judged to be tainted with these views. As a result, France's Alfred Loisy (1857–1940) and England's George Tyrrell (1861–1909) were excommunicated. Pius was also concerned, however, about Germany's theological trends, and, therefore, the Vatican persistently pressured scholars, whom it linked with Reform Catholicism, into modifying their views or resigning their academic appointments.

"Reform Catholicism" refers not to a single, organized movement but to a range of efforts to bring German Catholicism beyond the "ghetto mentality" that resulted from the Kulturkampf and into the mainstream of Germany's cultural and intellectual life.[47] The term *"Reformkatholizismus"* was introduced in 1898 by Joseph Müller, a priest and editor of the journal *Renaissance*, whose proposals for ecclesial change were condemned by the Vatican in 1901.[48] It was in the spirit of Reform Catholicism that in 1903 Karl Muth founded the famous Catholic journal *Hochland*, dedicated to theology, literature, art, and culture.[49] In the early 1900s the label "Reform Catholicism" was applied to scholarly efforts in Germany to incorporate contemporary ideas and historical methods into a Catholic understanding of the Christian belief. Three theologians whose writings were linked with Reform Catholicism were Franz Xaver Kraus (1840–1901), Hermann Schell (1850–1906), and Albert Ehrhard (1862–1940). Only the latter must be discussed here.

Albert Ehrhard, a patrologist, taught at the universities of Strasbourg, Würzburg, Vienna, Freiburg, and Bonn.[50] Of his many works, the one which directly expressed the vision associated with Reform Catholicism is entitled *Der Katholizismus und das zwanzigste Jahrhundert im Licht der kirchlichen Entwicklung der Neuzeit* (Catholicism and the twentieth century in light of the ecclesial development in modern times) (1902). According to Ehrhard, while the ideas and structures of the Middle Ages

have shaped much of Catholicism, they are not essential to the
church's life and mission. New ways of thinking and organizing
the church could be introduced into the Catholic church without
any loss of truth. Catholic scholars need to show, said the patrologist, that "there is no absolute contradiction between Catholicism
and the modern world." In fact, Catholicism and contemporary
society hold much in common, as seen in their respective efforts
to strengthen people's participation in community. But these over-
lapping concerns were being overlooked, and, therefore, tension
existed where it need not. In Ehrhard's judgment, "the actually
existing, intense opposition between the Catholic church and the
modern world. . . is not essential and absolute." Indeed, this an-
tagonism could be overcome, if the church and modern society
were to pursue the goal of mutual understanding and cooperation.

> This goal entails on the one hand the reconciliation of the modern
> world with Catholicism through [the church's] recognition of [the
> world's] divine character and substance and also of its pervasive reli-
> gious power. On the other hand, this goal requires the regeneration
> of the modern spirit itself by means of genuine, living Christianity.
> The missionary efforts of the Catholic church could effect this
> regeneration and result in the rescuing of modern society.[51]

In 1908, in response to *Pascendi*, Ehrhard spelled out one implication of his vision of Catholicism and culture. In his article "Die
neue Lage der katholischen Theologie" (The new situation of Catholic theology), he observed that the new encyclical would have
negative consequences for German Catholics, especially scholars.
Whereas Pius opposed contemporary thought and presented the
church as a critic of society, German Catholics had tried to contribute to their nation's thought, especially in the wake of the
Kulturkampf. The pope's encyclical *Pascendi* jeopardized the involvement of Catholic professors at German universities, because
it discredited the ideas and methods adopted by twentieth-century
scholarship and denigrated those Catholics who appropriated the
valid elements of the Enlightenment. In Ehrhard's judgment the
Oath against Modernism would have dire results for Catholic intellectuals: "If the practical norms of the encyclical were to be
imposed in Germany, then the life blood of theological research
would be cut off. . . ."[52]

Ehrhard's ideas about Catholicism and modernity in general and *Pascendi* in particular created tension between Ehrhard and the German bishops. Bishop Paul Keppler (1852-1926) of the Diocese of Rottenburg-Stuttgart had originally given his *imprimatur* to *Der Katholizismus und das zwanzigste Jahrhundert*, but he and Ehrhard eventually became embroiled in a controversy regarding the book.[53] Even after this specific conflict was resolved, Ehrhard was held suspect in Rome because of his views. In 1920, when Ehrhard was called to a chair at the University of Bonn, his appointment was nearly blocked by the Vatican.

Ehrhard's history is representative of those theologians who were associated with Reform Catholicism. The writings of Kraus, Schell, and others were closely examined by the Vatican during Pius X's papacy, and some were placed on Rome's Index of Forbidden Books. In the eyes of the Holy Office, scholarly efforts to bring together the ideas of the day and church doctrine were steps toward modernism. It was not until the pontificates of Benedict XV and Pius XI that Catholics could engage in a measure of theological renewal without being immediately accused of heterodoxy.

2.3 KARL ADAM AND REFORM CATHOLICISM

As a young scholar, Karl Adam was intent upon updating Catholic theology. He wanted to use modern historical methods in order to shed light on Christianity's abiding truths. That he should have been so definite about this aim as he began doctoral studies is not surprising, for he spent his youth amid a wealth of historical and archaeological research. In the 1700s Regensburg had begun to unearth and preserve its Roman ruins, and by the mid-1800s officials were charting the city's Roman walls, towers, and burial sites.[54] When Adam entered Regensburg's seminary in 1895, a museum had already been established and a book written on the city's archaeology. During his years in residence, excavations began on a Roman mill and buildings at the Alte Kornmarkt, and the digging of a canal revealed layers of the city's past. In his classes Adam studied the church's teachings, and on his walks he observed archaeological findings. When he completed his seminary studies, he was well aware of the question of continuity and change in ecclesiastical doctrine. As a graduate student, he pursued this issue in Munich, and, as a result, became connected with Reform Catholicism.

Adam's two graduate theses manifested his scholarly interest in history and doctrine.[55] Both books were in patristics, the arena in which ground-breaking Catholic theologians labored in the early 1900s. His doctoral dissertation *Der Kirchenbegriff Tertullians* (Tertullian's idea of the church), completed in 1904, treated Tertullian's understanding of church.[56] His *Habilitationsschrift*, published in 1908, explicated Augustine's teaching on the Eucharist. This book *Die Eucharistielehre des heiligen Augustin* (St. Augustine's teaching on the eucharist) was done under the direction of three internationally known scholars: Leonhard Atzberger (1854–1918), professor of dogmatics and apologetics, Otto Bardenhewer (1851–1935), professor of early church history, and Albert Ehrhard.

Adam employed historical-critical methods in *Die Eucharistielehre des heiligen Augustin*. He set Augustine's views within their historical context, in particular, in association with the writings of Tertullian, Cyprian, and other pertinent Greek and Latin Fathers. Also, he discussed Augustine's specific statements on the Eucharist in relation to the bishop of Hippo's entire body of thought, especially his ecclesiology. As Adam explained in the book's introduction, he deliberately adopted a historical approach to his study of Augustine.

> What results from the literary setting and background, when beneficial to the inquiry, is utilized as much as possible. So, too, special attention is given to the attitude to eucharistic problems in the whole of Augustine's notion of the church, especially in his teaching on the relation of things to persons. For the author [Adam] this was the way to attain secure results. Indeed the discipline of the history of dogma, when it is successful, has to provide intellectually fruitful associations.[57]

In his book on the Eucharist Adam staked out a position between historicism and neoscholasticism. On the one hand, he located Augustine's views on the Eucharist in their historical and literary context, and even cited the research of Adolf von Harnack, without adopting his thesis regarding the "Hellenization" of the kerygma. On the other hand, Adam highlighted the permanent value of Augustine's thought without assuming the ahistorical perspective of neoscholastic commentators. According to Adam, the early church's eucharistic teachings attained a new level of understanding in Augustine's work. In holding this interpretation of Augustine's thought, Adam conveyed an evolutionary view of doctrine: The changes in patristic thought on the Eucharist that culminated in Augustine's teaching express the church's deepening insight into the mystery of the Lord's Supper.

Die Eucharistielehre des heiligen Augustin revealed Adam's intent of shedding light on the wisdom of the Christian tradition with the help of contemporary ideas and methods. This scholarly orientation, which linked Adam with Reform Catholicism, became even more evident when Adam's essay opposing the implementation of the Oath against Modernism appeared in a German Catholic newspaper. Prompted by Pius X's *motu proprio* of 1910 requiring that all Catholic theologians profess the oath, Adam reiterated the point that Albert Ehrhard had made in 1908, as we have already seen, in response to *Pascendi*. In the article "Der Antimodernisteneid und die theologischen Fakultäten" (The Oath against modernism and the theological faculties) Adam observed that the intent of the *motu proprio* was sound: "It wants the historical theologian to uphold the ancient Catholic truth that sacred Scripture and tradition do not merely possess a purely profane character, but that they are to be valued as authorities of revelation and to be handled with proper respect."[58] However, he also pointed out that this pledge would have a negative impact upon the professional standing of Catholic teachers in Germany. It would be used against them by colleagues who would charge that Catholics lack academic freedom. As a result, the oath would function as "the official death notice regarding all Catholic scholarship." "The complete elimination of the [Catholic] theological faculty from the organism of the universities is then only a question of time." He concluded that theologians in Germany should be dispensed from the Oath against Modernism. Also, since many people remained unsure about Pius's intent in requiring the oath, the Vatican should explain his action: "A misunderstanding of the oath [should] . . . be forcefully met through an authoritative clarification by Rome."

Shortly after this article's appearance Adam learned that the Vatican was investigating his writings.[59] At the time, he held a faculty position at the Wilhelmsgymnasium and also served as an instructor at the University of Munich, teaching a course entitled "The Doctrine of Salvation and the Church."[60] As the Holy Office's inquiry progressed in secrecy, he feared that his budding theological career would soon be ended.

In 1908 Adam had seen Rome's condemnation fall upon his teacher Joseph Schnitzer. Schnitzer, professor of the history of doctrine, applied historical-critical methods to ecclesiastical documents and interpreted some of his results to mean that one had to question the permanence of some ecclesiastical teachings. He publicly disagreed with Pius X's condemnation of modernism, and, as a result, was forced to take a leave of absence from the university.[61] Eventually, Schnitzer resigned from the faculty of theology, earned a doctorate in philosophy, and received a chair in the university's faculty of philosophy.

In light of Schnitzer's situation, Adam anticipated the worst for himself. He weighed his options if the Vatican judged him unfit to teach. One was to join the Old Catholics, as had Ignaz Döllinger and Johann Friedrich (1836–1917). A second option was that he abandon his nascent career in theology and embark at the age of thirty-four upon a career in medicine. Neither option appealed to Adam. Fortunately, he was spared choosing between them when help arrived from an unexpected source.

In 1908 Karl Adam had been hired to tutor the sons of Crown Prince Rupprecht (1869–1955) of the Bavarian royal family, the Wittelsbachs. Through this teaching he earned the respect of Rupprecht.[62] When the crown prince heard that the Holy Office had initiated canonical proceedings against his sons' instructor, he made his esteem for Adam known to Cardinal Franciscus von Bettinger, archbishop of Munich, and Cardinal Franz Andreas Frühwirth, the Vatican's nuncio to Bavaria, and through them to officials in Rome. During this same period, Adam received an invitation to teach at Munich's prestigious academy for the Bavarian Cadet Corps. He accepted this position in 1912 and for the next five years taught Bavaria's future military officers.

Adam eventually learned that the Vatican had suspended the inquiry against him. Then there was even more good news: Rome had decided that Catholic theologians in Germany would be excused from professing the Oath against Modernism. It appeared that the controversial articles by Ehrhard, Adam, and others had paid off.

Adam's commitment to theological renewal was not only
evident in his doctoral thesis on Tertullian, his second thesis on
Augustine, and his article on the Oath against Modernism. It was
also expressed in his abiding, professional tie to Albert Ehrhard.
At the time that Ehrhard served as a reader of Adam's *Habilitationsschrift*, he held a chair in theology at the University of
Strasbourg. In 1917 Adam accepted a call to join that university's
faculty of theology, and he was welcomed there by Ehrhard. The
two scholars taught together for one year, and then, along with all
German professors, they were required to resign from the university. According to the armistice of 1918 all German citizens were
dismissed from the employment of the government in Alsace and
Lorraine. At this point the older priest agreed to an appointment
at the University of Bonn and the younger joined the faculty at the
seminary in Regensburg.

The colleagueship between the two scholars continued. In his
first major book, *The Spirit of Catholicism*, Adam made numerous
references to Ehrhard's *Der Katholizismus und das zwanzigste
Jahrhundert*. Then, in 1925, the University of Bonn invited Adam
to join its faculty of theology—an appointment which would have
brought Adam and Ehrhard together again. Adam declined the offer, however, for during the intervening six years he had accepted
a call to the University of Tübingen and had taken root there. In any
case, the two theologians had become close academic associates,
dedicated to the renewal of theology and thus connected with
Reform Catholicism.[63]

3. KARL ADAM AND THE CATHOLIC TÜBINGEN SCHOOL

At end of the Great War there appeared in Germany many
books concerning the transitory character of human existence
and its relation to the transcendence of God. Rudolf Otto in *The
Holy* (1917) analyzed humankind's way of relating in "fascination
and dread" to God, who is experienced as wholly other. Karl
Barth declared in his *Epistle to the Romans* (1918) that a gap,
indeed an opposition, exists between God and the world. Only
the act of faith can overcome this fissure. Romano Guardini in
The Spirit of the Liturgy (1918) described worship as communal
celebration in the mystery of God's presence. Awareness of the
flux of history prompted Otto Spengler to argue in *The Decline of*

the West (1918-22) that the Western world had begun its period of decay within the life cycle of a civilization. As this roster of books shows, amid the war's devastation reflective minds were intent upon making sense of the ups and downs of human affairs and, in many cases, locating an abiding point of reference outside of history.

In this milieu Karl Adam made a move that determined the rest of his life. Expelled from Strasbourg on December 10, 1918, he returned to Regensburg and taught at the seminary where he himself had studied for the priesthood. During the spring of 1919 he was invited by the University of Tübingen to fill the theological chair that had belonged to Paul Schanz (1841-1905) and then to Wilhelm Koch (1874-1955). Adam accepted this invitation.

Koch had withdrawn prematurely from the faculty in 1918.[64] He had begun teaching at the university and also at the diocesan seminary in Rottenburg an der Neckar in 1905. He was well received by his students, one of whom was Romano Guardini.[65] However, he made a less positive impression upon the seminary's rector, Dr. B. Rieg, who complained to Bishop Keppler regarding the professor's liberal views. Koch sought to clarify and qualify his teaching, and Keppler, a former theology teacher at the University of Freiburg im Breisgau, tried to mediate between the rector and the professor. But in 1913 a formal list of Koch's errors was drawn up by the rector, and in 1916 Koch took a leave of absence from the university. For the next two years, he served as a military chaplain on Germany's western front in France. When Koch returned to Tübingen, he found that he had not been assigned to teach any courses at the university. Choosing not to renew the conflict, he resigned from the faculty of theology and was made a pastor by Bishop Keppler. A few months later, the university issued its call to Karl Adam.

Moving to Tübingen at the age of forty-three, Adam turned his scholarly attention from historical study to systematic theology. During his fifteen years in Munich he had written books not only on Tertullian's ecclesiology and Augustine's eucharistic theology, but also on the forgiveness of sins in the early church.[66] But in accepting Tübingen's chair in dogmatics and apologetics, Adam shifted his academic focus from past documents to present issues. The titles of his courses for the 1919-1920 academic year display this focus: "The Doctrine of God and Creation," "The

Doctrine of the Sacraments and Eschatology," "Christology and Soteriology," and "Dogmatic Exercises."[67] Adam's turn to systematic theology was evident, too, in his publications, of which we will review three.

First, in his inaugural address "Glaube und Glaubenswissenschaft im Katholizismus" (Faith and the science of faith in Catholicism) (1919) Adam contended that the knowledge of faith, expressed in theology, originates in part out of the believing community's direct relationship with God. To be sure, it also relies upon the wisdom contained in Scripture, tradition, and the church's teachings. Nevertheless, theology is not solely dependent upon mediated insight. It springs, too, from faith's immediate awareness of God. According to Adam, this apprehension is communal. It comes not to an individual in isolation from other Christians, but arises within the believing community. Indeed, theology depends on the living church's experience and intuition of God. It develops out of the life of the Christian assembly and articulates the church's belief. In Adam's words:

> Not the "I," but the "we" is the bearer of the Spirit. . . . For the Catholic therefore the spiritually enlivened community, the church as the living unity of the faithful, is the mother of life and the "pillar and bulwark of truth" (cf. 1 Tm 3:15). Its faith and love, its living word is first; the letter in Scripture and tradition is next.[68]

This address was well received by Adam's colleagues in Tübingen, but it disturbed some Catholic theologians at other universities and seminaries.[69] In stressing the importance of experience and community for our knowledge of God, "Glaube und Glaubenswissenschaft im Katholizismus" bore a family resemblance to the longstanding theological orientation of the Catholic Tübingen School (which will be described below). Thus, it demonstrated that Adam, the newcomer, would undertake his systematic reflections according to the school's spirit and methods. However, after reading the lecture in Tübingen's journal, *Theologische Quartalschrift*, some Catholic scholars, including the respected Jesuit Erich Przywara, voiced concern about Adam's views. They were troubled by Adam's apparent de-emphasis of the role of Scripture and tradition, as mediated through the church, for our knowledge of God. They also mentioned the need for greater precision in Adam's use of such terms as "experience" and "knowledge." Adam responded to some of these criticisms in the second, revised edition of his book *Glaube und Glaubenswissenschaft im Katholizismus* (1923) and in articles on other theologians' books regarding human knowledge of God.[70]

A second publication representative of Adam's scholarly orientation was his essay on Protestant theology, "Die Theologie der Krisis" (The theology of crisis) (1926). A relatively ecumenical atmosphere had evolved at Tübingen since 1817, when the Catholic faculty of Ellwangen (northeast of Stuttgart) moved to the University of Tübingen (south of Stuttgart), where a Protestant theology faculty had existed since the Reformation. In 1926 Adam signaled that he valued Tübingen's ecumenism when he wrote on Protestant theology.

In "Die Theologie der Krisis" Adam expressed his empathy for some aspects of Karl Barth's "dialectical theology," as found in his *Epistle to the Romans*. He noted that whereas Martin Luther and John Calvin formed their theologies in opposition to Catholicism, Barth fashioned his thought in argument against liberal Protestantism. In Barth's judgment the turn to anthropology as theology's starting point—a turn which was initiated by Friedrich Schleiermacher (1768-1834)—resulted in Protestant theologians' neglect of divine revelation and the reduction of theology to "a phenomenology of religious consciousness." On this point, said Adam, Barth and Catholicism hold a crucial conviction in common, namely, that theology cannot begin at a subjective point. It must originate with that which is objective, God's revelation. Because the tendency toward subjectivism existed in both contemporary Protestantism and Catholicism, Barth's *Epistle to the Romans* and Pius X's *Pascendi* are comparable. According to Adam, each text had a salutary, chastening effect upon its readers.

> Just as this [encyclical] rescued Catholic theology from the ever increasing danger of immanentism and relativism and inscribed into its conscience the transcendence of revelation and the absoluteness and unchangeability of God's Word, so too it is Barth's pressing concern to lead [Protestant] theology back to its *theos* and its *logos* and to put to death a theology that is purely historical and psychological.[71]

Adam did not, however, end his analysis at this point. He went on to observe that Barth and Catholic theology differ in their views of the relationship between God and creation. From a Catholic vantage point, Barth went too far when he spoke of God uttering an unqualified "no" to all of creation. Catholic theology teaches that God's Word to humankind is not one of condemnation. Adam declared that Barth radically interpreted Luther's emphasis upon "faith alone" and Calvin's call to give "glory to God alone." Such an interpretation completely disassociates culture, ethics, and even religion from humankind's path to God. In contrast to Barth's dialectical view, Catholicism holds that God and creation bear an essential similarity, an "analogy of being." As a consequence, "a latent receptivity (*potentia obedientialis*) for God's visitation of grace belongs to humankind by nature—a receptivity which God's call alone can awaken and elevate to its goal and point of departure."[72] In Adam's judgment, Barth's statements about God and creation convey a "nihilism" and "cultural pessimism" that are alien to Catholicism. Thus, in the last analysis, "[T]he theology of crisis is not a theology of life [*Lebenstheologie*]."

A third text that manifested Adam's theology was the lecture "Die katholische Tübinger Schule" (The Catholic Tübingen School) that Adam gave to the faculty in 1927 on the occasion of the four hundred and fiftieth anniversary of the University of Tübingen.[73] In this address, he declared that the school is motivated by its commitment to renew Catholic theology, that is, "to examine and safeguard Catholic truth in the light of new problems and with the means which are made available through both a progressive histori-cal method and also rigorous thought, [which is] not afraid of flying to the [speculative] heights."[74] Each generation of the school's theologians provided its age with a fresh theological synthesis, that united historical research and contemporary philosophy.[75] The Catholic Tübingen School is defined, therefore, by

> the joining of a critically purified speculative thought, [which] inquires in the light of faith by means of a historical method [that] cleanly grasps what is given in Christianity and the church. The in-timate, *most intimate synthesis of speculative [theology] with his-torical theology* constitutes the *essence of the Tübingen School.*[76]

The theological synthesis that characterizes the Catholic Tü-bingen School is evident, said Adam, in the work of three of its early scholars: Johann Sebastian von Drey (1777–1853), Johann Adam Möhler (1796–1838), and Johann Evangelist Kuhn (1806–

1887). In his *Kurze Einleitung in das Studium der Theologie* (Short introduction into the study of theology) (1819) Drey insisted upon the theologian's reliance on the findings of historical research, and yet he simultaneously placed systematic, philosophical, and theological reflection at the high point of theological inquiry. Möhler demonstrated this kind of synthesis in his *Die Einheit in der Kirche* (Unity in the church) (1825), *Athanasius der Grosse und die Kirche seiner Zeit* (Athanasius the Great and the church of his time) (1827), and *Symbolik oder Darstellung der dogmatischen Gegensätze der Katholiken und Protestanten* (published in English, *Symbolism or Exposition of the Doctrinal Differences between Catholics and Protestants*) (1833).[77] By means of a "Platonic-Augustinian" approach to history, he discerned seminal ideas within the interactions of people and events. Kuhn took this "Platonic-Augustinian way of thinking" a step further in his lectures on dogmatic theology in which he applied Hegel's notion of dialectical movement to the development of church doctrine.[78] Kuhn, like Drey and Möhler, drew on the thought of the day, namely German Idealism, in order to reconcile the historical and speculative aspects of Christian faith.

Finally, the theological syntheses of Drey, Möhler, and Kuhn were more than academic endeavors, Adam asserted. They sprang from these theologians' participation in the church and were meant to enrich the Christian faith of women and men outside of the university. The same can be said, he insisted, of the work of the Catholic Tübingen School in general. Every generation of its theologians sought to integrate historical theology and speculative theology in such a way as to aid the church's worship and service. Time and again, the school's scholars crafted a *Lebenstheologie* addressed to contemporary believers.

> Their theology became a *theology of life*, not merely insofar as it, along with every Catholic theology, handed on the truths of life, but insofar as it sought to expose the flowing, inner life of these truths in their development as well as in their organic interaction with one another and in their unity in the highest, ultimate powers of revelation. For [Tübingen's theologians], Christianity is not a system of fixed formulas, maxims, and instruction; rather, it is a loose, streaming life, the mystical Christ who is realized in his church. . . .

For them, the church is not a sum of individuals, but an overarching community which creates faithful individuals.[79]

Since Tübingen's theology of life emerges out of the believing community, it possesses a quality not found in every theology, declared Adam. It radiates a spirit of piety. That is, it is more than a scholarly account of the object of Christian belief, and it is more than the articulation of "pure concepts and refined systems." The Catholic School at Tübingen communicates a reverence for God. When someone sets out to study a text by Drey, Möhler, Kuhn, or their successors, this reader "travels not through the stubbled field of abstract concepts, but on the Sea of Galilee where Jesus preached. And, one hears the fluttering wings of the Blessed Dove."[80]

This lecture and the other two that we have briefly reviewed revealed Adam's theological orientation in the early years of his tenure at the University of Tübingen. In "Glaube und Glaubenswissenschaft im Katholizismus" Adam affirmed that our knowledge of God depends in part upon the role of the living Christian community and its experience of God. He explained in "Die Theologie der Krisis" that theology must stay focused on its authentic object, God's revelation, and that it can do this without positing an opposition between God and creation. Finally, in "Die katholische Tübinger Schule" Adam claimed that the theology of the school is a *Lebenstheologie* that affords a synthesis of the historical and speculative elements of Christian belief. These themes are ones that would emerge time and again in Adam's writings for the remainder of his life.

Karl Adam stood at his life's midpoint when he began to teach at the University of Tübingen. During his forty-three years he witnessed the rise of the Wilhelmian Reich, the empire's fall in the Great War, the emergence of neoromanticism, and the shift in the Vatican's stance toward modernity when Leo XIII was succeeded by Pius X. Adam had matured into a priest-scholar, recognized for his scholarly writings on Tertullian and Augustine.

The events and accomplishments of the first half of Adam's life would eventually pale, however, in comparison to what was to take place in the second four and a half decades. Adam would live through the tumultuous years of the Weimar Republic, Hitler's

Reich, and the Second World War, and into the Cold War. He would publish articles and books on the church and Jesus Christ that were acclaimed around the world and censured by the Vatican. He would lose his personal investment in the *Lebensphilosophie* when this optimistic worldview went bankrupt through the disclosures of Dachau and Auschwitz. He would watch the emergence of scholars like Henri de Lubac, Karl Rahner, and Pierre Teilhard de Chardin, their suffering under the strictures of Pius XII's encyclical *Humani Generis* (1950), and their rehabilitation with John XXIII's convoking of the Second Vatican Council.

Karl Adam pioneered the way to the theological developments upon which Vatican II was built. How he did this in ecclesiology, christology, and theological method will become evident as we consider each of these topics in turn. It will become clear too that, like all forerunners, Adam was surpassed by those who followed him. When church leaders proposed Adam as a candidate for a preparatory commission for the council in 1959, they did so as a gesture of respect and gratitude for a faith-filled theologian whose time had passed.

2

In Search of Catholic Identity (1920-1925)

In 1930 a German book made a deep impression upon a priest at the Vatican's Secretariat of State. The book, recently translated from German into Italian, was Karl Adam's *Das Wesen des Katholizismus*, entitled in English, *The Spirit of Catholicism*.[1] The young cleric was Giovanni Battista Montini (1897-1978), who in 1963 became Pope Paul VI. Montini marveled at this text's account of the church's nature and mission, and urged his friends and associates to study it. However, officials in the Holy Office had also read the book and questioned its orthodoxy. As a result, they soon had it withdrawn from bookstores. This censure did not lessen the future pontiff's respect for the work. As Peter Hebblethwaite has reported, Montini "snapped up all the banned copies and stored them in his flat. He gave copies to those he thought would understand the historical method Adam followed."[2] In 1934, when the Vatican approved of the revised text, Montini resumed openly distributing the book to his colleagues.

What was it about *The Spirit of Catholicism* that won Montini's respect? The book was remarkable both for its thesis and its language. It presented the church as primarily a community, the fellowship of believers united in the body of Christ. This ecclesiology stood in sharp contrast to the prevailing view of the church as an institution whose members are bound together by a set of divine and human rules. Moreover, the book expressed this insight in engaging, nontechnical terms. It relied on such words as "community," "relation," and "genuinely human," instead of the usual ones like "office," "obligations," and "powers." This short,

29

readable text offered a fresh view of the essence, "*das Wesen*," of Catholicism.

The Spirit of Catholicism made an invaluable contribution to Catholic theology in the twentieth century. On the one hand, it brought in ideas from the past. It incorporated the theology of Johann Adam Möhler and the phenomenology of Max Scheler (1874–1928), thereby pulling together lines of thought that ran from the early 1800s into the 1900s. On the other hand, the book pointed toward the future. It strengthened the theological currents leading to Pius XII's *Mystici Corporis* in 1943, Paul VI's *Ecclesiam Suam* in 1964, and Vatican II's *Lumen Gentium* in 1965. Therefore, to quote Hebblethwaite again, *The Spirit of Catholicism* "had a significance that seems to have escaped everyone at the time and many subsequently."

1. CONTEXT: WEIMAR'S TURN TO LIFE'S "ESSENCE"

After the First World War, German thought made a "change in direction."[3] Writing at the end of the 1920s, Erich Przywara observed that during the decade there had occurred a significant turn "from the subject to the object, from the individual to the community, from (pure and autonomous) thought to 'nature,' from culture to religion, from interiority to the church."[4] In the late 1800s and early 1900s German intellectuals were interested in the neo-Kantian focus on the self and the categories of knowing, but in the 1920s they wanted to apprehend objective reality, life's essence.

In the aftermath of the war, Germans looked for new forms in which to grasp reality.[5] The majority of people labored to establish and maintain a constitutional government, the Weimar Republic, while militants on the left pressed for socialism and those on the right demanded a monarchy or a dictatorship. A socialist government ruled in Bavaria during the late spring of 1919, and on November 8, 1923, Adolf Hitler led his "beer-hall putsch" in Munich. Further, this struggle for new forms extended beyond politics to people's conduct. Women ventured to pursue careers outside the home, and in the cities many Germans experimented with a looser morality.

Unaccustomed ways of relating to reality were also manifested in literature and the arts. In 1919 Walter Gropius founded the Bauhaus school of art and architecture with its wholistic view of human structures. Vasili Kandinsky and Paul Klee took unusual, even disorienting perspectives in their paintings of ordinary objects. Even time was conceived anew, as people learned of Albert Einstein's theory of relativity (1905).[6] Thomas Mann expressed this new sense of time in his novel *The Magic Mountain* (1924), in which Hans Castorp experiences a day at the Alpine sanatorium Berghof differently from a day down below in Hamburg. During these years, too, *Die neue Sachlichkeit* (the New Objectivity or Matter-of-Factness) emerged in the movement to expose injustice and hypocrisy in society and the arts.

German philosophy also changed. The neo-Kantianism of Hermann Cohen and Paul Natorp at the University of Marburg was eclipsed by efforts to unite thought and experience in the *Lebensphilosophie*, which has similarities with today's "existentialism."[7] As was noted in chapter 1, distinct forms of this philosophy of life were articulated by Henri Bergson, Wilhelm Dilthey, Rudolf Eucken, Stefan George, Ludwig Klages, Friedrich Nietzsche, and Rainer Maria Rilke. Further, phenomenology, nurtured by the *Lebensphilosophie*, arose as a method for illuminating "objective realities."[8] During the early 1900s, it flourished under the leadership of Edmund Husserl (1859–1938) and his associates, Oskar Becker, Moritz Geiger, Alexander Pfänder and Max Scheler, all of whom assisted Husserl in editing the journal *Jahrbuch für Philosophie und phänomenologische Forschung* (1913–1930). In general, these scholars were not satisfied with strictly scientific methods which, they claimed, reduce reality to what can be empirically ascertained. They aimed at grasping the essence of human activity and historical situations by means of a process of intuition. Husserl examined human knowledge itself in his book *Ideas: General Introduction to a Pure Phenomenology* (1913). Scheler inquired into human feelings, commitments, and values in his texts, *Ressentiment* (1912), *The Nature of Sympathy* (1913), and *Formalism in Ethics and Non-Formal Ethics of Values*, two volumes (1913–1916).

Phenomenology's focus on human conduct and Weimar's yearning to reach life's essence led to widespread recognition of the importance of community.[9] This interest in communal forms of life was reinforced by Ferdinand Tönnies's *Community and Society* (1897), which had much appeal in the 1920s. Germans deliberately found ways to strengthen their "organic," "national" ("*völkische*") bonds, as distinct from their "artificial," institutional ties.[10] For tens of thousands of young people this longing for fellowship was satisfied by youth groups, *Wandervögel* ("migratory birds"), in which they went camping, sang folk songs, and recited poetry. This quest for community pointed some Germans toward Catholicism.[11] Converts to Catholicism included Max Scheler and Edith Stein (1891-1942), Husserl's student who eventually joined the Carmelites and died at Auschwitz. After the Great War, Germans differed among themselves about politics, war reparations, and morals, but they agreed on the necessity of belonging to a community.

This turn to life's essence touched Protestant theology. Karl Barth's *Epistle to the Romans*, appearing in its second edition in 1922, had become the clarion call for a return to orthodoxy. It set the direction for neo-orthodox or dialectical theologians like Barth, Emil Brunner, Rudolf Bultmann, Friedrich Gogarten, Eduard Thurneysen, and Paul Tillich. It was taken seriously, too, by more moderate theologians like Karl Heim (1874-1967), a Protestant colleague of Karl Adam at Tübingen. According to the dialectical theologians, Protestant theology erred when, following Schleiermacher, it focused on the believing subject and religious experience to the exclusion of God's revelation. The renewal of Christian faith and theology required, they asserted, a radical turn to faith's 'object', the divine Word. The neo-orthodox theologians accentuated God's transcendence in an even more radical way than did Rudolf Otto with his phenomenological approach in *The Holy*.[12]

The Protestant theologian Friedrich Heiler (1892-1967), relying as Otto did on phenomenology, also emphasized the objective basis of Christian belief.[13] Raised a Catholic, Heiler studied at the University of Munich, where he was taught by Adam. After receiving his diploma, he won recognition in 1918 for his book, *Prayer: A Study in the History and Psychology of Religion*. In 1919 he left the Catholic church and made a profession of faith within the Swedish Lutheran church, headed by Bishop Nathan Söderblom (1866-1931). Then, Heiler focused his attention on Catholicism as a phenomenon within the history of religions and published his observations in two books, *Das Wesen des Katholizismus* (The essence of Catholicism) (1920) and *Katholizismus* (1923).

These works became the immediate impetus for Karl Adam's book on Catholicism.[14] They were followed by Heiler's statement of his ecumenical vision in *Evangelische Katholizität* (Evangelical Catholicity) (1926).

According to Heiler, Catholicism is characterized by its universalism, its inclusion of the positive aspects of other religions.[15] It unites diverse and even opposing religious elements so that it stands as a "world church."[16] That is, it exists as a believing community in which many diverse peoples can find beliefs, symbols, and rituals with which they can identify. In a word, Catholicism is marked by "religious syncretism." It holds together a wide range of disparate, even contrary religious ceremonies and practices.

However, Catholicism risks being a *complexio oppositorum*, a complex of opposing forces without a genuine center point.[17] Heiler argued that Catholicism has only a weak interior point of unity. It neglects Christianity's inner truth, namely the testimony of the New Testament, and depends instead on rules and rituals for its synthesis. It relies on ecclesiastical laws, hierarchical structure, and ultimately the papacy to bind its centrifugal forces. For this reason, Catholicism must be authoritarian. It remains a single church because Rome imposes an external uniformity on the people's diversity.[18]

In Heiler's judgment, Catholicism could learn a great deal from Protestantism, and Protestantism could benefit from Catholicism. The churches of Luther and Calvin have stayed faithful to Christianity's authentic center. In their worship and theology, they have acknowledged the centrality of God's Word, as proclaimed in the New Testament. Protestantism could teach Catholicism to be faithful to the kerygma, so that the Catholic church could recover its true unifying point and lessen its reliance on authoritarian governance. In turn, Catholicism could teach Protestantism to become more receptive to the customs and beliefs of other cultures. Protestantism's exclusivity could give way to Catholicism's universality. If the two Christian communities were to learn from each other, they could eventually join in a community of "Catholic universality and evangelical concentration."[19] Indeed, there could evolve a single Christian church, imbued with an "evangelical catholicity."[20]

In *Das Wesen des Katholizismus* and *Katholizismus* Heiler responded in part to Adolf von Harnack's *Das Wesen des Christentums* (1900), whose title translates into English as "the essence

of Christianity," though, as previously mentioned, it was published under the titled *What Is Christianity?*. Heiler did not agree
with Harnack's contention that the early church had lost sight
of the gospel as the good news became subsumed into Hellenis-
tic categories. In contrast, he saw that the patristic period in-
volved a valid syncretism in which Christian belief was made
available to the world of its day. Whereas Harnack, employing neo-
Kantian thought, stressed the subjective and individual elements
of Christian faith, Heiler, relying on phenomenology, emphasized
the community as the locus of Christian belief in Jesus Christ.
These differences between Harnack and Heiler are significant, for
they set the stage for Karl Adam's *Das Wesen des Katholizismus*.[21]
Before reviewing Adam's text, however, we need to consider one
emerging trend in German Catholic theology in the 1920s.

Catholic thought also reflected the German people's desire
for a new way of relating to reality after the Great War.[22] Peter
Wust, one of Scheler's Catholic students, spoke of philosophy's
"turn to the object" in his *Die Auferstehung der Metaphysik*
(1920).[23] Theology too underwent this shift, as authors anchored
their discussions of the Christian faith in a fresh appreciation for
the objective aspects of human experience. That is, they spoke the
importance of community and played down personal autonomy.
This emphasis is evident in such works as Peter Lippert's *Von
Seele zu Seele* (1924), Engelbert Krebs's two-volume *Dogma und
Leben* (1921–25), Karl Eschweiler's *Die zwei Wege der neueren
Theologie* (1926), and Anton Rademacher's *Religion und Leben*
(1929). Also representative of this direction is Romano Guardini's
The Church and the Catholic (1922), which is comprised of five
lectures, "The Awakening of the Church in Souls," "Church and
Personality," "The Way to Human Becoming," "The Way to Free-
dom," and "Community." A brief summary of Guardini's first lecture will give us a sense of the Catholic orientation in the 1920s.

"The Church is awakening in souls," declared Guardini. A
new sense of God and the Christian fellowship was stirring in
people's lives. Why? Because men and women had come to see
the limitations of their neo-Kantian viewpoint. They had previously
assumed that reality existed primarily within themselves. Consequently they had adopted a "subjectivism" and "individualism,"
and they had suffered from the effects of this "solipsism." The
natural sciences reinforced this mentality, since they conveyed the

view that humankind lived "in an intermediate sphere between being and nothingness, among concepts and mechanisms, among formulas and systems, which sought to control objects, but which were not even coherent."[24] Religious belief had been regarded as an individual's attitude that lacked an objective referent, and, therefore, faith's common life, rituals, and rules simply made no sense.

The neo-Kantian outlook collapsed, judged Guardini, after the Great War. In the face of the war's devastation, people acknowledged the external world as "the primal fact." In the 1920s "a great awakening to reality is in progress."[25] This recognition of the objectivity of the world brought with it an awareness of a spiritual datum within the human person. Men and women now accepted the existence of their souls, which they had once regarded as figments of fanciful thinking. They also regained their appreciation for the spiritual ties that bind all people into communities. Individualism yielded to the desire for human solidarity. The motto "Stand on one's own" was replaced by a new one: "We belong together; we are brothers and sisters!" Finally, this consciousness led to the deliberate affirmation of a single, national community, a people. "'The people' ['*das Volk*']," said Guardini, "is the primary association of those human beings who by race, country and historical antecedents share the same life and destiny."[26] Germans realized that their customs, laws, and ceremonies were not constraints upon their individual lives but social forms that expressed their abiding, common life.

According to Guardini, this new outlook on community permitted a fresh understanding of religion and the church. It had become evident that belief is more than one person's feelings and speculative ideas. Belief requires a community within a tradition. Indeed, Christian faith involves "discipleship, obedience, receiving and giving." Therefore, as presented in the Epistle to the Ephesians and the Epistle to the Colossians, the church is the "mystical body of Christ." It lives in Christ, with its attention directed toward the Father.

Finally, Guardini noted that the view of the church as community had brought about a new appreciation of liturgy. People had discovered the value of their parish and, in particular, their parish's worship. A local congregation can be united in its common prayer, when this prayer is genuine liturgy. A parish's worship

can manifest a primary reality, namely, the unity that already exists
within the community. "In its essence," declared Guardini, "liturgy
is not well-organized religion, but the religion of the people [*das
Volk*]."[27] In summary, Germans' shift from an emphasis on the
autonomous self to an awareness of the self-in-community had led
to "the awakening of the church in souls."

Guardini's lecture "The Awakening of the Church in Souls"
was a visionary statement, a "programmatic formulation" for theology in the 1920s.[28] It described what was taking place in German
society and the church, and located this yearning for community
in relation to a Christian sense of human life in union with Christ.
At the same time that Guardini was articulating this ecclesiology,
Karl Adam was conveying a similar vision in a more detailed sketch
of Catholicism.

2. TEXT: "THE SPIRIT OF CATHOLICISM"

What is Catholicism? What is its identity, its *Wesen*? Adolf
von Harnack saw Catholicism as the "Hellenization" of the early
Christian belief. Friedrich Heiler presented it as the complex of
opposites, held together by papal authority. Neoscholastic theologians like Christian Pesch and Hermann Dieckmann viewed it as
the timeless institution founded when Jesus Christ declared Peter
to be the rock upon whom he would build his church (Mt 16:18).
Yet, Karl Adam was not satisfied with any of these answers. In
the thirteen chapters of *The Spirit of Catholicism* he presented
Catholicism as "the body of Christ," the community united with
the risen Christ.

According to Adam, Catholicism embraces all that is truly
human. It is "an affirmation of all values wheresoever they may be,
in heaven or on earth."[29] While the Catholic church may appear
to Heiler to be an institution composed of diverse and at times
divergent rules, rituals, and attitudes, it is at heart the community
that acknowledges the one 'person', Jesus Christ, who unites and
directs human existence. To be sure, the church does not always
live up to its inner reality, as when it fails to take a positive attitude
toward the contemporary world. But the existence of a gap between the church's essence and its historical expressions does not
invalidate its true identity. Attempts to understand the complex
reality of Catholicism must respect its "organic" character. That is,

Catholicism is not static but dynamic. It is alive, and thus it assumes new forms without betraying earlier ones. It is not so much like a "deposit" of precious metal that must be guarded against change as it is like the "tiny acorn" that grows into the "great oak."[30]

All aspects of Catholicism are linked to its center like a wheel's spokes running into their hub. This center is not of our making, but of God's. In fact, the church's center is Jesus Christ, "the real self of the Church." The church is the body of Christ (Col 1:18; 2:19; Eph 4:15 ff.). The ancient image of the church as Christ's spouse (2 Cor 11:2) reminds us, too, that the heart and mind of Catholicism are bound to its lover, Christ. This relationship with Christ is manifest in the church's life, that is, in its dogmas, morals, and worship as well as in its governance and sacramental activity. Christ meets us in all of these forms. If at times the church is reserved and seemingly "aristocratic," this stance is due to the desire to be faithful to Christ alone. "Her conservatism and her traditionalism derive directly from her fundamentally Christocentric attitude."[31]

The church's communal life shows its bond with Christ. The Christian assembly is not a collection of discrete individuals, nor does it depend on a social contract among believers. Catholicism is an organic whole, a community in which individuals participate for their well-being. "So the Church possesses the Spirit of Christ, not as a many [*sic*] of single individuals, . . . but as a compact, ordered unity of the faithful, as a community that transcends the individual personalities and expresses itself in a sacred hierarchy."[32] United in Christ, this community is similar to the human body in which each part has a function and a value in relation to the entirety. The church is Christ's body (Eph 1:23). Extending this metaphor, we can perceive the pope as the body's visible head, representing the invisible head, Jesus Christ. Also, we can see each bishop, in communion with a local church, as a symbol of a diocese's unity in Christ.

This view of the church as an organic whole, as the body of Christ, puts a number of key ecclesiological issues in the right perspective. Since the church makes Christ visible in the world, it is the avenue through which people know Christ and, through Christ, God. Also, the church stands in continuity with Jesus, who proclaimed the coming of the "kingdom." This kingdom is being realized in the church, though the church "is not as yet the whole and full kingdom of God."[33] Moreover, the church needs one person to stand as the visible expression of the invisible Christ, and, as a result, Catholicism in the West recognizes the Petrine office.

The church's communal nature is disclosed in a unity that is not constrained by the limits of time and space. The "communion of saints" includes not only "the saints on earth" but also "all those souls who have passed out of the world in the love of Christ, and who either as blessed souls enjoy in glory the Vision of their God, or as souls in the state of purgation await that Vision."[34] This human solidarity in Christ gives a singular place to Mary, who "gave the best of herself, even her whole being, to the service of God. . . . " Further, this fellowship of holy women and men is not a passive one, but one alive with "the traffic of love." The saints in heaven care for those persons still on their way to the Beatific Vision, and the saints on earth pray for the deceased who in purgatory are being purified for full life in Christ. The charitable works of one person—whether on earth, in purgatory, or in heaven—benefit the full body of Christ. No one need be isolated or bear life's sorrows alone. Instead each of us can share in the fellowship founded on Christ: "Streams of invisible, mysterious life flow thence through the Catholic fellowship, forces of fertilizing, beneficent love, forces of renewal, of a youthfulness that is ever flowering anew."[35]

The Christian fellowship is an inclusive one. It reaches out to all peoples; it is catholic. How can this be? As Friedrich von Hügel and John Henry Newman have pointed out, Catholicism upholds all genuine values. It accepts all that is true, regardless of national, racial, and denominational boundaries. In Adam's words: "Such is Catholicism: an affirmation of values along the whole line, a most comprehensive and noblest accessibility to all good, a union of nature with grace, of art with religion, of knowledge with faith, 'so that God may be all in all.' "[36]

Since Catholicism is universal, it makes assertions about itself that logically follow from its inclusiveness. One such claim is that "the Church is necessary for salvation." Catholicism sees itself as "*the* Church of Humanity." To stand apart from Catholicism is to exclude oneself from human solidarity, from the fellowship in which every individual learns to live for others and for God. A second claim concerns the church's symbolic character. The

Catholic church deliberately undertakes "sacramental action" in the world. It strives to reveal God's grace and to lead all people to God, "to make them like God." Unlike Protestantism, Catholicism acknowledges both God's initiative in justifying and sanctifying people and also our responsibility for cooperating with God. A third claim is that Catholicism possesses "special divine authority" for the preaching and teaching of the truth to all peoples.[37] The church has a duty to bring the good news "to all nations" (Lk 24:27).

Catholicism has not always manifested its best self, its acceptance of the entire human community, united in Jesus Christ. If a person asks "How does actual Catholicism fulfill the divine idea?" one must honestly answer "that actual Catholicism lags considerably behind its idea, that it has never yet appeared in history as a complete and perfect thing, but always as a thing in process of development and laborious growth."[38] Such a disparity between the ideal and the actual is bound to occur for two reasons. First, our finite forms and thoughts are simply inadequate vessels for God's infinite revelation. And, second, Catholicism embodies an inherent conflict between freedom and authority, "between the claims of personality and those of the community." At times it is difficult to live with Catholicism's inability to express its essence unambiguously in historical forms. Nevertheless, Catholics persist in their faith, since they are convinced that God's reign will be fully realized in the Second Coming.

In sum, Catholicism is the universal community formed in union with Jesus Christ. It is the body of Christ. Contrary to Harnack's view, the church's historical change has not distorted Jesus' message but has allowed the church to assume new, more inclusive forms. Contrary to Heiler's understanding, the church's diversity is not held together solely by external authority, but is united in the risen Christ by the Holy Spirit. This unity is then sacramentally expressed in the papacy. Finally, Pesch and Dieckmann are correct in describing the church as an organization with rules and lines of authority, but they need to perceive the church as an institution in relation to the more primary reality of the church as a community. Catholicism is the assembly of all people in Christ.

3. THE THEOLOGICAL METHOD

Karl Adam was intent on recovering an ancient ecclesiology, namely, the church as the body of Christ, and presenting this view of church in terms intelligible to his contemporaries, theologians and nontheologians alike.[39] He undertook, therefore, a theology that was both dogmatic (i.e., investigating tenets of Christian belief within the horizon of faith) and apologetic (i.e., explaining these tenets in categories relevant to the times). Toward this goal of dogmatic-apologetic theology, he drew on three sources: Scripture and tradition, historical research, and neoromantic thought with its philosophy of life. Let us examine Adam's use of each source.

The dominant scriptural motif in *The Spirit of Catholicism* is "the body of Christ." Similar to Guardini in "The Awakening of the Church in Souls," Adam appealed to Romans 12, 1 Corinthians 12, Colossians 1, and Ephesians 1 and 4. He depended on verses like "so we, though many, are one body in Christ, and individually one of another" (Rom 12:5) to support his conviction that the risen Christ lives in actual union with the believing community. In Adam's words: "As the Head of the body, Christ makes the organism of the Church whole and complete."[40] The church is Christ's tangible expression in the world. Even the church's institutional aspects manifest Christ; they are part of the church's sacramentality. As a result, people meet Christ in the church, not in individual, private visions. "Christ the Lord, as the Head of His members, never works on the individual believer in dissociation from His body, but always in and through it."[41]

Tradition contributed to *The Spirit of Catholicism*, for the book relies on patristic, medieval, and baroque sources such as the writings of Origen, Augustine, Pseudo-Dionysius, Thomas Aquinas, and Juan Cardinal de Lugo. Also, the decrees of the councils of Florence, Lyons, Trent and the First Vatican Council are cited in reference to the nature of faith, our knowledge of God, revealed truth, the natural sciences, and church polity. Of these sources, Augustine's thought played a major role.[42] According to Adam, "teachers delight to repeat in ever new forms those expressions of Augustine wherein he celebrates the mystical oneness of Christ and the Church: the two are one, one body, one flesh, one and the same person, one Christ, the whole Christ."[43] Explicit references to Augustine's writings abound. For instance, Adam appealed to the bishop of Hippo's "Commentary on John's Gospel" when he declared: "None of the Fathers sets forth the mystical unity of Christ and the faithful so clearly and impressively as does Augustine."[44]

Historical research shaped the book in two ways. First, the historical method determined the handling of texts from Scripture and tradition. Biblical testimonies are not conflated, as though they were timeless documents. Instead, on the one hand, each biblical text retains its distinctiveness and, on the other hand, each is seen as contributing to the unfolding of "an idea," that is, to the maturing of Christians' insight into the church's nature and mission. Second, the book's last chapter consists of an honest historical account of ecclesiastical abuses. Adam acknowledges that "the faithful Catholic" is upset "by the medieval Inquisition and by the auto-da-fé" as well as by the Counter-Reformation's "witch trials and their numerous victims." He even names specific cases of abuse, for example, Pope Innocent VIII's bull *Summis desiderantes* (1484), condoning the persecution of witches. This chapter is not a whitewashing of the church's history. A faithful Catholic "cannot but grieve that zeal for objective values in religion and society should have sometimes weakened men's understanding of personal values, especially of the rights and dignity of conscience, albeit erroneous."[45]

Adam's emphasis in the book upon experience and interpersonal relationships discloses his reliance on the *Lebensphilosophie*. *The Spirit of Catholicism* possesses themes and phrases taken from the writings of Friedrich Nietzsche. It stresses life, human dignity, and heroism, as Nietzsche did, but it casts these in a new light. Christian belief, Adam insists, strengthens people to embrace life in all of its manifestations. "Wherever there is life, there you must have conflict and contrary [*sic*]."[46] Since Christians make their journey to God in "semi-darkness," this difficult journey "gives our life of faith its nobility of spirit and its moral character."[47] Nietzsche was only one of the book's modern dialogue partners. Others included Döllinger, Ehrhard, Goethe, Harnack, Heiler, von Hügel, Bishop Keppler, Cardinal Newman, Schopenhauer, Bishop Söderblom, Johannes Weiss, and Julius Wellhausen.

Among the modern thinkers who particularly influenced *The Spirit of Catholicism*, two stand out: Johann Adam Möhler and Max Scheler. In the early 1800s Möhler made a lasting contribution to ecclesiology.[48] In an effort to overcome rationalism's reduction of Christian faith to universal principles, he employed romantic notions of historical development and community, as found in the writings of J. G. Herder, Schleiermacher and J. A. Neander, and presented a fresh understanding of the church in two major works. In *Die Einheit in der Kirche* (1825) Möhler viewed the church as an organic whole whose inner spirit is expressed in its outer forms.[49] This spirit consists of the stirrings of life and love, which allow people to set aside their selfishness and to participate in a reality larger than themselves. The inner dynamism is made concrete in laws and rituals, external forms that are meaningful and valid only so long as they communicate this interior vitality.

In *Symbolism* (1832) Möhler reviewed the doctrinal disputes between Catholics and Protestants, and argued that what Protestants see as contraries (e.g., nature *or* grace), Catholics perceive as complementaries (e.g., nature *and* grace). Catholicism presupposes that differences are reconcilable, said Möhler, because it sets apparent opposites in relation to the community in which these opposites are reconciled in believers' lives. In turn, Catholicism regards the community as the concrete embodiment of Jesus Christ. "Thus, the visible church, from the point of view taken here, is the Son of God himself, everlastingly manifesting himself among men in a human form, perpetually renovated, and eternally young— the permanent incarnation of the same, as in Holy Writ, even the faithful are called 'the body of Christ.' "[50]

Karl Adam built *The Spirit of Catholicism* on the foundation laid by Möhler. At the outset of the book, he asserts that the church is "organically united" with Christ, and he supports this claim by referring to the *Symbolism* of "our own unforgettable Möhler."[51] He reiterates Möhler's insight that in Catholicism the faithful relate to Christ not primarily in private, as Protestantism holds, but within the believing community. Further, Adam appeals to *Die Einheit in der Kirche* to support his contention that Christian belief and therefore theology rely on the church's "living tradition," expressed in part in the Scriptures.[52] Along with these two explicit references to Möhler, there are others: A bishop is meant to be a visible expression of a diocese's unity, and the church's laws should reflect and support life, not stifle it.[53] The differences between Adam's ecclesiology and Möhler's occur not in content but in form. That is, while Möhler cast his understanding of the church within the German romanticism of the nineteenth century, Adam adopted the *Lebensphilosophie*, especially as found in Max Scheler's phenomenology.

As noted in chapter 1, Max Scheler was one of the most respected phenomenologists of the 1920s.[54] Of his many writings, two directly pertain to Adam's ecclesiology. In *Formalism in Ethics and Non-Formal Ethics of Values* Scheler maintained that persons are not merely objects, known by empirical methods, for there is more to personal existence than can be quantified. Nor are persons solely knowing subjects. Such an account is reductionistic, for in fact persons engage in "judging, loving, hating, willing."[55] According to Scheler, to be a person is to be "a relation," that is, to be one who interacts with other persons and lives within commitments to other women and men. The relational character of personal existence means that persons exist not only as individual persons but also as members of communities and hence as "collective persons."[56] That is, persons become complete or fulfilled as they contribute to families, neighborhoods, parishes, and other "organic" associations—personal realities greater than individual persons—that ask them to become virtuous through their acts of generosity, fidelity, and honesty.

In his essay "Soziologische Neuorientierung und die Aufgaben der deutschen Katholiken nach dem Krieg" (The new orientation in sociology and the duties of German Catholics after the war) (1915-1916) Scheler applied his views on personal existence to postwar Germany.[57] He contended that individualism, fostered by Protestantism and dominating much of German life, must be balanced by a sense of community that Catholicism can nourish. The German people needed to attain a vision of the common life as found in Möhler's *Symbolism*, said Scheler. As a concrete expression of this understanding, they should celebrate the feast of Corpus Christi with its "idea" of the body of Christ. Moreover, since German Catholics have strong international ties, they had the responsibility to tell other nations about the German people's positive qualities.[58] In Scheler's judgment, Catholicism could provide the resources for the regeneration of Germany's "*völkische*" community.

Scheler wrote *Formalism in Ethics* and "Soziologische Neuorientierung" during his "middle period" (1911-1921), after he had become a Catholic. They were read by both Protestants and

Catholics who found that Scheler had identified their longings and intuitions. The essay alone made such a profound impact on its Catholic readers that it immediately propelled the idea of the mystical body of Christ into the forefront of German Catholic thought.[59]

Karl Adam incorporated many of Scheler's views regarding modernity and community into *The Spirit of Catholicism*.[60] He felt that society was being eroded by individualism, by the belief that persons are discrete entities who contract to live together. As a result, Germany was comprised of "the autonomous man" who "has renounced the fellowship of the Church, the *communio fidelium*, the interrelation and correlation of the faithful." This autonomous man "has severed the . . . root of his life, that is to say, his fellowship with other men."[61] The church cannot accept this individualism, for it recognizes the solidarity of all people and seeks to realize this unity in the Christian life. The church is not a conglomerate of "many single individuals" but "a community that transcends the individual personalities." The body of Christ is an organic whole in which all persons participate "as one single man."[62]

In 1927, in his address to the faculty on the occasion of the University of Tübingen's 450th anniversary, Adam observed that the Catholic Tübingen School was characterized by its "intimate synthesis of speculative [theology] with historical theology."[63] In offering this insight, Adam was describing not only the works of Drey, Möhler, and Kuhn, but also his own book *The Spirit of Catholicism*, which had appeared three years previously. This text correlates Scripture and tradition, historical research, and the *Lebensphilosophie* and phenomenology. Therefore, it is the kind of synthesis that Adam attributed to the school. What Adam pinpointed as the aim of the Catholic School at Tübingen, he himself had already realized in his ecclesiology.

4. RECEPTION: AN INTERNATIONAL BEST-SELLER

The Spirit of Catholicism was published during a slight thaw in Rome's attitude toward modernity.[64] Benedict XV (1914-1922) had a broader vision of the church than his predecessor, for he wanted the church to interact in positive ways with society. He

labored to end the Great War by speaking on behalf of its victims and promoting negotiations among the warring nations. He
established the Pontifical Oriental Institute in order to teach the
West about the East and to strengthen communications between
Rome and the Eastern churches. And, in an effort to improve the
church's inner workings, he published the first Code of Canon
Law. Benedict's orientation was sustained by his successor, Pius XI
(1922–1939), who deliberately stood in the heritage of Leo XIII.
Pius, who had known Leo, was an accomplished paleographer.
He had taught dogmatic theology at Milan's seminary and served
as the prefect of the Ambrosian Library. As pope, he instituted
the feast of Christ the King in 1925, celebrating Christ's primacy
over all political and social powers. In 1931 he renewed the social
teachings of Leo XIII's *Rerum novarum* (1891) with his encyclical
Quadragesimo anno. Further, he set a reconciliatory tone with
Catholic scholars, some of whom he knew from his earlier scholarly activities, and tried to move the church beyond the modernist
controversy.

It was within this more open milieu that theologians and
the Vatican's Holy Office assessed *The Spirit of Catholicism*. Erich
Przywara immediately gave the book high praise, observing that "it
is the greatness of this monograph about the church that it avoids
all one-sidedness."[65] This balance is evident, said Przywara, in four
ways. First, regarding our knowledge of God, the book values both
the church's immediate intuition of God and the mediation of
Scripture and tradition. In Przywara's judgment, this presentation
of human knowledge of God is, therefore, more well-rounded
than the one presented in Adam's essay "Glaube und Glaubenswissenschaft im Katholizismus." Second, the book unites charismatic
and hierarchical views of the church. Third, it describes Catholicism in its ideal form and also in its actual expressions in history.
It manages to be frank while also conveying the author's love for
and belief in the church. Finally, according to Przywara, *The Spirit
of Catholicism* stresses the fact that a person lives his or her faith
within the church. It expounds, therefore, ideas which Guardini
discussed in "The Awakening of the Church in Souls" and the other
lectures in his book *The Church and the Catholic*.

Hermann Dieckmann wrote a lengthy, careful review of the
second edition of *The Spirit of Catholicism* (1926). After noting
that the revised edition includes approximately twenty new pages

on the communion of saints, he summarizes each chapter and then appraises the text, questioning the text's vocabulary. While the book uses a "living, warm language that penetrates to the height and depth of thought," it would better attain its goal "if the most important doctrines defined by the church, which are pertinent to the discussion, were presented in the language of the church."[66] The book's statements on the sacraments, for instance, "presuppose familiarity with Catholic doctrine." Its handling of the church's nature would be stronger if reference were made to the Code of Canon Law, for if the appropriate canons were discussed, there could be a more adequate account of "the relationship of Christ to the powers handed over to the church." More could be said in particular about papal primacy. The description of Christ as the church's "ensouling spirit" requires more precise expression in order to clarify the relationship between Christ and the Holy Spirit. Finally, according to Dieckmann, the text would offer a fuller treatment of the church's teachings, if it included more of the church's official formulations, as in Krebs's *Dogma und Leben.*

The focal point of Dieckmann's review is the issue of theology and culture. Dieckmann observes that neoscholastic terminology, which he calls the "church's language," is not employed in *The Spirit of Catholicism.* Rather, the text depends upon the language of the day, language that can be found in writings by such scholars as Henry James, Traugott Oesterreich, Max Scheler, and Anton Scholz. Thus, Dieckmann asks, "To what extent may and should a Catholic work which is meant to clarify religious, theological thought adopt the terminology of other schools, worldviews and confessions?" The book's reliance on contemporary discourse has yielded statements like these: "I apprehend God through Christ in His Church." Religion is "something originally given, . . . a fundamental datum of the human spirit. . . ." These sentences show that Karl Adam is trying to carry "the Christian truth" into the promised land along with "the gold and within the vessels of the Egyptians." This endeavor entails a great risk. Without the church's normative language, namely neoscholasticism, Adam's book can be misconstrued to give greater weight to recent ideas than to the longstanding truths of Scripture and tradition.

In concluding, Dieckmann commends Adam for his lucid account of Catholicism: "The author has the gift of succinctly presenting controversial concepts." Adam has also appropriately stressed the church's unity amid diversity, "the one in the many." "The author's predilection is directed toward this unity, filled with life; and rightly so." This same theme of unity embracing diversity has appeared, notes Dieckmann, in the works of Augustine, Thomas Aquinas, J. B. Franzelin, and M. J. Scheeben. In bringing this topic again to the attention of readers, Adam has increased the life of the church. "To have worked out and promoted these reflections is the service of this book. For this, heartfelt thanks are expressed to the author!"

The Spirit of Catholicism caught the eye of Protestants as well as Catholics. Karl Barth regarded the book as a significant presentation on Catholicism. In the spring of 1928 he quoted the text before audiences in Bremen, Osnabrück, and Düsseldorf when he lectured on "Roman Catholicism as a Question to the Protestant Church."[67] According to Barth, Protestants should allow themselves to be challenged by the theological views of Catholics like Karl Adam, Romano Guardini, Hugo Lang, and Erich Przywara. In hearing the claims of these theologians, Protestants could ask themselves whether they have maintained appropriate notions of divine revelation and the presence of God in human life. At the same time, Protestants should note the deficiency of Catholic theology. It is more interested in "the supernatural" than in "the Word of God." For instance, Karl Adam is not saying all that must be said when he describes Christ as "the inflowing stream of life." He is watering down the Christian faith when he declares that Catholicism is "the affirmation of the whole, full life of men." Statements like these, insists Barth, lose sight of God's transcendence and freedom. The notion of "vitality" has shaped too much of Catholic theology.

In 1932 George Orwell, the famous British writer, wrote a laudatory review of *The Spirit of Catholicism* on the occasion of its third printing in English. This is a refreshing book, says Orwell, for the author "is not trying to prove any particular adversary a fool but rather to show what goes on inside the Catholic soul, and he hardly bothers to argue about the philosophical basis of faith."[68] This text is not so much a polemic as a description of the Catholic self-understanding. As such, it respects the reader's ability to decide whether or not to accept what is described. *The Spirit of Catholicism* talks about a community. The church is the visible expression of the fellowship of people in union with Christ.

However, the book's language is problematic. What words mean
is not always clear. He cites Adam's statement that "the visible
organism of the Church postulates for its visibility a real principle
of unity in which the suprapersonal unity of all the faithful ob-
tains perceptible expression and which supports, maintains and
protects this unity." According to the British writer, the density
of sentences like this one can make the reader hesitate to go on,
though persistence is rewarded.

Along with reviews of *The Spirit of Catholicism* by a variety
of independent readers, there was also a report on it done for
the Vatican's Holy Office.[69] During the 1927–1928 academic year
the faculty at the University of Breslau proposed Adam as their
first choice for a professorship. His name was removed from the
list of candidates, though, when word circulated that the Holy
Office was scrutinizing his writings. This rumor seemed to lack
substance until September 1931, when Mario Bendiscioli, who
had translated *The Spirit of Catholicism* from German into Italian,
learned that official proceedings were in fact underway against the
book.[70] Aided by Bendiscioli and Guardini, Adam tried to prevent
a decision regarding the book, but in vain. On August 1, 1932,
the Holy Office reached the tentative conclusion that *The Spirit
of Catholicism* might contain doctrinal errors, and thus it had
to be withdrawn from bookstores. On August 27, Bishop Michael
Buchberger of Regensburg informed Adam of the Holy Office's
judgment and, on September 2, Adam wrote a letter of compliance.

Adam immediately began negotiations with the Vatican. He
was assisted by Eugenio Cardinal Pacelli, Bavaria's papal nuncio,
who would become Pius XII. Also, Cardinal Michael Faulhaber,
Archbishop of Munich, advised the Holy Office that the source
of the problem was not the book's ideas but its translation into
Latin, as required for examination by the Holy Office. On June 10,
1933, Archbishop Conrad Gröber of Freiburg im Breisgau, acting
on behalf of the Vatican, told Adam that Rome had softened its
evaluation of the book. The Holy Office was not placing the work
on the Index of Forbidden Books but only requiring that linguistic
ambiguities be remedied on twenty-nine pages of the text. During
the next few months Adam made alterations in the book and
submitted them to Rome.[71] They were accepted by the Vatican
in December 1933, and the revised text appeared in book stores
in January 1934.

What changes in *The Spirit of Catholicism* were required by the Vatican? The report of the Holy Office made four major points.[72] First, the book's language needed to be more precise. For example, the phrase "the divine" was ambiguous. It could mean either God or a reality apart from God in which other beings could participate. Also, "the divine" referred in some places to something in human beings in general and in other places only to something in Jesus Christ. It was not clear whether "the divine" functioned in the same sense as "divinity." Ambiguity surrounded, too, the expression "likeness to divinity" which was applied to Jesus Christ.

Second, the discussion of human knowledge of God and faith did not coincide with the Vatican's teaching. The book emphasized that our apprehension of God depends on God. Yet the church has taught that humankind possesses a natural ability to know God. The text needed to explain that human beings can know God by means of their ordinary cognition.

Third, the book's ecclesiology was at times misleading. Its presentation on the church as the body of Christ could be misunderstood to mean that the church is solely interpersonal and not institutional. There should be more discussion of the church's external unity, as maintained by confessions of faith, the consistent practice of the sacraments, and the authority of the bishops, especially the bishop of Rome. In particular, it was wrong to declare that "the divine" has become objectivized in the believing community. Also, the book identified Christ too closely with the Christian community; it needed to qualify its claim that Christianity is Christ. The text failed, too, to give sufficient regard to the church's teaching office. The account of the church's history overlooked the theological principle that Christ would not create an imperfect church.

Fourth, the book's christology should be developed further. The incarnation was emphasized at the expense of the crucifixion. God's saving work appeared to consist primarily in God's becoming a human being, as though Jesus' death and resurrection were not central in salvation. Further, the book needed to clarify that God's "becoming flesh" in Jesus Christ is singular; it does not repeat itself in every human life. The author's stress upon the incarnation had resulted in an overly optimistic view of humankind.

Adam responded positively to the recommendations of the reviewers and the Holy Office.[73] In the foreword to the fourth printing of *Das Wesen des Katholizismus* (1927), he thanked Hermann Dieckmann for his review's "worthwhile pointers" and added that he could not make the structural changes suggested by Dieckmann (i.e., rearranging the chapters and including ecclesiastical texts) because these modifications would threaten the book's character as a short text written for the general reader. Adam also said that he retained "all modernizing turns of expression" in the text, because Catholic theology, since the time of St. Cyprian, has rightly sought "to bring 'the gold of Egypt' into the promised land." Finally, he pointed out that the book was meant to be both dogmatic and apologetic. It is "no dogmatic manual, proceeding with pure concepts and bold theses, but an awakening call, born from love, to those who more or less stand apart from the life of the church."[74]

Linguistic changes in areas specified by the Vatican are evident in comparisons between the sixth (1931) and seventh (1934) printings of *Das Wesen des Katholizismus*.[75] Two points of comparison will be given here. First, Adam clarifies statements regarding natural knowledge of God and knowledge of God based on faith. The sixth printing reads: "I apprehend God through Christ in His Church. I come to know the living God through Christ active in His Church." The seventh printing states: "I come to *living faith* [italics mine] in the triune God through Christ in His Church. I come to know *the effects* [italics mine] of the living God through Christ active in His Church." In other words, the later version explicitly affirms our natural knowledge of God and faith's role in extending this. It makes clear that our minds do not actually grasp God.

Second, in the later version Adam adds that natural knowledge of God must be nurtured by reverence of God. The sixth printing declares: "If there really is a living, personal God, this [reality] exists not in me and my conditions of being but exists in God alone, whether [or not] I acknowledge Him. The question is not: Can I know God?, but: Am I permitted to know God?" By contrast, the seventh printing says: "For although God has clearly manifested Himself in His creation of human reason, such natural knowledge of God can ignite truly living religiosity only if it is sustained by humility and reverence."

For nearly three decades *The Spirit of Catholicism* was an international best-seller.[76] Despite the Vatican's reservations, Catholic readers confirmed the reviewers' positive assessments. First published in 1924, the German text went through thirteen more printings, the last being in 1957. By the mid-1930s it had been translated into Czechoslovakian, Dutch, English, French, Hungarian, Italian, Japanese, and Lithuanian. And by 1955 it had also appeared in Chinese, Danish, Portuguese, and Spanish. In all of these languages, the book had numerous printings. In sum, *The Spirit of Catholicism* was read in at least thirteen languages from the mid-1920s until the 1960s.

5. Legacy: Church as Community

Writing in 1947, the American theologian Joseph Bluett observed that after the Great War the literature on the church as the body of Christ flourished in a "period of phenomenal growth."[77] Interestingly, the amount written during the early 1920s "equalled that of the twenty previous years," and in the late 1920s "the output was doubled." The early 1930s "saw a volume of literature five times that of the corresponding years of the preceding decade." This flood of books and articles crested in the late 1930s. *The Spirit of Catholicism* was one book among the many that appeared over two decades. Yet, it stands out as one of the few books to which later ecclesiological texts have frequently referred.

On June 29, 1943, Pope Pius XII issued *Mystici Corporis*, concerning the institutional and charismatic dimensions of the church as the body of Christ.[78] The encyclical points out the merits of the ecclesiology of the body of Christ and warns against the ways in which it can be carried to extremes. The theological works that directly shaped this encyclical letter are *Le Corps mystique du Christ* (1933) by Emile Mersch and *Corpus Christi quod est Ecclesia* (1937) by Sebastian Tromp. Nevertheless, one cannot help but link Pacelli's attempt in 1943 to safeguard the notion of the church as body of Christ with his efforts in the early 1930s to stop the Holy Office from placing *The Spirit of Catholicism* on its Index of Forbidden Books. Moreover, Adam's insistence on the union of the risen Christ with the faithful is echoed in Pius XII's claim that what distinguishes the church is "the Spirit of our Redeemer, who penetrates and fills every part of the Church's being and is active within it until the end of time as the source of every grace and every gift and every miraculous power."[79]

Commentators have noted the importance of *The Spirit of Catholicism* in preparing the way for *Mystici Corporis*. In 1946 the church historian Roger Aubert pointed out that Adam and Guardini "played an important role" in the ecclesiology of the mystical body of Christ.[80] Twenty years later Aubert reiterated this point when he said that *The Spirit of Catholicism* "fashioned a true theological revolution for a half century."[81] In 1948 the French theologian Louis Bouyer noted that *The Spirit of Catholicism* and Peter Lippert's *Die Kirche Christi* (1931) "stimulated" the theological movement leading up to *Mystici Corporis*.[82] Recently, the German theologian Gotthold Hasenhüttl has credited Adam with setting the stage for *Mystici Corporis* by promoting the idea that Christ meets us not solely as individuals but as members of the Christian community.[83] Finally, the German theologian Walter Kasper, now the bishop of Rottenburg-Stuttgart, affirmed modern ecclesiology's indebtedness to Adam when he wrote:

> In *The Spirit of Catholicism* Adam taught [us] to understand anew the church as the mystical body of Christ, as the living community pulsing with the life of Christ, as the Catholic Church in the encompassing sense of the word because [Catholicism] speaks a full yes to the whole of scripture, to the whole person, to one's body and to one's soul, to nature as to culture.[84]

In the years after *Mystici Corporis*, *The Spirit of Catholicism* continued to have a strong impact upon Catholic thought. The French theologian Yves Congar, in his book *Lay People in the Church* (1953), insisted that the church's institutional form is inseparable from its communal life, its fellowship of women and men committed to Jesus Christ. In emphasizing church as community, Congar relied heavily upon Möhler's writings, but he also appealed to Adam's *The Spirit of Catholicism*.[85] Later, in his book *Tradition and Traditions* (1960–63), Congar again referred to *The Spirit of Catholicism*. He specifically cited Adam's understanding of the "living tradition," the vital dynamism in which the truths of divine revelation are continually being passed on, discovered anew and realized more fully in the church's life.[86]

Commenting on the emergence of ecclesiologies like Congar's in the twentieth century, the German theologian Leo Scheffcyzk has credited *The Spirit of Catholicism* with prompting the shift from an apologetic to a dogmatic presentation of the "mysterious essence" of the church. Inspired by Adam's example, contemporary views of the church rely, Scheffcyzk has noted, on a biblical understanding of the body of Christ, phenomenology, and the psychology of religion.[87]

According to the British theologian Peter Hebblethwaite, *The Spirit of Catholicism* influenced Pope Paul VI's encyclical *Ecclesiam Suam* (1964). As already mentioned, in the 1930s Giovanni Battista Montini so valued Adam's book that he gave it to colleagues who would be able to appreciate the book's historical perspective on the church. Montini's use of this text did not, however, stop here. In his first encyclical, Paul VI presented a vision of the church that has deep similarities with Adam's ecclesiology.[88]

In *The Spirit of Catholicism* Adam distinguished between the ideal church and the real church, and so too did Paul VI in *Ecclesiam Suam*. The pontiff pointed out that any modern attempt to reflect on the church's nature and mission must give serious consideration to both "the ideal image of the Church as Christ envisioned it" and to "the actual image which the Church presents to the world today."[89] In 1924 Karl Adam observed "that actual Catholicism lags considerably behind its idea, that it has never appeared in history as a complete and perfect thing. . . ."[90] Four decades later, the pontiff expressed this same idea when he wrote: "But the actual image of the Church will never attain to such a degree of perfection . . . that it can be said to correspond perfectly with the original conception in the mind of Him who fashioned it."[91] Further, knowledge of the real church is reached, insisted Paul VI with Adam, through persistent and balanced historical research.[92] The bishop of Rome was convinced that reflection upon the church's historical development allows the Christian assembly to gain "a renewed discovery of its vital bond of union with Christ."[93]

Four months after *Ecclesiam Suam*, the Second Vatican Council promulgated its Constitution on the Church, *Lumen Gentium*, and this text, too, bears the mark of ideas that Adam promoted. As the American theologian John Thiel has observed, Adam's thought is evident in at least two ways in the conciliar document.[94] First,

Lumen Gentium emphasizes the church as community, especially through its use of the metaphor of the people of God. This image is reinforced when the church is presented as the body of Christ. The Constitution resembles Adam's ecclesiology when it states: "For by communicating his Spirit, Christ mystically constitutes as his body those brothers of his who are called together from every nation."[95] With this use of "people of God" and "body of Christ," Vatican II subsumed institutional and juridical views of church within the more primary context of the church as community.

Second, Adam's impact appears, also, in the understanding of history that is manifest in *Lumen Gentium*. Adam insisted upon the developmental character of the church. With Möhler and the Catholic Tübingen School, he spoke of the living tradition. *Lumen Gentium* communicates this understanding of church and tradition through its use of the image of the "pilgrim church."[96] An appreciation of history is expressed, too, in the document's language. Just as Adam had avoided propositional speech and adopted more descriptive, pastoral language, so does *Lumen Gentium*. The constitution's discourse attests that the wisdom of Christian faith needs to be restated in language appropriate to the time and place of its hearers.

Theologians who were students of Karl Adam have mentioned the affinity between *The Spirit of Catholicism* and the Second Vatican Council's teachings. In the judgment of moral theologian Bernard Häring, Adam was "one of the theologians who contributed in an outstanding way to the preparation of the Second Vatican Council though he was never present at any of its commission meetings."[97] In this same vein, Tübingen theologian Fritz Hofmann has written: "Much from *The Spirit of Catholicism* may seem to us today as an anticipation of the realizations which Vatican II first brought about for the whole church. Or, was it possibly rather a seed which, planted worldwide in receptive soil, took root, grew and brought forth fruit?"[98] This question was answered by the Munich theologian Heinrich Fries, who has described his teacher as a "forerunner" of Vatican II. In remarks on *The Spirit of Catholicism* Fries has stated that "the contemporary understanding of church, as well as that to which the Second Vatican Council gave testimony, would not have been possible without such preparations and struggles [as Adam's]. Therefore, this council is a confirmation of the theology and theological impulse of Karl Adam."[99]

Talk about the church as community is common today. Contemporary ecclesiologies presume Pius XII's *Mystici Corporis*, Paul VI's *Ecclesiam Suam*, and Vatican II's *Lumen Gentium*. But at the start of the twentieth century Catholics were unfamiliar with the view of the church articulated in these texts. Even though the notion of church as community had been recovered by Möhler in the early 1800s, it was shunted aside in the second half of the century, especially when, on July 18, 1870, the First Vatican Council promulgated its Constitution on the Church, *Pastor Aeternus*, with its institutional ecclesiology.[100] The language of the mystical body of Christ lay dormant for decades and came to life again only after the First World War. One of its strongest implementations was in *The Spirit of Catholicism*.

Book reviews and the Vatican's report on *The Spirit of Catholicism* speak of the book's strengths and weaknesses. On the one hand, its merits include an encompassing vision of Catholicism, its emphasis upon the centrality of Christ in the church's life, the recovery of the ancient motif of the body of Christ, its historical consciousness, the notions of person and community, and its engaging, descriptive language. On the other hand, the book's language could be more precise, and its emphasis upon the incarnation could be balanced by more reflection upon Jesus' suffering, death, and resurrection. These shortcomings are significant and, as we will see, they raise a question regarding Adam's reliance on Germany's neoromanticism.

Soon after writing *The Spirit of Catholicism*, Karl Adam embarked on a disciplined inquiry into the mystery of Jesus Christ. Within nine years he had produced two major books, *Christ Our Brother* and *The Son of God*. Why did he shift from ecclesiology to christology? Though he did not say, one reason can be deduced from the logic of his theology. If the church is the body of Christ, then our understanding of the "body" as a whole will improve as we become clearer about its "head." The church's nature and mission become clearer as more light is shed on its Lord's "person" and "work." For Adam, ecclesiology takes its bearings from christology.

After 1925 Adam made christology one of his major concerns.
In doing so, he stressed an understated theme within the theology
of the Catholic Tübingen School. By and large, the school's theologians of the nineteenth century, with the exception of Johannes
Kuhn, did not elaborate on their christological views. What they
left unsaid Adam made explicit beginning in 1926. In the words of
Fritz Hofmann: "Karl Adam's theology developed beyond that of
the earlier Tübingen School nowhere so much as where it treated
Christ, his person and work, the mystery of our salvation through
him."[101] Adam's christology, therefore, is the focus of the next
two chapters.

3

Doing Christology "From Below" (1926–1930)

Two major trends have shaped Catholic christology since the Second World War.[1] One current has highlighted the humanity of Jesus Christ. Since the fifteen-hundredth anniversary of the Council of Chalcedon in 1951, scholars have illuminated the way in which Jesus Christ was "truly man." Key figures in the early years of this endeavor were Alois Grillmeier, Felix Malmberg, Karl Rahner, Edward Schillebeeckx, Piet Schoonenberg, and Bernhard Welte. A second stream has appreciated the theological value of historical study regarding Jesus of Nazareth and the formation of the New Testament. Christology has increasingly drawn on the results of biblical research. Catholic scholars who have joined in this effort include Josef Rupert Geiselmann, Franz Mussner, Rudolf Pesch, Rudolf Schnackenburg, and Anton Vögtle.

These currents regarding the humanity of Christ and scriptural witness to Jesus did not spring up overnight. They emerged in the second half of this century because of labor done in the first half.[2] To be sure, this early work was undertaken with caution, due to the restrictions imposed in 1907 with Pius X's condemnation of modernism. It developed with a degree of freedom only after 1943, when Pius XII's encyclical *Divino afflante Spiritu* permitted the limited use of historical-critical methods in the study of the Bible. Nevertheless, some pioneering efforts in Catholic christology did take place during the 1920s and 1930s. One of the theologians engaged in this ground-clearing was Karl Adam.

Both of the themes that guide so much of today's christology were central to Adam's thought. *Christ Our Brother* and *The Son*

57

of God stress the humanity of Jesus Christ. "For the mystery of
Christ does not lie," said Adam, "in the fact that he is God, but
that he is God-man."[3] Also, these two books are anchored in the
New Testament, especially in the synoptic Gospels. They rely, for
example, on the evangelists' testimony that Jesus addressed God
as "Abba." In Adam's words: "With this little word Father, Jesus
sheds the warmest, sunniest light on the relations of mankind to
God and dispels all those gloomy shadows with which the savage
demonolatry of the pagans and the cold, rigid belief of the Jews in
the *lex talionis* had overcast the image of God."[4] Statements like
these in the 1920s prepared the way for the inquiries of the 1960s.
They led to systematic reflections upon the mystery of Jesus Christ
that begin with his humanity. In short, Adam's work contributed
to the development of christology "from below."[5]

In this chapter and the next, we will look at Adam's books
on Jesus Christ and the ways in which they prepared the way
for recent christology. This third chapter displays the emphasis
upon the humanity of Christ in *Christ Our Brother*, entitled in
German, *Christus unser Bruder*. Chapter 4 examines the use of
Scripture in *The Son of God*, which appeared in German with the
title *Jesus Christus*. While these two books possess virtually the
same theological content, they differ in their historical setting and
their form. Thus, we will consider each book's context, the text
itself, its method, reception, and theological legacy.

1. Context: The Liturgical Movement

Life in the Weimar Republic became relatively stable by the
mid-1920s.[6] Germans were having their first experience of democracy. Coalitions formed among the major parties, the Social Dem-
ocrats, the Catholic Center Party, and the German People's Party,
and the government operated according to Germany's new constitution. Paul von Hindenburg, elected president in 1925, supported the efforts of the various cabinets to give direction to
the nation. Hjalmar Schacht, the president of the Reichsbank,
succeeded in stabilizing the reichsmark, and the nation gradually
returned to modest economic prosperity. Gustav Stresemann, the
foreign minister, negotiated a reduction of the war reparations and
brought Germany into the League of Nations. As internal order
and international respect were restored, the nation's intellectual

and cultural life regained vitality. In philosophy, Ernst Cassirer published his three-volume *Philosophy of Symbolic Forms* (1923-29), and Martin Heidegger completed his *Being and Time* (1927). In literature, Hermann Hesse wrote his novel *Steppenwolf* (1927).

During the 1920s, through the convergence of religious ideas and ecclesial events, liturgical renewal became a creative force among German Catholics.[7] At the turn of the century, Pius X played an instrumental role in the updating of Catholic worship through his decrees on sacred music (1903), daily Communion (1905), and children's Communion (1906). These instructions coincided with a growing awareness of the nature of liturgy, which Benedictine abbeys throughout Europe were promoting. In the 1830s Prosper Guéranger (1805-1875) had restored the Abbey at Solesmes, near LeMans, and sparked new thought about the liturgy with his *Institutions liturgiques* (3 volumes, 1840-1851) and *L'Annee liturgique* (9 volumes, 1841-1866). He also influenced Maurus Wolter's restoration in 1868 of the Abbey of Beuron, not far from Freiburg im Breisgau. Beuron quickly flourished as the first center of liturgical revival in Germany. Here Anselm Schott (1845-1896), inspired by work at the Abbey of Maredsous in Belgium, published a missal in German for the use of the laity at Mass. Beuron stimulated the renewal and study of worship at the Abbey of Mont César in Louvain and at the Abbey of Maria Laach near Coblenz. From Mont César, Lambert Beauduin (1873-1960) directed the rebirth of parish liturgy and edited the review *Questiones Liturgiques et Paroissiales*. At the Catholic Congress in Mecheln on September 23, 1909, Beauduin delivered a paper, "The Proper Prayer of the Church," that became the keynote address of the worldwide liturgical movement.

After the First World War the renewal of worship blossomed in Germany and Austria. Under the leadership of Abbot Ildefons Herwegen (1874-1946), the Abbey of Maria Laach held liturgies at which worshippers participated through the use of hymns and German missals. Further, it supported research on the history and theology of liturgy by such scholars as Anton Baumstark, Odo Casel, and Kunibert Mohlberg. Much of this work appeared in the abbey's series of monographs, *Ecclesia orans* (1918-), and its journal, *Jahrbuch für Liturgiewissenschaft* (1921-). Another wellspring of the liturgical renaissance was the Abbey of Klosterneuburg, outside of Vienna, where Pius Parsch (1884-1954)

took steps to recover the church's liturgical year and the appreciation of the Mass as a sacrificial meal celebrated by the entire
Christian community, not the priest alone. Of the wealth of literature generated by the liturgical movement in the 1920s, two books
immediately pertain to our study. One is by Romano Guardini; the
other is by Josef Jungmann.

In his *The Spirit of the Liturgy* (1918), the first volume in
the series *Ecclesia orans*, Guardini clarified the eucharistic liturgy's
view of Christ. While the gospels portray Jesus "walking about the
streets and among the people" and hence "so entirely one of us,"
at Mass he appears in a different light. Guardini observed: "There
[at Mass] He is the Sovereign mediator between God and man, the
eternal High Priest, the divine Teacher, the Judge of the living and
of the dead; in His Body, hidden in the Eucharist, He mystically
united all the faithful in the great society that is the Church; He
is the God-Man, the Word that was made flesh."[8] This view of
Jesus is produced in the liturgy as the gospels function within the
context of worship and the liturgical year. It gains its validity from
the fact that the liturgy is "no mere commemoration of what once
existed" but is itself "the enduring life of Jesus Christ in us, and
that of the believer in Christ, eternally God and Man." The church
is enriched when the liturgy's representation of Christ as mediator
complements the gospels' earthly figure of Jesus.

In 1925 the Jesuit scholar Josef Jungmann (1879–1975) shed
more light on the liturgy's presentation of Jesus Christ. In his
The Place of Christ in Liturgical Prayer, Jungmann argued that
the ancient representation of Christ as mediator and high priest
became increasingly blurred in the liturgy, especially in the East,
beginning in the fourth century. Clement of Rome expressed the
ancient view of Christ as mediator when he prayed, "we praise
thee [God] through the high priest and advocate of our souls,
Jesus Christ. . . ."[9] The Council of Hippo (393) affirmed the view
of Christ as mediator when it established the rule that liturgical
prayer "was not to be addressed to Christ instead of the Father;
and equally, in the mediatory formula, the Father was not to be put
in the place of Christ."[10] Despite this instruction, prayers at Mass
were increasingly directed to Christ himself, thereby challenging
the subordinationism of the Arians. The traditional doxology, giving praise to the Father "through the Son in the Holy Spirit," was
changed to accentuate Christ's equality with the Godhead: "Glory

be to the Father and to the Son and to the Holy Spirit." According to Jungmann, over the centuries the church's appreciation of the Eucharist as the sacrament of love within the body of Christ— the view held by Augustine—shifted to the view that the Mass is a ritual of awe and fear.[11] This attitude is manifest, observed Jungmann, in the monophysite liturgies of the East. By contrast, it appears only to a small degree in the Roman rite, which was not greatly affected by the church's reaction to Arianism. The Roman liturgy upholds the early church's view of Christ as mediator, for it offers prayers to the Father "through Christ our Lord."[12]

Jungmann's study highlighted and strengthened a thread that ran through the writings of the liturgical movement. Pius X's decrees stressed union with Christ. Guardini's *The Spirit of the Liturgy* presented the Eucharist as the sacrament of communion in the body of Christ, and therefore it recovered the sense of Jesus Christ as the head of the body, as the mediator between God and creation. *The Place of Christ in the Liturgy* secured this understanding of Jesus Christ as mediator and high priest by demonstrating both the centrality of this view in the early Christian church and its eclipse in reaction to Arianism's subordinationist christology.

The Place of Christ in the Liturgy had a strong impact upon the liturgical movement. It had such lasting value that in 1962 Jungmann made minor revisions in the text and published a second edition. One reason for the book's importance was that it indirectly pointed to the need for the renewal of preaching based on the scriptural readings at Mass. Since in the Eucharist the Christian community is united with Christ in giving praise to the Father, the congregation should hear the kerygma, the Word of God. For centuries, Catholics had neglected this understanding of liturgical preaching. A second reason for the significance of *The Place of Christ in Liturgical Prayer* was its implication for christology.

The neoscholasticism of the Latin manuals determined most Catholic christology in the 1920s. According to today's classifications, it generated a christology "from above" within a pre-Enlightenment horizon of meaning. Presuming an understanding of the triune God, it employed ahistorical categories to reflect upon the testimony that "God became man" (Jn 1:14). The nine-volume *Praelectiones dogmaticae* (1894-99) and the four-volume *Compendium theologiae dogmaticae* (1923-25) by Christian Pesch

exhibit this descending christology.[13] At the start of his discussion
on Jesus Christ, Pesch posits that "Jesus Christ is true God." He
"proves" this claim by employing scholastic categories, for example, types of causality developed from Aristotelian metaphysics.
At the same time, he appeals to isolated statements in the Bible
and patristic texts. After this exposition, he moves to the second
proposition that "Jesus Christ is true man." Here, too, he "demonstrates" his assertion by adopting scholastic categories and relying
on proof texts taken from biblical and patristic writings. Finally,
Pesch asserts that "Jesus Christ is true God and true man" and
defends this proposition by referring to what he already "proved"
regarding the first and second propositions and also by employing
the same kind of arguments operative in his defense of these
propositions. He concludes this deductive process by repeating
key words from the doctrine of Chalcedon, namely, that Jesus
Christ is one "person" who possesses both a "divine nature" and
a "human nature."

The writings of Guardini and Jungmann on the figure of
Christ in liturgy indirectly exposed the limitations of neoscholastic christology. The christology "from above" of Pesch and the
other neoscholastic theologians was not necessarily wrong, but it
assumed knowledge of an intellectual framework with which the
modern mind is unfamiliar. Since the scholastic perspective was
ahistorical, Christ appeared more as an idea than as a person.
In its technical terms, propositional reasoning, and static view
of history, neoscholasticism conveyed a notion of Christ which
a reader might intellectually grasp, but it failed to present Christ
as a living person. While the scholastic representation of Christ
may have been appropriate in a former age, this account was easily misunderstood in a world shaped by historical consciousness.
Neoscholasticism's Christ seemed not to be human, and therefore
it could be unwittingly construed as monophysitic. Since Guardini
and Jungmann highlighted the need for christologies that retrieve
the ancient church's sense of Jesus Christ as a person, indeed as
the mediator between God and creation, they displayed the need
for a new kind of christology.[14]

Karl Adam was aware of this need. Shortly after Jungmann
published *The Place of Christ in Liturgical Prayer*, Adam wrote
the essay "Durch Christus, unsern Herrn" (1926) in which he
explained that, in the light of Jungmann's work, Catholics had to

regain their appreciation of Jesus Christ as the one through whom and in whom people are united with God and with one another.[15] This essay increased the interest in Jungmann's work, and in 1962 it was mentioned by Jungmann himself in his foreword to the book's second edition: "[T]he treatment of the subject seemed already at that time to be demanded by the religious situation. In fact very soon no less a person than Karl Adam, in a much noticed essay, 'Through Christ, Our Lord,' . . . referred to the book and to the importance of the questions raised therein."[16]

The essay by Adam became in fact the seed from which sprang his first book on christology. Adam was so convinced of the accuracy of Jungmann's thesis that he enlarged his essay, "Through Christ, Our Lord," into the book *Christus unser Bruder* (1926). This first edition consisted of four chapters. In 1930 Adam expanded this text in a new edition of seven chapters, which we shall review. It is this edition that was published in English under the title *Christ Our Brother*.

2. TEXT: "CHRIST OUR BROTHER"

The thesis of *Christ Our Brother* is straightforward. According to Adam, Jesus Christ is not only truly God, he is also truly a human being. Christ is fully united with God, and yet he is also completely united with us. He is both God's Son and our brother. "Why is the Incarnation of God the decisive thing?" asks Adam. "Because we now have among us a Man who is God. We have a Brother who is God."[17]

The gospels portray Jesus as a man who affirmed both God's will and God's creation, says Adam. Jesus gave himself completely to God. He lived out of "his unconditional surrender of his whole being to the divine will: 'My meat is to do the will of Him that sent me.'"[18] And Jesus embraced life in all of its manifestations, including corrupt tax collectors and prostitutes. "There was in Him no world-weariness, no strengthless melancholy, no timid shrinking from the fray."[19]

Prayer, Adam contends, was the central dynamism of Jesus' life. His personal dialogue with God, whom he addressed as "Father," gave Jesus strength and direction. As the Bible attests, in his last days Jesus manifested his "unconditional surrender" to God even though this meant succumbing to apparent tragedy.

In the Garden of Gethsemane Jesus displayed "the supreme type of Christian prayer."[20] It did not lead to passivity, to "a weak, languishing love," but to courage in the face of hardship, to "the greatest heroism."

Explicitly building on the work of Jungmann, Adam argues that Christians have "one-sidedly" stressed the divinity of Christ. This one-sideness is evident in the practice of private prayers taking priority over the community's worship at Mass. The faithful see themselves as individuals before God, not as members of the mystical body of Christ. Implicit here is an attitude similar to that of gnosticism and monophysitism. In praying primarily to Christ in private prayer, Catholics have forgotten that our prayers are in fact made in union with Christ, who shares in our humanity. A person's individual devotional practices can imply that Christ's humanity was a mere guise. The church's reaction to Arianism has reinforced the devotional emphasis upon Christ's divinity. Out of fear of making too little of Christ's equality with God, Catholics have lost their sense of Christ as the mediator in union with whom, in the power of the Spirit, people give praise and thanks to God.

As Jungmann has shown, the Roman liturgy preserved the early tradition of praying in union with Christ to God. It retained, for instance, the practice of ending orations with the expression "through Christ our Lord." The Synod of Hippo upheld this theology when it declared that liturgical prayers should be addressed to God the Father. In Adam's words: "We are instructed to pray, not to Christ, but through Christ to the Father, through God Incarnate to the Triune God."[21]

Adam notes that liturgical practice in the Roman rite expresses a dogmatic principle: Jesus Christ is the head of the mystical body. In Christ we meet God, not because we have somehow left behind our human nature and been lifted up to God, but because in Jesus Christ God has entered totally into our humanity.

> And therein lies the mystery and the miracle of Christ. It is not that a human nature was taken up into the divinity, but that the divinity became a full and perfect man. It is not the ascent of the human to the divine, but the condescension of the divine to the human. It is not that flesh became God, but that God became flesh.[22]

Our liturgical prayers must be joined, therefore, to the prayer of Jesus Christ. He is our mediator, our high priest, with whom we are united by virtue of our humanity. "Whatever part of the liturgy we examine, we find Christ represented as our Head who binds us together into one whole and offers us with thanksgiving to His Father."[23]

One key aspect of Jesus' "redemptive work," observes Adam, was his "redeeming word." Jesus' teaching, in proverbs and parables, was marked by a "simplicity" and "naturalness" that reflects his soul. The content of this teaching concerned God's "utter supremacy and His fatherhood." Consider Jesus' prayer: "Our Father, who art in heaven." This understanding of God sheds light on "the mystery of man" as the one whose fulfillment is realized only in God. Jesus' "redeeming truths" are "that the Triune God is the true and sole meaning of my life, and that God is my Father; that my soul has an infinite value; that my love for God should be manifested in love for my fellow men."[24]

Another crucial aspect of Jesus' redemptive activity is his "work." Humankind had to be saved from "a twofold servitude," namely, "from the bonds of merely natural being" and "from attachment to sin." This release has occurred in the incarnation. By entering fully into the human condition, God has bridged the gulf that existed between God and ourselves. "Our own flesh and blood, our human nature, is no longer cursed of God, but blessed." We have not accomplished our reconciliation with God, rather God has brought this union about by coming near to us in Jesus Christ. "To be Christian means to be redeemed, not through one's own strength, but 'through Christ our Lord.' "[25]

All of creation is being drawn into Jesus Christ's saving work, Adam explains. This is the activity of the Holy Spirit, who is "that divine Union, wherein Father and Son meet in an unending commerce of superabundant life."[26] The Spirit is not confined to the flow of love within the Godhead, but reaches into the depths of creation and inflames everything with the love of God. In the case of humankind, the Spirit not only seeks to fill all hearts with divine love but also desires to bestow on people the gift of Christian faith, so that everyone can join even more fully in the divine communication. This means concretely that all programs in religious education can only nurture what the Holy Spirit has first graciously given.

In conclusion, three insights into the mystery of Jesus Christ come about when we meditate on the scriptural readings of the

Christmas liturgy, especially on the infancy narratives of Matthew
and Luke and also on Isaiah's proclamation that "a child is born
to us." First, God is "a living, personal God" who surpasses our
natural speculations about divinity.[27] Second, God has revealed
God's very self in the life, death, and resurrection of Jesus, who
"displays the ideal of a pure, holy, wise, good, courageous, perfect
humanity in so luminous and impressive, yet so simple and plain
a fashion, that he is for always the ideal man." As the risen Christ,
Jesus continues to make God known to the faithful. Third, Christ
meets us in the believing community which is "His body." The
Catholic church is "the on-moving life of the Risen Christ; it is
Christ unfolding himself in history; it is the fullness of Christ."[28]
According to Adam, these three insights form "the sacred triad:
God, Christ, the Church."

3. THE THEOLOGICAL METHOD

In *Christ Our Brother* Adam relied on the same theological
method that he followed in *The Spirit of Catholicism*.[29] *Christ
Our Brother* was written within the horizon of faith, and it was
meant to shed light on a primary element of Christian belief.
More specifically, it was intended to retrieve the early church's
understanding of Christ as mediator and to present this understanding in terms intelligible to modern readers. Adam designed
the book, therefore, to be both dogmatic and apologetic. With this
orientation, he drew on Scripture and tradition, historical research
and the *Lebensphilosophie*. I will examine Adam's use of these
three sources.

The book's dominant motif, Jesus Christ as mediator, is rooted
in the New Testament. Adam appeals to 1 Timothy 2:5b: "[T]here
is one mediator between God and men, the man Christ Jesus."
This representation of Christ is complemented with the images of
Christ as the high priest (Heb 4:14; 7:25) and the "head of the
body."[30] The latter motif depends on quotations from Pauline and
deutero-Pauline texts: "For just as the body is one and has many
members, and all the members of the body, though many are one
body, so it is with Christ" (1 Cor 12:12). "[A]nd [God] has made
[Christ] the head over all things for the church which is his body,
the fullness of him who fills all in all" (Eph 2:22-23). Through
their human nature, Christians are joined to Jesus Christ, who was

a human being. Adam fills out this emphasis upon the "body" of Christ by introducing the kenosis hymn of Philippians 2:6-11. Since Christ "emptied himself, taking the form of a servant, being born in the likeness of men," Christ has made it possible for all people to be united to God through Christ, with whom we share our human nature. In Adam's words: "The vital fact is not that God dwelt bodily among us and that we can see the glory of God in the face of Christ Jesus, but that this God is our brother, that He is of one blood with us, that He is the Head of our body."[31]

Adam links these biblical motifs of Christ as mediator, high priest, and head of the body to Augustine's view of Christ as mediator.[32] Augustine, declares Adam, held that "[t]he communion with the flesh and blood of Christ which we celebrate in the liturgy is a real communion with Christ our Head, and therefore a real communion with all His members."[33] The bishop of Hippo acknowledged the primacy of grace in human life before God and the character of human response to grace in Christ. "I cannot call my cooperation my own work," says Adam; "it is the working of Christ in me."

Adam amplified his reading of Augustine in his book, *St. Augustine: The Odyssey of His Soul* (1931), which was published immediately after the expanded edition of *Christ Our Brother*. According to Adam, Augustine initially understood Christ to be humanity's "true exemplar," who has shown us the way to authentic wisdom.[34] But as Augustine matured in the Christian faith and devoted himself to the study of Scripture, he replaced his moralistic view of Jesus Christ with a more profound, ontological one. Adam summarizes this more profound understanding when he writes: "Since mankind is corrupted in its very nature, there is only one redemption possible, viz., that we should get a new nature by incorporation in a new and sinless humanity. . . . This new man is Christ." Christ has transformed creation so that all people by virtue of their humanity can be united with Christ's transformed human nature. According to Adam, Augustine came to hold that "[r]edeemed humanity is to be regarded as an unfolding in space and time of the humanity of Jesus."[35]

Christ Our Brother rests, however, on more than biblical motifs and the writings of Augustine. It depends, too, on the results of historical research. This is evident not so much in what is said, as in what is not said and also in what the book's design shows.

Little is made of Jesus' miracles, and there is no mention of Jesus' titles in the New Testament. These omissions are glaring when one recalls that Jesus' miracles and titles are important elements in the christologies of the Latin manuals. Further, *Christ Our Brother* does not offer a biography of Jesus, nor even a chronology of his ministry. In this, it stands in contrast to Ernest Renan's book *Vie de Jésus* (1863).

Christ Our Brother presents various aspects of Jesus' life: his teaching about God's compassion, his affirmative outlook on life, and his intimate prayer to "Abba."[36] This emphasis upon Jesus' implicit attitude about God and human life anticipates the "new quest" for the historical Jesus, in which attention focuses not so much on the details of Jesus' life as on Jesus' concept of God and his self-understanding.[37] Adam's approach differs from the new quest, however, in that it highlights Jesus' actions as these are portrayed in the gospels, a feature that we will consider in the next chapter. The book is silent regarding the details of Jesus' birth. This silence is noteworthy, since Adam's emphasis upon the incarnation could have resulted in an uncritical rendering of the infancy stories of Matthew and Luke. Rather, Adam relies on these narratives only insofar as he needs them in his meditation to make the three points mentioned above. *Christ Our Brother* concentrates on Jesus' ministry, especially those events mentioned in all four gospels, such as Jesus' association with society's outcasts and his preaching. Given both what Adam says about Jesus and what he does not say, it is evident that the theologian has taken seriously some of the results of historical-critical research into Jesus' life and the formation of the New Testament.

Adam relies, too, on the philosophical ideas of his day. Throughout the book, he carries on a dialogue with Nietzsche. On at least two occasions he explicitly refers to Nietzsche's view of human dignity, and in each case he stresses that Christian belief agrees with Nietzsche's call for humankind to attain its full stature. He observes, however, that Christian faith and Nietzsche part ways on what constitutes complete humanity, and on the role of Christian faith and the church in the process of human self-actualization. In Adam's judgment, humankind can reach its true end only in union with Christ.[38] Of Adam's other references to modern thought, there are two that require comment. These are his ties to the writings of Johann Adam Möhler and Max Scheler.[39]

In his *Symbolism* (1833) Möhler argued for a Catholic understanding of the God-given goodness of human life.[40] He insisted
that the source of this goodness is divine grace at the heart of
creation. According to Möhler, the biblical account of "the fall"
should be interpreted to mean that while we no longer bear a
"likeness" to God, we are still made in God's "image." This divine
image within humankind is the basis in humanity for the incarnation and, hence, for the regeneration of all people in Christ.[41]

Christ Our Brother reiterates Möhler's theological anthropology. Adam holds that original sin, though devastating to humankind, did not completely eradicate the human longing for and
receptivity to God. "So faith in the Incarnation is not a miraculous flower growing in me without root; it has its root in my
natural capacity for God, in what the theologians call a *potentia
obedientialis*, and it is evoked therein by God."[42] God's "image"
remains in human nature, though it cannot be renewed by our
own efforts. The communion of humankind with God is possible
only in Christ, in "the God-man." Thus, all men and women are
drawn by the Spirit to acknowledge Jesus Christ as the "new
foundation" for their very humanity. Interestingly, even though
Adam was a student of Augustine's thought, he did not adopt the
bishop of Hippo's pessimistic assessment of humankind. Adam's
understanding of creation and grace closely resembles the more
optimistic thought of Möhler.

Adam also drew on the philosophical anthropology of Max
Scheler. As we noted in chapter 2, according to the phenomenologist, persons are not isolated selves but relational beings linked
to one another in many conscious and unconscious ways.[43] In his
Formalism in Ethics and Non-Formal Ethics of Values Scheler
contended that we only become persons in relation to one another, and a person becomes individuated only within relationships to other persons. The self realizes itself as it maintains its
commitments to others and lives in community. Moreover, because
of the mutuality among persons, one person's moral character
is shaped by the moral fiber of the community to which he or
she belongs. Indeed, personal existence is determined by "the
principle of the moral '*solidarity of all persons*.'" Scheler writes:

> The principle of solidarity in good and evil, in guilt and merit, states
> that there is a *collective* guilt and a *collective* merit in addition to

and independent of the guilt of which an individual is guilty and the merit that is 'self-merited'. . . . This principle further states that every person is not only responsible for his own individual acts but also originally *'coresponsible'* for all acts of others.[44]

Christ Our Brother presupposes Scheler's understanding of human solidarity. According to Adam, there is no such reality as an isolated "I." Insofar as we are separated from one another, this estrangement is a product of original sin. The primary reality of human life is the "we" whose source and goal is Jesus Christ. In union with Christ we are united with God and simultaneously become true persons and mature into the authentic human community. Jesus Christ abides, therefore, as the mediator between God and creation. Our communion with Christ is manifest at the Eucharist. In Adam's words:

> The Mass is never an individual act, but always a community act; and this not merely in the sense that the whole community should take part in it, but also and emphatically in the sense that participation in the one Bread gives the community its true cohesion and unity, and builds it up into the supernatural organism of the Body of Christ, in which form it is presented to the Father by the hand of the divine High Priest.[45]

Christ Our Brother is a theological synthesis of Scripture and tradition, historical research and phenomenology. Adam brought together biblical testimony regarding Christ as the head of the body, Augustine's vision of Christ as the mediator, Möhler's theological anthropology, and Scheler's understanding of personal existence. He accomplished this correlation while implicitly incorporating a critical sense of the formation of the New Testament. The end product of this synthesis is a text that forcefully attests to the unity of human life in Jesus Christ. For this reason, Fritz Hofmann has said, "One must reach back to theologians like Augustine and Johann Adam Möhler, if one wants to find such an intensive consciousness of the solid association of humankind in guilt and grace as encounters us in Adam."[46]

4. RECEPTION: ANOTHER BEST-SELLER

Christ Our Brother was well received by its readers, both German and non-German. Within two years, the 1930 edition was

translated into Dutch, English, French, and Italian. By 1940 it was
also available in Spanish and Portuguese, and by 1957 in Japanese.
In total, the book appeared in seven languages.[47]

Reviewers agreed with the praises of general readers. Short,
positive statements appeared in German periodicals. *Hochland*
declared that the book "outweighs in spiritual weight and religious
merit many serious scholarly and pious books."[48] The reviewer
judged that the book's thesis is correct: "Private devotion too easily
forgets [the mediation of Christ], for it runs the danger of moving away from the new Arianism of liberal theology to an actual
monophysitism which stays with Christ [as] God." Personal prayer
must "always renew and deepen itself in the liturgical piety of the
praying church." *Theologie und Glaube* observed that "[b]ecause
Adam calls attention to life's meaning and value in the eternal
truths, his text is above all timely."[49]

Evelyn Underhill, the respected authority on Christian prayer,
endorsed Adam's book in a review that also treated Karl Barth's
The Christian Life. Describing Barth as "an explosive theocentric
genius," she alerted readers to his "extreme transcendentalism," to
a theology "which ignores the corporate and incarnational aspects
of religion. . . ."[50] Then, turning to *Christ Our Brother*, she lauded
Karl Adam for shedding light on the reality that Barth neglects.
"Thus, by a strange turn of fortune's wheel, we find Professor
Adam—perhaps the most influential Roman Catholic writer of
modern Germany—insisting on the human side of the Christian
revelation, once regarded as the peculiar stronghold of Evangelical
piety." In Underhill's judgment, *Christ Our Brother* could be more
lucid, however, when treating some technical matters: "I am not
sure that I understand all that Professor Adam is trying to say in
this book, for his thought often seems muffled in the theological
clichés with which he has clothed it."

American journals also had words of praise for *Christ Our
Brother*. According to the *Catholic World* Adam stood "in the
vanguard of Catholic thought," along with Romano Guardini, Dietrich von Hildebrand, Jacques Maritain, and Giovanni Papini. "Of
all German interpreters of Catholic thought Karl Adam is the most
appreciated in English-speaking countries." He has demonstrated
"a penetrating intellect and an unusually clear mind," which mines
the riches of Scripture and tradition. "No source, ancient or modern, is ignored in this life of Christ, and the whole is presented

in a synthetic vision, in which each detail lights up the whole."[51] A similar assessment was presented in *Thought* which said that *Christ Our Brother* is an outstanding work, similar in importance to Léonce de Grandmaison's *Jesus Christ* (1928) and Archbishop Alban Goodier's *The Public Life of Our Lord Jesus Christ* (1930). In the reviewer's words: "With a power of synthesis like [Hilaire] Belloc's, Dr. Adam draws from St. Augustine, his master, and just as boldly, but humbly, interprets the very mind of Mother Church."[52]

While general readers and theologians responded with enthusiasm to *Christ Our Brother*, church officials were cautious.[53] The Diocese of Regensburg held a formal hearing on the book but reached no consensus as to whether revisions were required. The matter was referred to Rome. On June 10, 1933, Archbishop Conrad Gröber of Freiburg im Breisgau told Adam that the Holy Office wanted him to modify twenty-six pages of *Christ Our Brother*. It was at this same time that the bishop also informed the theologian of the Vatican's specific concerns regarding *The Spirit of Catholicism*.

Adam immediately went to work on both texts, which were temporarily withdrawn from bookstores. As noted previously, in the autumn of 1933 he submitted his changes for *The Spirit of Catholicism* to Rome. Prior to Christmas, 1933, he received formal approval of the modified text and then released the new edition to bookstores. In the spring of 1934 the professor presented the revised manuscript of *Christ Our Brother* to Bishop Johannes Sproll of the Diocese of Rottenburg-Stuttgart, the diocese with ecclesiastical jurisdiction over the Catholic faculty at the University of Tübingen. The revised text was given Sproll's imprimatur in April 1934, and it soon appeared at bookstores. Thus, within one year after the Vatican's censure, both *The Spirit of Catholicism* and *Christ Our Brother* were again available to readers.

The Holy Office's predominant criticism of *Christ Our Brother* was that the book neglects the divinity of Christ.[54] According to Rome's censors, this lacuna occurs because of a lack of conceptual clarity, and thus more precision is required in the text. These criticisms were taken seriously by Adam, as a comparison of the book's second and third editions shows. For example, whereas the second edition (1930) speaks of Jesus' "unique divine-human I-consciousness," the third edition (1934) talks about Jesus'

"I-consciousness uniquely rooted in God."[55] The earlier version declares that "the sure guarantee . . . of new life" is found "in the blessed humanity of Christ," but the later version contends that this guarantee resides "in the God-man and his creative powers as Savior."[56]

Once *Christ Our Brother* returned to the bookstores, it resumed its strong sales in Germany and around the world. Its presentation of Jesus Christ as the mediator between God and humankind struck a deep chord in its readers. The book quickly became a standard text to which other theologians like Yves Congar referred.[57] It left to these theologians the task of developing more precise ways of speaking about the humanity of Jesus Christ.

5. LEGACY: REGAINING CHALCEDON'S BALANCE

Almost forty years after the first edition of *Christus unser Bruder*, the Second Vatican Council promulgated a decree that emphasizes Jesus Christ as mediator. According to *Gaudium et Spes*, Christ is "the new man," "the perfect man," who restored humankind and raised our human nature to "a dignity beyond compare." Christ has mediated between God and creation. "For, by his Incarnation, he, the Son of God, has in a certain way united himself with each man. He worked with human hands, he thought with a human mind. He acted with a human will, and with a human heart he loved." Christ is indeed a member of the human family. "Born of the Virgin Mary, he has truly been made one of us, like to us in all things except sin."[58]

These words resemble those of Karl Adam.[59] "Jesus has a purely human consciousness," said Adam, "a purely human will, a purely human emotional life. He is a complete man."[60] Whether or not the writers of *Gaudium et Spes* were consciously drawing on *Christ Our Brother* need not concern us. What can be shown is that the conciliar text belongs to the current of thought which Adam had strengthened four decades earlier.

A watershed essay for the development of Catholic christology is Karl Rahner's "Chalkedon—Ende oder Anfang?" (1954). Though this essay appeared in English entitled "Current Problems in Christology," it is best represented by the German title's literal translation "Chalcedon—End or Beginning?"[61] This essay was first published in the three-volume collection, *Das Konzil von Chalke-don*, which commemorated the fifteen-hundredth anniversary of the Council of Chalcedon.[62] The work as a whole and Rahner's essay in particular prepared the way for the view of Christ as "the new man" that is articulated in *Gaudium et Spes*. Interestingly, "Chalcedon—End or Beginning?" builds on the ideas presented in Adam's *Christ Our Brother*.

According to Rahner, every correct statement of a truth prompts a fresh articulation of this same truth. Once we say something right about God, we seek to find another way to express this same insight. In Rahner's words: "The fact that every formula transcends itself (not because it is false, but precisely because it is true) is due . . . [to the] transcendence [that] is at work precisely in the movement of the formula itself."[63] This principle of "self-transcendence" means that, if we want to preserve the truth of the doctrine of Chalcedon, we must repeatedly express the doctrine's content in new terms. When we merely repeat the original formula, we likely distort it. Why? A correct formulation of a truth depends in part upon its historical context, which the truth itself transcends. When a doctrine is simply recited within a new setting, it can mean something different from what its writers intended. Therefore, to retain this timeless truth the old formulation must be balanced by a new formulation within language of the current situation.

In light of this thesis, how does "Chalcedon—End or Beginning?" build on *Christ Our Brother*? Adam's work of 1926 and Rahner's of 1954 are similar in their common concern to overcome a latent monophysitism in Catholic theology. In *Christ Our Brother*, Adam argued against "gnostic and monophysitic sects," for they "have removed all human features from the image of Jesus, or at least have not let His substantial likeness with us men stand forth in its full strength and emphasis."[64] Unfortunately, this disregard for Christ's humanity has occurred not only among explicitly monophysite Christians, Adam observed, but also among mainline Catholics. Thus, theologians must counter this one-sided tendency by calling attention to the humanity of Jesus Christ. As Fritz Hofmann noted, Adam deliberately set out to correct "a pull to monophysitism at work in modern devotion to Christ—a pull which was frequently not only unobserved by theology but also even accelerated by it."[65]

Thirty years after Adam, Rahner addressed the same concern. He criticized neoscholastic theologians for presenting the doctrine of Chalcedon in such a way that they unconsciously fostered a distorted view of Jesus Christ. In their desire to be faithful to the Council of Chalcedon, they often merely recited its formulations, thereby inadvertently allowing them to be misconstrued. In spite of their good intentions, the neoscholastic theologians conveyed a dehumanized view of Jesus Christ. Their mere recitation of the dogma thus fueled one of the falsehoods that Chalcedon was speaking against, namely, an emphasis on the divinity of Christ at the expense of his humanity. "And is it not true," noted Rahner, "that the almost unavoidable consequence of all this is a conception, which undoubtedly dominates the popular mind . . . and which could be put rather as follows: 'When our *Lord* (= *God*) *walked on earth* [italics mine] with his disciples, still humble and unrecognized . . . '?"[66] Rahner deliberately left the quoted sentence incomplete, for no matter what else is said the initial clause conveys the distortion. It indicates that Jesus Christ is God in the livery of a human being.

In "Chalcedon—End or Beginning?" Rahner called for a new attentiveness to the humanity of Jesus Christ. Chalcedon's statement regarding Christ's "unconfused and unchanged real human nature . . . implies," declared Rahner, "that the 'human nature' of the Logos possesses a genuine, spontaneous, free, spiritual, active centre, a human self-consciousness. . . . " Chalcedon's understanding of Christ's human self-agency ought no longer be overlooked. Indeed, if Christian faith and theology could regain a sense of the "active centre" of Christ's humanity, they could renew the church's appreciation of Christ as mediator. "Thus by maintaining the genuineness of Christ's humanity, room is left within his life for [human] achievement, and the possibility of a real Mediatorship and thus—if you will—of a real Messiahship is preserved."[67]

In 1957 Alois Grillmeier, the renowned patrologist, illumined the connection between Adam's christology and Rahner's. Adam worked within "the Scotist-Tiphanic school of Christology, whose principal concern is the loyal defense of Christ's humanity," observed Grillmeier.[68] Within the christological heritage of Duns Scotus (d. 1308) and Claudius Tiphanus (d. 1641) Adam's writings were "the most significant presentation of this Christology in German" in the first half of the twentieth century.[69] In fact, Adam represented a theological orientation that had preceded

Scotus and Tiphanus, namely, the *"Logos-anthropos"* christology of ancient Antioch. According to Grillmeier, Rahner too wanted to recover the wisdom of the *"Logos-anthropos"* school and of Duns Scotus, and—going beyond Adam—to incorporate it with the *"Logos-sarx"* christology of Cyril and the Alexandrian school.

We cannot say with certainty that Rahner studied *Christ Our Brother* with an eye to its *"Logos-anthropos"* christology. We do know, however, that Rahner read Adam's writings, for in 1956 he wrote an article on the Tübingen theologian's contribution to theology.[70] (We will review this essay in chapter 6.) Also, near the end of his life, Rahner spoke of Adam as one of the most important Catholic theologians of the 1920s and 1930s.[71] These statements by Rahner and the close similarity between "Chalcedon—End or Beginning?" and *Christ Our Brother* lead to the conclusion that Adam's work regarding the humanity of Christ served as one of the inspirations for Rahner's emphasis upon Jesus Christ as truly human.

Rahner differed from Adam, however, in his way of conceptualizing Christ's unity. To be sure, both Adam and Rahner were intent upon upholding the "hypostatic union." But they adopted different perspectives on this mystery. Adam asserted that Jesus Christ is one, uniting both a "divine nature" and a "human nature," but he did not explain how this is the case. In Adam's words: "Without investigating in detail the character of [Christ's] personal union, we may nevertheless say this much: that it involves such an intimate and essential conjunction of the human nature with the divine Word that this nature belongs essentially to the divine Word, that it is His humanity, and that the divine Word can say, 'I am this man.' "[72] This statement is representative of the Antiochene and Scotist-Tiphanic schools, both of which spoke of the hypostatic union as a *"unified unity."* In this view, human nature is united with the Logos, but the character of this unity is not open to philosophical and theological investigation. According to Grillmeier, this heritage "sees the humanity of Christ as being one, indeed as being personally one with the *Logos*, bypassing any further inquiry into the metaphysical structure of the unity."[73]

In contrast, Rahner used the notion of Christ's *"unifying unity"*—a notion employed by the Alexandrian school—within his dialectical understanding of personal identity. Love and independence relate to one another, said Rahner, in "direct proportion."

The greater a person's love of God, the greater the person's independence in relation to God. In other words, union with God does not destroy the self, rather it strengthens the self to move toward "genuine self-coherence" in the presence to God. Roughly speaking, then, Jesus Christ is the singular instance in history of the perfect union of grace and freedom, of "radical proximity" and authentic "independence." Rahner stated: "We must conceive of the relation between the Logos-Person and his human nature in just this case, that here *both* independence *and* radical proximity equally reach a unique and qualitatively incommensurable perfection, which nevertheless remains once and for all the perfection of a relation between Creator and creature."[74] In the hypostatic union, Jesus Christ is the perfect instance of unity with God and personal individuation.

In the light of Rahner's refined philosophical and theological account of Christ's unity, one shortcoming in Adam's christology becomes evident. Adam lacked any explication of the unity of Christ's divinity and humanity. This was Grillmeier's assessment.[75] It was also Rahner's criticism of the Scotist-Tiphanic school in general and implicitly of Adam's christology. "The weakness of the Christology associated with Scotus and Tiphanus," said Rahner, "is that it cannot distinguish these two concepts [nature and person]: it declares that the human nature and the divine nature are united in the Person of the Logos. When it is asked by what (i.e., by what uniting unity) they are united (i.e., in the united unity) the original formula is repeated, so that in fact no answer is forthcoming."[76] The theologian Robert Lachenschmid has explicitly applied Rahner's appraisal to Adam's work: "In our time in the German-speaking arena, the theory of pure unity, which stresses the unity of Christ,—though it brings no clarity to the unifying— found [its] most significant presentation in Karl Adam."[77]

Adam's christology stood within Antioch's *"Logos-anthropos"* heritage. As such, it possessed the strength of accentuating Christ's humanity and the weakness of not elaborating sufficiently on the hypostatic union. Having observed this, we must immediately distinguish Adam's thought from another twentieth-century attempt to recover the valid insights of Antiochene christology. Adam did not adopt the *Homo-Assumptus* theology of the Franciscan theologians Déodat de Basly and Léon Seiller, who sought to restore the ancient understanding that the divine Word assumed the full humanity of Jesus Christ.[78] Insofar as some expressions of their *Homo-Assumptus* theology may have implied a Nestorianism or adoptionism, these expressions were condemned in 1951 by Pius XII in his encyclical *Sempiternus Rex Christi*.[79] However, this judgment did not pertain to Adam's work, for he did not discuss Christ's unity in such a way as to suggest that Christ possessed two wholly independent "natures."[80]

In conclusion, Adam and Rahner were critical of the implicit monophysitism in Catholic theology and piety. Both theologians accentuated Christ's humanity, but they differed in their ways of thinking about Christ's personal unity. This difference can be attributed in part to their respective places in the history of recent Catholic theology. It is fair to say that Rahner picked up where Adam left off in christology. He elaborated on what the Tübingen theologian had reclaimed, namely, the humanity of Christ, and he tackled the issue which Adam left unresolved, that is, the character of the hypostatic union.

This continuity between the work of Adam and that of Rahner points beyond itself to the resemblance between Adam's christology and that of *Gaudium et Spes*.[81] The conciliar decree stresses the humanity of Christ in the title for article 22: "Christ the New Man," and this article upholds the completeness of Christ's humanity when it insists that human nature "was assumed, not absorbed" in Christ. It also describes Christ as "the perfect man," who "worked with human hands," "thought with a human mind," "acted with a human will," and loved "with a human heart." It points out that "by his incarnation" the Son of God "has in a certain way united himself with each man." In short, *Gaudium et Spes* allows no hint of monophysitism as it accentuates Christ's human nature. In this, it confirms what Adam promoted in the late 1920s and what Rahner accentuated in the 1950s: Jesus Christ is not only truly one with God, he is also truly one with us. Christ is our brother.

In 1934 the church historian Alec Vidler called attention to the fact that the Holy Office had not condemned *Christ Our Brother*, and he interpreted Rome's toleration of the book as a positive sign. Ten years earlier the Vatican had signaled the continuation of its restrictions against historical-critical research by condemning the revised edition of the scriptural commentary

Manuel biblique (1905-11, 1923) by Fulcran G. Vigouroux and Louis Bacuez. However, something had changed between 1923 and 1934, for the Holy Office had not placed *Christ Our Brother* on the Index of Forbidden Books. Vidler declared that the acceptance of Adam's christology could only be taken to mean that Pius X's "pronouncements and decisions are being less rigorously applied" by Pius XI.[82]

In Vidler's judgment *Christ Our Brother* was a bold work. It did not conform to the two dominant forms of Catholic theology. It was neither the "cold and rigid intellectualism" of the neoscholastic manuals, nor was it the "sentimental piety" of Catholic spiritual writings. In addition, it "protests against 'the one-sided prominence given to Christ's divinity and the obscuration of His humanity' in traditional orthodoxy as commonly interpreted." In his book, observed Vidler, Adam introduced an incarnational theology that highlighted the self-emptying of Jesus Christ: "The tendency of his own Christology, if we may judge rather from what [Adam] leaves unsaid than from what he says, seems to be towards a position that is equivalent to, though formally distinct from a kenotic theory of the Incarnation."

More than fifty years after these comments, we know that Vidler was correct on two points. First, Pius XI permitted a less theologically restrictive atmosphere between the wars, and, as a result, theologians took up neglected issues. Adam, Guardini, Jungmann, and others set out to recover Chalcedon's insight that Jesus Christ is truly human.[83] Subsequently, this emphasis on Christ's humanity was pursued in sophisticated philosophical and theological categories by Rahner, and it was eventually confirmed in *Gaudium et Spes*. In 1934 Vidler had predicted that "the process of neutralizing the anti-modernist excesses will be a long and delicate one." This process was indeed gradual, but it did occur in a movement that runs from Guardini, Jungmann, and Adam through Rahner to Vatican II.

Second, Vidler was correct too when he noted that *Christ Our Brother* has similarities to a kenotic christology, for it "does not say that Christ during his life on earth was omniscient."[84] Also, it explicitly stresses Christ's "condescension" to assume human nature. In the incarnation there has occurred "the condescension of the divine to the human."[85] Appealing to Philippians 2:7, Adam conceived of the incarnation as the event in which Christ had in some sense relinquished his divine stature.[86] However, Adam left much "unsaid," as Vidler has noted. He offered no explication of his notion of condescension, just as he gave no explanation of his concept of the hypostatic union.

A christology "from below" begins with the man Jesus. It develops out of an understanding of the humanity of Christ. Adam did this in *Christ Our Brother*. Moreover, an ascending christology is somehow anchored in the testimony of the New Testament. Adam's christology possessed this feature, too, as we will see in our study of *The Son of God*.

4
Using Scripture in Christology (1931-1933)

In an interview in 1982 Edward Schillebeeckx recalled an incident from his life that is pertinent to our study of Karl Adam's christology. Soon after beginning his theological studies at the University of Louvain in September 1939, Schillebeeckx found himself bored. In his words: "Theology—and theology at Louvain in those days was Thomas Aquinas' *Summa Theologiae*—meant nothing to me."[1] When his disinterest in his courses became known to the Dominican director of studies, Schillebeeckx was called to the director's office, where he acknowledged that theology was much less exciting for him than philosophy. The director, a professor of philosophy, admonished Schillebeeckx, saying " 'That is quite wrong. You must really try to work your way into theology. If the *Summa* doesn't mean anything to you, begin with Karl Adam.' " Immediately afterwards, Schillebeeckx began to read Adam's books and, as a result, became increasingly engaged in theological inquiry.

What was it about Adam's work that helped to ignite Schillebeeckx's love of theology? Three things. First, Adam did not rely on "neoscholastic rationalism." Schillebeeckx has stated: Adam "analysed and expounded all the dogmas of the Church from the Trinity to the Immaculate Conception and didn't use a single scholastic term in all his work." Second, the Tübingen theologian provided a synthesis of theology and philosophy. Schillebeeckx has remembered: "When I read Karl Adam's books, however, I began to realize that it was certainly possible to form a solid link between theology and philosophy, with its references to the religious question." Third, Adam incorporated the findings of biblical

research into his texts on Jesus Christ. Regarding Adam, Schillebeeckx has written:

> He was one of the first Catholic theologians to make use of [biblical
> research]. But Catholic exegesis did not have much to offer in those
> days and Catholics did not read the work of Protestant exegetes.
> They only began to do that after the war. Karl Adam, though,
> studied the Bible. There are splendid pages in his books on the
> 'psychology' of Jesus, containing elements of concern for the *man*
> Jesus that was to develop later.[2]

Schillebeeckx's reminiscences set the stage for our study of
Adam's use of Scripture in christology. At the start of the previous
chapter, I recalled Walter Kasper's observation that recent Catholic
christology has experienced two major trends, the recovery of
Chalcedon's doctrine regarding the humanity of Christ and the
inclusion of the results of biblical study. Chapter 3 treated Adam's
contribution to the first of these currents through his publication
of *Christ Our Brother*. Now, this fourth chapter examines Adam's
pioneering efforts in regard to the second movement. It focuses
on Adam's scriptural interpretation in *The Son of God*, entitled in
German, *Jesus Christus*.

Beginning in the late 1920s, Adam wanted to provide Catholics with a fresh understanding of the person and work of Jesus
Christ. He was intent on presenting a living reality, a 'person' who
walks with people on life's way and leads them to the fullness of
life. He did not want to present Jesus Christ as primarily an idea,
as a conceptual construct. Such a representation was conveyed,
he believed, by neoscholasticism. Adam aimed at directing Christians' attention to the risen Christ disclosed in the gospels. Hence,
Adam wrote:

> An awe-inspiring figure is the Christ of the Gospels, planted like a
> *tremendum mysterium* in our midst. He stands forth challengingly,
> a riddle which must be solved, a question which must be answered.
> He stands before us as our fate. . . . We cannot look away or close
> our ears, we must watch and listen. "Lord, incline my heart unto
> Thy testimonies" (Ps 118:36).[3]

To reach his goal of discussing the living Christ, Adam relied
on the Bible as the written source of the church's images and stories about God and Jesus Christ. Twenty years of patristic research

had sharpened Adam's historical consciousness and his use of critical methods. But he did not want his biblical interpretation to be primarily historical. If he depended solely on historical-critical methods, he could follow the route of the "original quest" for the historical Jesus and end up where the liberal Protestants had.[4] Adam needed a different way of using the Bible in his theology. He required an approach that regarded Scripture as testimony to the risen Christ, who is present to the people of every age. He adopted, therefore, a literary hermeneutics, a way of reading the New Testament that elicited its images and narratives of Jesus Christ.

This fourth chapter shows that in his christology Adam employed what we would now call a postcritical hermeneutics.[5] To be sure, there are moments when Adam's comments suggest that his scriptural interpretation is precritical, as though he viewed the gospels as biographies of Jesus.[6] But these statements do not represent the theologian's central intention.[7] Adam was aware of the conclusions of historical-critical research but viewed the Bible as more than a source for historical information. He aimed at apprehending the "subject matter" of the New Testament and, thus, attempted to take an approach to these texts that would capture their verbal sense. In order to develop this thesis, I will discuss the context of *The Son of God*, especially in terms of precritical, critical, and postcritical forms of biblical hermeneutics, and then review the text itself. Subsequently, I shall explain the book's theological method, its reception, and finally its theological legacy in the works of Walter Kasper and Edward Schillebeeckx.

1. CONTEXT: THREE KINDS OF INTERPRETATION

In the 1930s scholars utilized many of the historical-critical methods on which we rely today.[8] They accepted in general the canons of modern historiography, which in the early 1900s Ernst Troeltsch specified as the principles of correlation, analogy, and criticism.[9] They were familiar in particular with source criticism. Julius Wellhausen had used it in his study of the Pentateuch, and H. J. Holtzmann depended on it for his two-source theory of the gospels. Also, scholars were gaining familiarity with form criticism. Hermann Gunkel undertook this "research into literary types" in his studies of the Pentateuch at the turn of the century, and beginning in 1919 Karl Ludwig Schmidt, Martin Dibelius, and Rudolf Bultmann applied form criticism to the New Testament.

What was lacking in the 1930s was redaction criticism and methods in literary analysis. It was not until the 1950s that Günther Bornkamm, Hans Conzelmann, and Willi Marxsen treated each gospel as a literary unit shaped by an editor in order to convey an understanding of God and Jesus Christ to a specific Christian community.[10] In addition, the use of "literary-hermeneutical approaches" in biblical studies has emerged only within the past twenty years.[11] Some of these works build on the efforts of René Wellek and Austin Warren in "new literary criticism," and others rely on the studies of Ferdinand de Saussure and A. J. Greimas in structuralism. The adoption of methods such as these in biblical hermeneutics since the time of Karl Adam is significant, for it means that we are better equipped to comment on Adam's scriptural interpretation than Adam himself was.

Adam provided little commentary on his use of the Bible in theology. He was clear about his goal. He wanted to discuss the risen Christ, the Christ of dogma. "In history," he said, "it is the 'dogmatic' Christ, the God-man who lives and works in continuous existence."[12] The professor insisted, too, that he was not depending primarily upon the application of historical-critical methods to the Bible. According to Adam, the hermeneutics of Adolf von Harnack and other liberal theologians produced a picture of an individual who never in fact existed. "There was," he said, "no such thing in history as a purely 'historic' Jesus—that is to say, a merely human Jesus. Such a figure is pure fiction, a literary phantom."[13] But having said what he was not doing, Adam did not explain his means for reaching his goal of a christology devoted to the living reality, Jesus Christ.

Why did Adam say so little about what was so important to his christology? Why did he not explain his interpretation of the Bible? One of the reasons was most likely that Adam could not explicitly comment on scriptural hermeneutics without risking censure by the Vatican. For almost forty years Pius X's 1907 condemnation of modernism prevented open discussions among Catholic Scripture scholars and theologians regarding their interpretations of the Bible. It was only in 1943, when Pius XII issued *Divino afflante Spiritu*, that Catholics were permitted the limited use of historical methods in the study of the Bible.[14] Adam could not explain, therefore, that he wanted to employ some of the methods and conclusions of biblical research and then to go beyond these to another kind of biblical interpretation.

A second reason for Adam's silence on his use of Scripture is that he lacked the conceptual categories to talk about how he intended to appeal to Scripture in theology. He did not have a language in which to talk about a biblical text as a literary whole whose meaning depends more on factors internal to the text—for example, genre, plot, and characterization—than on external factors—for instance, an editor's situation and intention. Today, we can give this commentary by distinguishing among precritical, critical, and postcritical forms of biblical interpretation.

Precritical interpretation regards biblical accounts as descriptions of what actually occurred.[15] It assumes a direct correspondence between the Bible's words and a state of affairs in history. In other words, it connects a text's verbal sense with a historical referent, just as one would do with a newspaper's report. For example, a precritical view treats the pericopes about Jesus' transfiguration as eyewitness recollections of how Jesus appeared and what was said on a mountain in Palestine. It assumes that the disparities among these pericopes can in principle be resolved. In a precritical view, the same event is being described when the accounts say that the disciples were "afraid" (Mk 9:6), that the disciples "were heavy with sleep" (Lk 9:32), that Jesus said, "Rise, and have no fear" (Mt 17:7). Inconsistencies in the biblical accounts are reconciled in order to provide an "exact" report of an occurrence and then to line up these occurrences so as to yield a chronology of the life of Christ. In the 1920s a precritical hermeneutics was operative in the Latin manuals like Christian Pesch's *Compendium Theologiae Dogmaticae*.

Critical interpretation perceives the Bible to be a collection of communities' attempts to express the transcendent meaning of relatively commonplace events. By means of the canons and procedures of critical methods, this approach endeavors to locate a biblical text in its earliest setting and to highlight the intention behind the text in this context.[16] By distinguishing between facts and their interpretation, this type of hermeneutics assumes that the state of affairs which prompted a biblical testimony can be known apart from this testimony itself and that this state of affairs can be described in nonreligious terms. Critical interpretation regards the pericopes about Jesus' transfiguration, then, as primarily post-Easter testimonies in which Jesus' followers read their experience of the risen Christ back into Jesus' life.

Critical interpretation was subtly adopted by Catholic scholars in the 1920s and 1930s, in spite of the Vatican's prohibition. During the years that Adam wrote *Christ Our Brother* and *The Son of God*, other Catholics published books on Jesus and the gospels in which they implicitly relied to varying degrees on the results of historical-critical research.[17] These books include such works as *L'Evangile de Jésus-Christ* (1928) by Marie Josef Lagrange, *Jésus-Christ, sa personne, son message* (1928) by Léonce de Grandmaison, *The Public Life of Our Lord Jesus Christ* (1930) by Alban Goodier, *La vie et l'enseignement de Jésus-Christ notre Seigneur* (1931) by Jules Lebreton, *Jésus-Christ, sa vie, sa doctrine, son oeuvre* (1933) by Ferdinand Prat, and *Das Leben Jesu im Lande und Volke Israel* (1933) by F. M. William.

Postcritical interpretation follows the verbal sense of a biblical text, especially of narratives.[18] It rests on the conviction that what a narrative like a gospel is about can be determined, in the last analysis, by neither its supposed historical referent nor the surmised intention of its editor or early communities. Rather, a narrative's meaning must be ultimately judged on the basis of elements internal to the text itself. In short, a story must be read on its own terms. Such an approach directs the reader to enter into a narrative's world in order to know its main characters through their interaction with one another and their world's circumstances and events. If we want to understand the meaning of Jesus' transfiguration in Mark's Gospel, we must see this event in relation both to other events within the story—for instance, Jesus' baptism and the empty tomb—and also to the pattern of Jesus' interaction with other key figures in the story—for instance, God, Satan, and the disciples. In sum, postcritical hermeneutics assumes that a text's meaning is primarily a function of its literary form.

Postcritical interpretation was born at the turn of the century with the recognition of the importance of biblical eschatology for understanding Jesus and the gospels. Scholars like Johannes Weiss, Wilhelm Wrede, and Albert Schweitzer undermined the quest for the historical Jesus, for they insisted that Jesus and his post-Easter followers proclaimed a reality outside of history. The effort to move beyond historical-critical methods was secured with the publication of Barth's *Epistle to the Romans* (1918) and *Church Dogmatics* (1932-1967).[19] Barth was committed to an approach to the Bible that attended to the literary sense of a text so that the witness to God's Word might be faithfully conveyed.[20]

Karl Adam concurred with Barth on the use of the Bible in theology. He judged that the Scriptures are more than a resource for historical reconstructions of Jesus' ministry and early Christian communities' beliefs about Jesus. While he was aware of the conclusions of source criticism and form criticism, he held that these findings need not detract from the Bible's integrity and witness to God and Jesus Christ. Even though Adam disagreed with Barth on natural theology and the *analogia entis*, he agreed with the Reformed theologian in wanting to focus theology on the transcendent reality to which the Bible attests.[21] This intention is evident in *The Son of God*. As my summary will show, Adam constructed this book's christology by means of scripturally based images of Jesus Christ.

2. TEXT: "THE SON OF GOD"

The incarnation is the central mystery of the Christian faith, says Adam in *The Son of God*. In Jesus Christ, God has become a human being. What is extraordinary is not just that God has lifted up humankind to join in the divine life, but that God has stepped down to assume the human condition. "The Christian gospel announces primarily," Adam insists, "not an ascent of humanity to the heights of the divine in a transfiguration, an apotheosis, a deification of human nature, but a descent of the Godhead, of the divine Word, to the state of bondage of the purely human."[22] This thesis is pursued in eight chapters.

A comprehensive understanding of Jesus is threatened on two sides, declares Adam. On the one side, it is challenged by liberal Protestantism's "invention" of the historical Jesus. On the other side, it is jeopardized by the persistence of "monophysite tendencies" in the church. For a christology to be a balanced presentation of Christian belief it must treat the "God-man," the "Christ of dogma," who shares in human life as well as divine life. It must show that Christ has brought about the "new humanity" of all people.

Christology depends on a self-involving method that allows for singular events in human affairs. As the "Phenomenological School" has pointed out, some kinds of investigation require not a "neutral method" but one that recognizes an "essential relation" between the knowing subject and its object.[23] This is the case in theology, which must be a "reverent inquiry" as well as a "critical" one. Theology displays respect for its object in an "open-mindedness" that acknowledges the occurrence of miracles. Therefore, it cannot be strictly bound by the historian's criteria of correlation and analogy as these principles are spelled out by Troeltsch. Theology places demands upon the whole person, upon the inquirer's mind, heart, and will. It is not content with "truth out there" but includes "truth as experienced," truth that requires a corresponding way of life.[24]

It is inappropriate, states Adam, to distinguish between the "historical Jesus"—the picture of Jesus produced by modern historiography—and the "Christ of faith." To be sure, this distinction may seem applicable to the New Testament because of the way the Scriptures were formed. As source criticism has shown, Paul's writings were the earliest; the Gospels of Matthew, Mark, and Luke came about in such a way that today we speak of the "synoptic problem"; and the Gospel of John possesses a unique literary style which makes it stand apart from the goals of the others. Also, as form criticism has demonstrated, biblical texts are based upon oral traditions which have been gathered and edited into written forms. Because of the findings of source criticism and form criticism, modern critics beginning with H. S. Reimarus (1694–1768) have questioned the truthfulness of the New Testament. These people have erred, however, in that they have failed to recognize the value of the living tradition, the church's process of handing on the truth from one generation to the next.[25] When one acknowledges the validity of tradition, one sees that the testimonies which led to the New Testament must be true, for the early Christian communities would have had ways to check their veracity. As a result, what was faithfully passed on orally within the earliest Christian assemblies has come to us in the Pauline letters and the gospels. If we want to increase our knowledge of the person attested to in the New Testament, therefore, we must not analyze the Scriptures on the basis of modern historiography's criteria, but must work with the New Testament's images of Jesus.

According to Adam, the gospels present Jesus as a "born leader" who drew people to his mission and himself.[26] In the gospels he is an attractive individual, possessing exceptional health as exhibited in his lengthy walks away from the villages. He is bright, as is evident in his debates with the authorities. He is decisive, as revealed in his insistence that one either say "yes" or "no." He radiates a deep love for ordinary life, as his parables and miracles demonstrate. In sum, the gospels present Jesus as a whole person, indeed "the complete man."[27] More than this, he is a "hero" who refuses to succumb to Satan's temptations and is ready to assume the suffering of others. He is "a regal figure" who "washes the feet of his disciples." Given that he is simultaneously regal (divine) and humble (human), he is the singular individual in whom "two sets of lines meet to form a living unity."[28]

The gospels depict Jesus as a man who obeyed God and died out of faithfulness to God. Jesus is the son who was motivated by his "unreserved surrender to his Father's will." Indeed, he calls God "Abba" and often withdraws to a solitary place in order to pray. For Jesus, this "Abba" is an "all-operative, creative God."[29] God is "all-holy" and, hence, above human affairs. Yet, God is "infinitely gracious," committed to human well-being.

The gospels' depictions of Jesus prompt one to ask, Who is this individual? The answer, given by Adam, is that Jesus is both "the son of man" and "the Son of God." Jesus is the son of man, for he proclaims the coming of "the kingdom of God" and welcomes it by such actions as healing the sick. He is not, however, solely an apocalyptic figure, as Albert Schweitzer contended in *The Quest of the Historical Jesus* (1906). Jesus, the son of man, is not only the "world judge in the future," he is also the "redeemer in the present." Therefore, he is the Son of God. When Jesus announces the coming of God's kingdom, "he makes his own person the central point of his teaching."[30] His disciples decide in favor of the kingdom when they follow him and confess that "Jesus is the Christ." Jesus himself implies his "divine nature" when he declares that "no one knows the Father except the Son and anyone to whom the Son chooses to reveal him" (Mt 11:27).

Jesus' self-understanding as the Son of God is confirmed when Jesus is raised from the dead. All that Jesus had proclaimed and all that he lived and died for was endorsed by God in Jesus' resurrection. At the resurrection God set "his unbreakable seal

upon the life of Jesus."[31] And, with Jesus' appearances the disciples began to understand his mission and identity. Throughout
Jesus' life, the disciples had awaited their leader's earthly triumph,
and they were distraught when Jesus was put to death. But they
came of age when they encountered the risen Jesus. According to
the vision theories of David Friedrich Strauss and Ernest Renan,
the disciples underwent something wholly subjective when they
met Jesus beyond death. But these theories have no basis in the
testimony of the New Testament. St. Paul linked Jesus' resurrection
with the disappearance of Jesus' body. He would not have done
so if he held that the resurrection appearances had no basis in
the material world. In the resurrection appearances, the disciples
experienced something that had both subjective and objective
elements. They changed their lives in response to an objective
reality. Then, at Pentecost, they were drawn by the Holy Spirit to
a fuller comprehension of Jesus' person and work.

But why did Jesus die on the cross? Adam argues that Jesus'
death was a matter of justice. Someone had to make amends for
the wrong done to God, and this person had to be one who
could freely bring human nature before God's "wrath." It was not
enough that the divine nature had been united with humankind
in Jesus. The incarnation had to culminate in the Son of God's
expiatory sacrifice. The Son "accomplishes [this sacrifice] by an
act of supreme moral freedom, a spiritual act of heroism past all
conception, for the honour of the Father and for the salvation
of mankind."[32] Justice has been served and harmony restored to
creation, which had been disordered by sin.[33] God's justice and
mercy met when the incarnation came to completion in Jesus'
suffering, death, and resurrection.

In *The Son of God* Adam developed his insight that Christianity's central truth concerns God's entrance into human life. The
heart of the mystery is that "the Word became flesh" (Jn 1:14).
Adam summed up his view in a statement that conveys the kenotic
thrust of his incarnational christology:

> We are asked to believe in the incarnation of God, that is to say,
> we are asked to accept the fact that God so humbled himself as
> to "empty" himself, to use St. Paul's words, of his Divine majesty
> (Phil 2:6,7). In that he thus "emptied himself" of his own power

and glory in order to become one of us, he manifests his own unconditioned, absolute freedom—the freedom of God.[34]

3. THE THEOLOGICAL METHOD

The Son of God is an intriguing book. On the one hand, it presents such a coherent, concrete picture of Jesus that even today it can engage its reader. On the other hand, it seems too coherent. It appears to be too synthetic and not sufficiently analytic. One cannot help but judge that the book smooths over a variety of methodological issues. These impressions prompt us to ask about Adam's use of Scripture, his reliance on the doctrine of Chalcedon, and his description of Jesus as "the complete man."

To understand the biblical hermeneutics in *The Son of God* we must consider not only what Adam says about Scripture but also the way he actually uses it. His comments are confusing, for he acknowledges the results of source criticism and form criticism, but he rejects the distinction between the historical Jesus and the Christ of faith. Moreover, throughout the book, Adam cites historical-critical studies of the New Testament such as those by Bultmann, Dibelius, Gerhard Kittel, and Hermann Strack. Nevertheless, he does not ultimately depend on these studies' results for his presentation of Jesus. Given these ambiguities in Adam's commentary, we must examine how Adam has actually utilized the New Testament.

The Son of God is not a biography of Jesus. It does not even propose a rough chronology of Jesus' life. Instead, it gives sketches of Jesus' ministry and his passion—sketches consisting of scriptural images—and it weaves these together in such a way as to convey the coherence of Jesus' ministry, suffering, death, and resurrection. Further, *The Son of God* does not appeal to christological titles like "Lord," "Christ," and "Son." It works only with the titles "son of man" and "Son of God." In the case of the latter, it does not presume either that Jesus explicitly called himself the "Son of God" or that this title was applied to Jesus during his life. Rather, the book associates Christians' ascription of "Son of God" to Jesus with Jesus' addressing God as "Abba." With these emphases alone, the book evinces a historical critical appreciation of the New Testament.

But *The Son of God* also displays Adam's effort to move beyond critical hermeneutics to a more literary interpretation of the gospels. He maintains that christology must work with the testimony of tradition. This recognition means in practice that the central chapters of *The Son of God* are a tapestry of images of Jesus—images derived in part from the gospels. Jesus is depicted walking with Peter on Galilean paths, healing the centurion's son, and telling the parable of the good Samaritan. With this attentiveness to biblical descriptions, Adam exhibits a postcritical hermeneutics.

This understanding of Adam's use of Scripture has been corroborated by Adam's former student Heinrich Fries, now professor emeritus at the University of Munich. According to Fries, Adam did not want to give a historical reconstruction of Jesus' life, but rather aimed at illumining images of Jesus in the New Testament. In the words of Fries, "Adam did not present a life of Jesus, but he tried to sketch out the figure of Jesus Christ, as it is to be lifted up out of the New Testament and was articulated in the faith of the church."[35] Adam was intent on crafting this kind of scriptural account of Jesus because, notes Fries, he wanted to bring his reader to "a decision" about Jesus Christ.[36] He intended to direct the reader's attention to Christ alive in the Spirit.

Fries has supported his view of Adam's scriptural interpretation by quoting the following passage from *The Son of God*:

> More than this, there was once a man, within historical times, who, as a child of the Jewish people, knew only of one God of heaven and earth, of a unique Father in heaven, and stood in reverential awe before this heavenly Father: a man whose meat was to do the will of this Father, who from his earliest youth in good and bad had sought and loved this will alone, whose whole life was one prayer; a man, further, whose whole being was so firmly united with this Divine will, that by its omnipotence he healed the sick and restored the dead to life; a man, finally, who was so intimately and exclusively dedicated to this will, that he never swerved from it, so that not even the slightest consciousness of sin ever oppressed him, so that never a cry for penance and forgiveness passed his lips, so that even in dying he begged pardon not for himself but for others. And this man from the intimacy of his union with God could say to afflicted mortals, "Thy sins are forgiven thee". And it

was this holy man, utterly subject as he was to God throughout his whole life, absorbed as he was in God, awestruck as he stood before him, who asserted, as if it were the most natural and obvious thing in the world, that he was to be the judge of the world at the last day, that he was the suffering servant of God, nay more, that he was the only-begotten Son of God and consubstantial with him, and could say of himself, "I and the Father are one."[37]

According to Fries, this passage displays Adam's kind of writing in general and his use of Scripture in particular. It recalls details of the gospels' testimony and inserts scriptural verses into this recollection. It is descriptive to the point of being lyrical. As a result, it is also engaging and evokes the gospels' images of Jesus in the reader's imagination. Of course, admits Fries, in the second half of the twentieth century we may not be struck by Adam's figuration, for we now speak in ways that are more "prosaic, flat, technical and sparing." Furthermore, critical exegesis has made us uneasy with the weaving of biblical phrases and allusions into a theological text. But in Adam's day things were otherwise. Ordinary language was more poetic, contends Fries. In this context, Adam could make imaginative associations that may puzzle us now.

I wish to expand on Fries's comments by calling attention to two aspects of the passage quoted above from *The Son of God*. First, we should note the passage's figuration. Adam writes that Jesus, "a child of the Jewish people," "stood in reverential awe" before his Father. From "his earliest youth" he made his life "one prayer" to God. He "healed the sick and restored the dead to life," and, as he was dying, "he begged pardon not for himself but for others." He said then what he had previously stated to others, " 'Thy sins are forgiven thee.' " This "holy man" was "the judge of the world"—the judge who was "the suffering servant of God." Moreover, this holy man, judge, and servant, was "the only begotten Son of God." These imaginative statements and others like them are woven into *The Son of God*.

Second, we should observe that not only is this passage descriptive, it is also laden with biblical allusions. This "child of the Jewish people" was the son of Mary and Joseph, of the house of David (Mt 1:18). He stood before God "in reverential awe" like Isaiah before the heavenly throne (Is 6). In "his earliest youth" he had remained with the teachers in the temple, his " 'Father's house' " (Lk 3:49). He "healed the sick," including Simon's mother-in-law (Mk 1:30-31) and the centurion's servant (Mt 8:5-13), and he "restored the dead to life" in the persons of the son of the widow of Naim (Lk 7:11-17) and Lazarus (Jn 11). Jesus "never swerved from" God's will, as he underwent the temptations in the desert (Lk 4:1-13) and anguished in the Garden of Gethsemane over his impending death (Lk 22:39-46). On the cross, he "begged pardon" for his executioners (Lk 23:34), just as he had said, "Thy sins are forgiven thee" to the paralytic (Mk 2:5) and to the adulterous woman (Lk 7:48). He was the world's "judge" who would come as the son of man (Mk 13:26) and separate the sheep from the goats (Mt 25:31-46). He was the "suffering servant" who had foreseen his death (Mk 8:31) and been led like a sheep to slaughter (Mk 14:53; 15:1,16). He was the "Son of God" who declared, " 'I and the Father are one' " (Jn 10:30). Each of Adam's images has an implicit tie to a biblical passage.

Having seen the descriptive language and biblical images in the above passage from *The Son of God*, we can better appreciate Fries's explanation of why Adam opted for this kind of writing. According to Fries, Adam was intent on reflecting on the risen Christ so that Christians could renew their commitment to and understanding of their Lord. He wanted to link christology to his readers' experience, to their actual Christian faith. Therefore, he did not allow the results of historical-critical research to determine the aim and scope of his christology, but chose to employ biblical images to provide an account of the 'person' whom Christians worship at the Eucharist and follow in their everyday service of their neighbors.

From today's vantage point, however, we can see inadequacies in Adam's literary reading of the gospels. The emphasis in *The Son of God* upon Jesus' health and vitality indicates that Adam has imposed upon the New Testament the *Lebensphilosophie* of the 1920s. This imposition is evident, too, in Adam's talk about Jesus as "the hero" and the "heroic" qualities of the Christian life. With this kind of language, Adam is not so much highlighting scriptural testimony as he is responding to Nietzsche's criticism of Christianity. Further, in light of the development of literary-hermeneutical approaches to the Bible, Adam's simultaneous treatment of the entire New Testament is unsophisticated. It disregards differences in literary genre and in the theology conveyed by each text as a coherent unit. In hindsight we can see that Adam's attempt to take a postcritical approach to the New Testament could be better executed by means of interpretive methods that are now available to Scripture scholars and theologians.

But there is more to Adam's theological method than a literary approach to the Bible. It also draws on the Christian tradition, in particular, the doctrine of Chalcedon and Anselm's satisfaction theory. Adam does not, however, directly discuss the formulations of Chalcedon or Anselm, nor does he employ their technical terms. Instead, he simply alludes to these teachings and relies on commonplace words to express complex theological notions.

For example, Adam concludes his description of Jesus' activities by applying an intriguing, though not entirely lucid metaphor to Jesus. Adam describes Jesus speaking with inner authority in his debates with the Pharisees and simultaneously identifying with ordinary people in his outreach to prostitutes and tax collectors. Then, the professor says that Jesus' actions manifested two "lines" that come together at a single point. In Adam's words: "[I]t is quite impossible to determine the point where these two sets of lines meet to form a living unity. A dominating nature, a regal figure is Jesus, and yet he washes the feet of his disciples."[38] This statement alludes to Chalcedon's teaching that Jesus Christ is two "natures" in one "person."

This reference to Chalcedon's doctrine has both a strength and a weakness. On the one hand, the simple image of two lines joining at one point is easy to remember. Readers can recall it when they are reflecting on the mystery of Jesus Christ. Hence, the metaphor provides a quick entry point into the formulation of Chalcedon. On the other hand, talk about two lines and a point of unity glosses over difficulties in understanding what Chalcedon meant in its talk about two "natures" and one "person." As Robert Lachenschmid has pointed out, Adam proposes a "theory of pure unity" regarding Jesus' divine and human natures, but "brings no clarity to the oneness."[39]

The Son of God is also grounded in Anselm's satisfaction theory. Adam asks, Why was it necessary that the Son of God die on the cross? And, he answers that it was a matter of justice which can be best understood in terms of the metaphor of self-emptying, kenosis. The wrong done by the first Adam could not be simply forgotten, it had to be rectified. "Somehow or other the way of redemption had to be a way of justice, of the creature's reparation and expiation." Divine justice had to be satisfied on behalf of humankind, but a human being could not make the appropriate amends. Thus, God stepped in, "emptying himself" out of love for creation. The divine Word became a human being, Jesus of Nazareth, and Jesus chose to make infinite amends to God by dying on the cross. Jesus poured out his very self in his passion and death, and this act by the God-man fulfilled the requirements of justice. "If justice demands an infinite expiation, love gives an infinite expiation. Justice and love meet in the Incarnation of the Son of God."[40]

This presentation of Anselm's satisfaction theory is, on the one hand, easy to follow. It reads well and on one level makes sense. The image of giving one's self away for another person is one that can be grasped by anyone who is committed to a spouse, friend, or parent. Thus, it seems intelligible to say that since God's justice was violated by humankind, it had to be restored by a human being capable of self-emptying to the point of displaying total dedication to God. On the other hand, Adam does not fully explain this notion of self-emptying as applied to God and divine justice. We are left unsure as to why God required this act of kenosis. In short, Adam has provided more of a summary of Anselm's theory than a fresh insight into it.

Questions persist after a reading of Adam's text as they do after a reading of Anselm's *Cur Deus Homo*. Is it appropriate to speak of God as "angry" and needing to be "satisfied"? Why was an absurd death a repayment? What does it mean to speak about the kenosis of God? the kenosis of Jesus? By not delving into these kinds of issues, Adam avoided the limitations of Anselm's theory. He relinquished theological precision on this matter for the sake of a presentation that is accessible to a wide range of readers.

Adam did indeed draw on the riches of the Christian tradition in his christology. He brought the doctrine of Chalcedon to bear upon his presentation of Jesus' "person," and he has made use of Anselm's satisfaction theory in his account of Jesus' "work." And, Adam did this in an imaginative way. But he left some tough questions unanswered and, therefore, crafted a text that requires greater theoretical exactness.

Finally, one other aspect of Adam's theological method must be noted. Adam labored to incorporate contemporary ideas into *The Son of God*, and, in particular, he worked with the thought of Max Scheler. In his *Formalism in Ethics and Non-Formal Ethics of Values* Scheler argued that there exist universal values by which all people should live so as to become full persons.[41] Honesty, fairness, and holiness have been prized in all societies, and when they have shaped people's lives, they have guided men and women toward full personal existence. According to Scheler, it does not suffice to promote only a formal ethics like Kant's. We must possess an ethics with a content, with norms about right and wrong, truth and falsehood.

Learning values consists not just in knowing them in one's mind but also in practicing them in one's day-to-day activities, Scheler observed. For this reason, all of us depend on role models who by their very example teach us how to conduct ourselves. By their behavior, role models introduce us to such values as honesty, fairness, and holiness. Because we love and respect these people (e.g., our parents and teachers), we imitate them, thereby learning those properties that are most beneficial to human life. Scheler insisted: "Nothing on earth allows a person to become good so originally and immediately and necessarily as the evidential and adequate intuition of a good person in his goodness."[42] The virtuous person can motivate us to pursue the virtues. The honest person can strengthen us to tell the truth, and a holy man or woman can inspire us to seek God.

According to Scheler, the central place of religious figures in world religions makes sense when they are explained in the language of role models. Jesus, Buddha, Muhammad, Confucius, and Lao-tse embody the values that each of them proclaimed. Each lived what he taught and, as a result, became an exemplary figure for his people. That is, each of these men came to be regarded as a religion's central "saint," the exemplar of the loftiest human qualities. Jesus, Buddha, Muhammad, Confucius, and Lao-tse are best called the "primordial saints," the role models who inspire other women and men to become saints. In his essay "Vorbilder und Führer" (Typology of religious role models and leaders) Scheler pointed out that the "primordial saint" sets a community's pattern of religious belief. He or she demonstrates the proper way of life and motivates others to live according to this paradigm. In Scheler's words: "The followers 'believe', what [the saint] 'shows', and what they themselves cannot 'show'."[43]

This understanding of values and role models runs through *The Son of God*. The book conveys an ontology of values, the greatest of which is holiness. Adam quotes, for instance, Jesus' beatitude "Blessed are they who hear the word of God, and keep it" (Lk 11:28) and then includes a statement that echoes Scheler: "With these words Jesus reveals his attitude towards the values of our existence. They hold the solution to what constitutes the highest value for man. In the order of precedence of personal values the religious man takes the highest place."[44] This emphasis on an ontological, ordered set of values is also presupposed when Adam speaks of Jesus as "the holy man," the embodiment of "sanctity."[45]

As we have seen, *The Son of God* presents Jesus as "the complete man." He appears as the human being who possesses all those qualities for which we yearn. He is healthy, rational, upright, faithful to others, and above all holy. According to Adam, "Jesus is in every respect an heroic, epic figure, heroism incarnate. And it was this heroic spirit, this unconditional staking of their lives for the known truth, that he demanded also of his disciples."[46] In this account, Jesus stands as Christians' role model. He reveals that the goal of human life is holiness, namely, the fullness of life and total union with God, and he also gives his followers the strength, namely, the Spirit, so that they can follow Jesus' example and become their best (i.e., holiest) selves before God. As depicted by Adam, Jesus is what Scheler calls the "primordial saint," the one who sets the standard for life and provides the inspiration for people to live up to this ideal.

Karl Adam produced the christology of *The Son of God* by tapping three major sources. First, he implicitly recognized the findings of historical-critical research into the Bible. Second, he attended to the witness of the New Testament by employing a literary interpretation of the gospels, and at the same time he made use of the doctrine of Chalcedon and the satisfaction theory of Anselm. Third, relying on Scheler's phenomenology of human values, he presented Jesus as the primordial saint who stands as the norm and source of personal existence. Adam's threefold correla-tion of historical study, Scripture and tradition, and contemporary thought is succinctly described by Hans Kreidler when he writes that Adam's "image of Jesus Christ is exegetical and dogmatic. The source of this Christ-image is the faith of the church, but this image is presented through a careful exegesis of the scriptural text and the expressions of theological tradition as well as through the medium of a language adapted to the people of the day."[47]

4. Reception: Another Best-Seller

The Son of God developed out of lectures that Adam gave at Salzburg's *Hochschulwochen* in the summer of 1930 and presented at the University of Tübingen in the early 1930s. These lectures were well received. According to Fritz Hofmann, students were touched by "the elegance of [Adam's] speech," "the liveliness of his gestures," and his "personal emotion." They agreed: "Here speaks not simply a learned professor about the object of his scholarship, here is the theologian as preacher."[48] Recalling these same lectures, Heinrich Fries has said that Adam conveyed more than facts and ideas, and more than a way to think critically about Jesus Christ. His lectures introduced an "existentially represented subject" in a language which was "living, colorful, powerful, original and full of poetic beauty."[49] In Fries's judgment, "what Adam communicated with his Christ books to an entire generation, above all in the difficult years of the Third Reich—[to an audience] far greater than the circle of theologians—is immortal."[50]

This strong, positive response occurred, too, when these lectures appeared as a book. The first edition was published in January 1933, and the second edition, with minor revisions, came out two months later. But by late summer the Holy Office had the text withdrawn from bookstores and required Adam to make revisions.[51] In September, Adam wrote Archbishop Conrad Gröber of Freiburg im Breisgau that he would comply with the Vatican's demands. He swiftly made the required changes and submitted them for Rome's approval, which came in early December. Thus, the third edition appeared in early 1934. Later in that year, the book was published in English, and soon it was translated into French, Dutch, Italian, Portuguese, Spanish, and Japanese.[52] Subsequently, as an international best-seller for at least two decades, it went through six to eight printings in German, French, and Italian.

The reviews in German journals were laudatory. *Stimmen der Zeit* noted three merits in the book. First, the book is based on a critical exegesis of the Bible. Second, it is grounded in the history of dogma. In particular, it respects Chalcedon's doctrine of the two natures and their unity in one person. Third, the book utilizes phenomenology in its effort to convey a profound respect, indeed an "original childlike attitude," for the mystery of Jesus Christ. With these three qualities, *The Son of God* speaks to "the whole man."[53] The journal *Der katholische Gedanke* pointed out that *The Son of God* provides "the outline of the figure of Christ" as this form emerges in an interaction between doctrine and modern theology, including the history of religions. It conveys how a "dogmatic theologian" has united his critical reflections about Christ with his love for Christ. Therefore, the book is worthwhile for use by catechetical teachers as they try to reach youth who "yearn for a deep experience of the Christ-figure." It speaks to youth, for it is able "to free Christ from all rubble and painting over and to show him as the one who he was—manly, austere, purposeful, solitary, profound."[54] *Theologie und Glaube* observed that while liberal Protestant theologians have investigated the historical Jesus, Catholic theologians have inquired into the mystery of the "God-man." Among these theologians, Adam has given personal witness to Jesus Christ in a way that is also a "scholarly defense" of Christian belief. The reviewer added: "Regarding christological problems, academics have in Adam a learned Catholic leader, to whom they may join themselves with their own christological journeys, which no one is spared today." Finally, mention is made of the book's literary character. "We intentionally want to call special attention to the warm, solemn style which is in general experienced despite the high scholarly character of the work."[55]

The reviews in English were also positive. The *Tablet* declared that "*The Son of God* is the work of a master." The book treats the historical and biblical material so carefully that when it is finished, the reader senses the mystery of Jesus Christ. It makes good use of history, psychology, and philosophy, and, as a result, it illuminates Jesus' human nature and divine nature. Readers "will see in the portrait [of Jesus] presented by Karl Adam a depth and a truth which stamp it as orthodox."[56] In the same vein, *Thought* commended the book's presentation of "a humanly attractive Christ." As the head of the mystical body, Christ embraces all that is human and extends God's grace to all people. He is spoken of with a "deep reverence" and described "with a power of synthesis like Belloc's." Reliance on the Bible and the thought of Augustine yields an account which acknowledges the "fullness of Christ." "This gift of creative synthesis, a sense of men and movements similar to Christopher Dawson's, gives life to Dr. Adam's works." The review concludes: "Dr. Adam is not only theologically safe, but is called the greatest of living German-speaking theologians, a staunch propagator of the '*Corpus Christi Mysterium*' doctrine, and standard-bearer of that Apologetic, which, in his own words, wishes 'to render the spirit of Catholicism intelligible to the contemporary mind.' "[57]

The Holy Office did not condemn *The Son of God*, but, as Kreidler has reported, it judged that the book possessed theological flaws which demanded immediate correction.[58] According to the Vatican, the book needed to provide a clearer discussion of the act of faith, so that it would distinguish between revelation and belief, and also between natural and supernatural knowledge of God. Also, some of the ideas expressed about Christ were ambiguous. For example, the comments about Christ's self-emptying should explicitly uphold Jesus' knowledge of God. The book should specify, too, that the soul of Jesus Christ remained in union with God throughout his earthly life. The Holy Office observed that the vocabulary created some of the text's difficulties. The book states that the incarnation springs from "the eternal triune movement of love, which breaks forth from the depths of the divine life and reveals itself in space and time as the becoming flesh of the divine Word." Just what this means is not evident. Ambiguity arises, too, when the adjectival expression "the divine" is used to refer to God.

Adam addressed Rome's concerns without modifying the book's basic ideas. He revised a number of sentences to uphold the supernatural aspect of our knowledge of God. For instance, the first and second editions (1933) state: "This faith is entirely God's act, supernatural in its whole essence, *fides infusa*."[59] In contrast, the third edition (1934) explains: "This faith is God's act, supernatural according to its origin and object, a 'gift of God' (Eph 2.8)." Further, Adam refined his comments on the incarnation. In speaking about "an eternal triune movement of love," he added that God "has revealed" this movement "in his Son."[60] Whereas the early editions speak of Jesus as "God's will become flesh, become

human," the third edition states that Jesus is "the embodied will
of the most holy God."[61] The account of human consciousness
and Jesus' intimacy with God no longer talks about Jesus' "intuition bringing together the present and the future into one."[62]
Instead, it asserts that Jesus' "prophetic and Messianic purpose of
salvation required the revelation not so much of the chronological
sequence of the two ages as of their essential correlation and
mutual implication."

The Vatican's report of fifteen pages did not demand substantial changes in *The Son of God*. However, it came at an unfortunate
moment. It arrived while Adam was already making revisions in
The Spirit of Catholicism and *Christ Our Brother* so as to comply
with the Vatican's censure of these two texts. More significantly,
the Holy Office's statement reached Adam while he, like all Germans, was trying to assess Germany's new chancellor, Adolf Hitler.
In particular, in the summer of 1933 Adam was attentive to the
German bishops' negotiations with the government for a concordat between the Vatican and Germany. Nevertheless, he set his
mind on the Holy Office's new censure, completed his textual
revisions, and had them approved by Rome.

5. LEGACY: BIBLICAL STUDIES AND CHRISTOLOGY

In 1974 three continental, Catholic theologians wrote major
books in christology that depend on the conclusions of biblical
research. Walter Kasper of Tübingen completed *Jesus the Christ*,
Hans Küng also of Tübingen finished *On Being a Christian*, and
Edward Schillebeeckx of Nijmegen published *Jesus*. Kasper, Küng,
and Schillebeeckx did not set out together to write their respective
christologies, and they differ in their use of the results of scriptural
exegesis in christology. Nevertheless, they have at least one thing
in common. Their books are the fruits of a major trend that was underway before Kasper (1933-), Küng (1928-) and Schillebeeckx
(1914-) began their fruitful careers. Their christological texts
came about in part because of the efforts of previous generations
of theologians. We cannot review here the history of Catholic
theologians' reliance on historical-critical studies of the Bible in
their systematic reflections on Jesus Christ.[63] We can observe,
though, some of the connections between Adam's work and the

christologies of Kasper and Schillebeeckx, both of whom have acknowledged their indebtedness to Adam.[64]

Walter Kasper, formerly professor of theology at the University of Tübingen and since June 1989 the bishop of Rottenburg-Stuttgart, has mentioned that his christology has been influenced by Adam's. At the outset of *Jesus the Christ* Kasper explains that he has followed a synthetic method which is patterned after the approach of Adam and Adam's student, Josef Rupert Geiselmann (1890–1970), who taught Kasper. He states: "Methodologically this book is indebted to the Catholic Tübingen School, and in particular the Christological approaches of Karl Adam and Josef Rupert Geiselmann."[65] This method, he adds, is characterized by its attentiveness to "the origins of Christianity in Jesus Christ"— origins which are accessible to us "only through biblical and ecclesiastical tradition." Kasper, like Adam, upholds the Catholic Tübingen School's concern to draw on the persistent handing on of wisdom that has occurred within the church. He has indirectly reiterated this point in other writings, where he has described his theological method and Adam's in the very same words: Kasper and Adam adhere to a synthetic method that produces "the unity of scientific thoroughness, ecclesial-mindedness and openness to the times."[66] By bringing together these three elements, each theologian has produced a theology that flows out of the church's living tradition.

In 1976 Kasper gave the major address at the dedication of the Karl Adam House, a student center and residence in Stuttgart. On this occasion, he depicted Adam as a pioneer in the use of biblical studies in christology. We assume today, noted Kasper, that christology depends on the New Testament in order to highlight the humanity of Jesus Christ. But this view was unusual in the 1920s and 30s, and therefore Adam's books, *Christ Our Brother* and *The Son of God*, were extraordinary. Kasper observed: "The human existence of Jesus is for us the way, the medium and the sacrament of salvation. This insight led Adam to design a biblically oriented christology that for its day was astounding."[67]

One other point of similarity between Kasper's christology and Adam's is the way these theologians actually use Scripture in their respective reflections on Jesus Christ. As we have seen, Adam's knowledge of the findings of critical research is reflected in his silence regarding the infancy narratives, for example, and his fashioning the image of Jesus Christ as "the complete man" by means of a literary approach to the gospels. Kasper's *Jesus the Christ* also evinces a reliance on both critical and postcritical hermeneutics.[68] The book's second major section, "The History and Destiny of Jesus Christ," depends on the conclusions of biblical exegesis in its historical reconstruction of Jesus' preaching, actions, and implicit sense of his mission. The book's third and last major section, "The Mystery of Jesus Christ," includes literary interpretation of the New Testament. Kasper works with images of the servant (Phil 2:6–11), the new Adam (Rom 5:12–21) and the mediator (1 Tm 3:16) in order to shed light on the person of Jesus Christ, alive in the Spirit. Kasper, like Adam, has done christology with an eye to the biblical witness to the risen Christ. To sum up, in his theological method in general and more specifically in his use of Scripture in christology, Kasper has built on the work of Karl Adam.

Edward Schillebeeckx's christology also has points of similarity with Adam's. At the start of this chapter, we reviewed Schillebeeckx's reminiscences of reading *Christ Our Brother* and *The Son of God* in the 1930s. As the Flemish theologian has recalled, he was struck by the fact that, unlike other Catholic theologians, "Karl Adam . . . studied the Bible," and he brought this research to his christology. As a result, *Christ Our Brother* and *The Son of God* have "splendid pages" on "the 'psychology of Jesus,' containing elements of concern for the man Jesus that was to develop later."

One could apply these same comments to Schillebeeckx's reflections on the person and work of Jesus Christ. His book *Jesus* exhibits the fact that Schillebeeckx has "studied the Bible" with exegetical thoroughness. Moreover, the text itself is marked by its "concern for the man Jesus." Schillebeeckx is intent upon illuminating the concrete figure of Jesus. In the opening pages, he writes: "That the man Jesus, in the sense of 'a human person,' is for me the starting-point of all my reflection I would call a sort of palisade that needs no further proof or justification. It is a truism."[69] It is fair to say, therefore, that in his study of the Bible and his focus on Jesus of Nazareth, Schillebeeckx has pursued a theological orientation similar to the one that he lauds in Adam's work.

One further point of similarity between Schillebeeckx and Adam is their biblical hermeneutics. Just as Adam wanted to direct readers' attention to the risen Christ, so too in *Jesus* Schillebeeckx has aimed at more than a sketch of the historical Jesus.[70] He has said that, on the basis of historical research, christology can foster a "disclosure" in which Christians experience the presence of God and receive a fresh insight into the mystery of Jesus Christ. In this vein, he defines the theologian's job in christology: "to gather together elements which may lead to a new, authentic 'disclosure' experience or source experience."[71] He reaches for this same idea when he writes: "The result of historical investigation is objectively observed material in which the believer sees more, experiences a disclosure. The believer does indeed see God's saving activity realized in Jesus' life, which without the material about Jesus recovered by the historical method would not be possible."[72]

To achieve his goal of facilitating new disclosures of God Schillebeeckx relies in *Jesus* upon both critical and postcritical hermeneutics. By means of historical-critical research he gathers the data, the "objectively observed material," about Jesus' preaching, actions, and last days, but does not stop here. Rather he assembles these exegetical findings into a coherent whole, into a loose story not unlike a biography. According to Schillebeeckx, this literary unit, specifically, the second major section in *Jesus*, is "a post-critical, narrative history."[73] This narrative is "post-critical," for it possesses an overall shape which, while not violating the results and canons of historical-critical research, is not strictly speaking derived from critical inquiry. Rather, it is determined by the theologian's faith in a "living person," Jesus Christ. Further, such a narrative is crucial for Schillebeeckx's program, because it is the coherence of the literary unit that promotes new disclosures or insights into the mystery of Jesus Christ.

Both Schillebeeckx and Adam, therefore, adopted a postcritical hermeneutics. However, they executed this kind of interpretation in different ways. In *The Son of God* Adam moved beyond the conclusions of critical research by taking a literary approach to the New Testament. He tried to work with images of Jesus Christ in the gospels. In *Jesus* Schillebeeckx has gone beyond the results of exegesis to order these conclusions into a quasi-historical narrative that may generate new images of Jesus Christ. We cannot say that Schillebeeckx had Adam's work clearly in mind when he wrote *Jesus*, but there are significant similarities between Schillebeeckx's work and Adam's, and since Schillebeeckx has spoken highly of the impact of *Christ Our Brother* and *The Son of God* upon his life, we can conclude that at a minimum Adam's books initially inspired Schillebeeckx to do what he has accomplished in *Jesus*.

Two major (but unopposing) trends run through contemporary Catholic christology: emphases upon the humanity of Jesus Christ and on the place of the Bible in systematic theology. In the third chapter and this fourth chapter, we have seen that both of these themes were central to Adam's christology in the 1920s and 30s. *Christ Our Brother* challenged the implicit monophysitism in much post-Reformation Catholic piety and theology, thereby taking seriously the Council of Chalcedon's claim that Jesus Christ is "truly man." Further, *The Son of God* is anchored in the New Testament. It aims at a postcritical reading of the Bible that elicits the synoptic Gospels' images of Jesus Christ. In short, Adam's christological books were forerunners of today's emphasis on the humanity of Jesus Christ and the centrality of the Bible for christology.

The Son of God was published at a tragic turning point in history. It appeared in January 1933, the month in which President Paul von Hindenburg named Adolf Hitler as Germany's new chancellor. Amid the national turmoil and tyranny that ensued, Adam spoke out regarding the controversial leader. How could he remain silent when his christology reiterated the value of being human, of being a "complete man"? In July 1933 and again in January 1934 Adam made public statements on the relationship between Catholicism and Hitler's National Socialism. As we shall see, the theologian's efforts to build a bridge between Christian faith and German nationalism in the Third Reich raise the question of whether Germany's neoromanticism had too strong an influence upon Adam's theology.

5

Confronted by Nazism
(1933-1945)

1933 and 1934 were difficult years for Karl Adam. At the age of fifty-seven he should have enjoyed his accomplishments: three internationally acclaimed books, dozens of scholarly and pastoral articles, a prestigious academic chair and the esteem of bishops, professors, and Catholic readers around the world. However, what should have happened did not. By late 1933, at the Vatican's request, Adam had withdrawn each of his texts from bookstores and revised them. But there was more than this. As he was resolving his differences with Rome, he found himself at odds with Berlin.

Karl Adam tried to be a bridge-builder in politics as well as in theology. As we have seen, he adopted a method of synthesis in his writings on the church and on Jesus Christ. In national affairs too Adam, though politically naive, wanted to bring together what stood apart. Amid the tensions between the Catholic bishops and Adolf Hitler, he attempted to point the way toward a synthesis acceptable to both sides. Adam was not a Nazi. Yet, he thought he saw a point of contact between Catholicism and National Socialism in Hitler's public espousal of traditional German values concerning marriage, family, and the German *Volk*. According to Hans Kreidler, Adam wanted "to reconcile the National Socialist outlook with the Catholic and perhaps even to purify National Socialism from within by means of Catholicism."[1]

When we hear that Adam spoke out in favor of Hitler during the early months of 1933, we cannot help but ask why. Why was an insightful theologian not astute regarding a demagogue? Why was his criticism not as immediate, strong, and persistent as we would expect?

The reason for Adam's initial support for Hitler can be found in German neoromanticism. This body of thought disposed Adam, as it did many of his contemporaries, to hear the National Socialist talk about community and not to weigh the actions of Hitler and his associates. The *Lebensphilosophie* directed Adam to say yes to whatever seemed to bring life, even if at times violent. "Wherever Adam believed he caught the scent of healthy life," observed Fritz Hofmann, "there he declared this yes, even if such life still bubbled up with ambiguity, including danger as well as hope."[2] The neoromanticism that had nurtured Adam's vibrant vision of the church and Jesus Christ also obscured his perceptions of the Third Reich.

This chapter describes the failure of one theologian's good intentions as he tried to aid in a dialogue between Catholicism and National Socialism.[3] In particular, it reviews four of Adam's political statements.[4] First, in July 1933, Adam endorsed Hitler as the new chancellor. Second, he condemned National Socialism's German Faith Movement in January 1934. Third, in February 1935, he criticized the ideology of Alfred Rosenberg. Fourth, soon after Germany's invasion of Poland, he advocated the military conscription of Catholic seminarians. Our study ends in 1939 when, because of the war, it became even harder for Germans to express openly their true thoughts on Hitler's policies and actions.[5] I will compare Adam's views to those of other Catholics but, because of a lack of space, not to those of Protestants,[6] and will endeavor to set each of Adam's statements in its respective context. The link between Adam's neoromanticism and his stance toward National Socialism will be explicitly made in chapter seven.

1.1 CONTEXT: THE BISHOPS' STANCE IN 1933

In the winter and early spring of 1933 the Catholic bishops in Germany faced a difficult political and religious issue: Should they maintain their ban against the National Socialist German Workers party? Or, should they now permit Catholics to join the National-sozialistische Deutsche Arbeiterpartei (NSDAP) or Nazi party? This question urgently required a reconsidered, clear answer.[7]

The issue was unsettled because of the rapid flow of political events. On January 30, President Paul von Hindenburg named

Hitler chancellor. In his radio address on February 1, Hitler defused some criticism from bishops by declaring that his government regarded "Christianity as the foundation of our national morality and the family as the basis of national life."[8] After the Reichstag building was destroyed by arson on February 27, he promulgated the "Reich President's Edict for the Protection of People and State," which suspended the personal rights granted by the Weimar Constitution and established concentration camps for "political dissidents" (e.g., at Dachau). The elections on March 5 gave the Nazis the strongest voice of any single party in the Reichstag and seemingly demonstrated the chancellor's widespread backing among Germans. Two weeks later, on March 23, in a speech to the Reichstag, Hitler gave a broad range of assurances regarding his proposed authoritarian rule, one of which was that he would respect the churches' rights. In response, the Reichstag passed the Enabling Act, which transferred legislative power from the Reichstag to Hitler's cabinet and cut the government's ties to the Weimar Constitution. Hitler immediately initiated his *"Gleichschaltung,"* his "synchronization" or enforced conformity, of all aspects of German life. He began to purge the civil service of non-Nazis, hence of Jews and also of Catholics, who were forbidden membership in the NSDAP by the bishops. These events forced the Catholic bishops to rethink their public opposition to National Socialism.

There were theoretical and practical reasons for the bishops to uphold their prohibition against the Nazi party. National Socialism embraced an ideology, a worldview, directly at odds with Catholic teaching. Its spokesman Alfred Rosenberg advocated a return to Teutonic mythology, denigrated Christian doctrine and church teachings, and called for a "positive Christianity," subordinated to the German state.[9] Also, National Socialism espoused racial views contrary to the Judeo-Christian tradition. It denounced Jews because of their race, contrary to the Catholic church's insistence that its differences with Judaism were not racial but strictly religious. Further, in practice the bishops had a precedent of condemnations against National Socialism—a precedent which dated to the early 1920s and had been stated in sharp terms since 1930. It would be inconsistent, therefore, to lift the ban against the NSDAP, and it would leave vulnerable those Catholics, especially in the Center party and the Bavarian People's party, who had courageously acted on the hierarchy's rejection of National

Socialism.[10] Priests had denied Nazi Catholics the reception of the Eucharist and also a Christian burial, and Catholic political leaders like Adam Stegerwald had vigorously criticized Hitler and his movement. There was the question, too, of how the bishops could reconcile their differences with a man who had condoned lawlessness. In August 1932 Hitler had sent a supportive telegram to five Storm Troopers condemned to death for the sadistic murder of a Communist in the Silesian village of Potempa.[11] As a result of Hitler's intervention, the five were released. Prudence as well as Christian doctrine spoke in favor of sustaining the Catholic ban against the NSDAP.

At the same time, there were compelling reasons for accommodating National Socialism. Hitler was Germany's legitimate chancellor, and he was showing signs of becoming more responsible for the common good. In his speeches on February 1 and March 23, he declared his commitment to the inherited values of the German people. Hitler seemingly held common ground, too, with Catholicism in opposing atheism, Bolshevism, and liberalism, which appeared to be immediately greater threats to the church than National Socialism. There were also informal signals that the Nazi regime was disposed to negotiate a concordat with Rome—an agreement which had been sought for many years by Eugenio Cardinal Pacelli, who had served as the Vatican's nuncio to Germany from 1920 until 1929 and then had become Pius XI's secretary of state.[12] The Vatican had worked out a suitable *modus vivendi* with Italy's totalitarian ruler, Benito Mussolini. Could not something be possible with Hitler, especially since his government would likely be short-lived?

There were pragmatic reasons for ending the ban against Catholic membership in the NSDAP. German society was on the verge of chaos. The daily outbreaks of street violence had to be stopped, and Hitler appeared capable of doing this. High unemployment still persisted from the worldwide economic depression of 1929 and subsequent crisis of July 1931. Because of Hitler's newly instituted government programs, people were returning to work at such a quick pace that by the end of the year there would be a 40 percent decrease in unemployment, from six million to approximately three and a half million, out of a total population of approximately sixty-six million.[13] Simultaneously, however, many Catholics were being dismissed from their civil service jobs, and, as a result, they were complaining to the bishops about their plight. Some were even leaving the church so that they could retain their jobs. Unless the prohibition against the NSDAP were dropped, there would seemingly result another Kulturkampf, of which some bishops still had painful memories. The exigencies of the situation pressed for some kind of working relationship with Hitler.

In late March the bishops made their decision. The Fulda bishops' conference, led by Adolf Cardinal Bertram of Breslau, and the Bavarian bishops' conference, chaired by Munich's Michael Cardinal Faulhaber, announced on March 28 that they were lifting their prohibition against National Socialism. After explaining that the ban had been imposed in order to protect the church's rights, the bishops observed that it was no longer required, since the conditions which prompted it had seemingly ended.

> It has now to be recognized that public and solemn declarations have been made by the highest representative of the nationalist government, who at the same time is the authoritative leader of that movement, through which due acknowledgement has been made of the inviolability of Catholic doctrinal teaching and of the unchangeable tasks and rights of the Church. In these declarations the nationalist government has given explicit assurances concerning the validity of all provisions of the Concordats concluded by individual German states with the Church. Without repealing the condemnation of certain religious and moral errors contained in our earlier measures, the episcopate believes it may trust that the above-mentioned general prohibitions and warnings need no longer be considered necessary.[14]

This announcement reversed the bishops' stance, but it also urged Catholics not to tolerate any actions that violated the law: "Catholic Christians . . . do not require at this time a special admonition to be loyal to the lawful authorities and to fulfill conscientiously their civic duties while rejecting on principle all illegal or subversive conduct." The announcement reiterated the rights of the Catholic church and Catholic organizations (e.g., newspapers, schools, and youth groups). It repeated the bishops' condemnation of the Nazi insistence that German citizenship be determined by race, and it opposed a national policy of sterilization.

Representative of the divergent views among the German bishops were the positions of Faulhaber and Archbishop Conrad

Gröber of Freiburg im Breisgau.[15] Faulhaber opposed National Socialism on principle, but judged that an accommodation had to be worked out, since Hitler was the legitimate chancellor. By disposition, Faulhaber was a monarchist who had condemned the revolution of 1918 and lacked enthusiasm for the Weimar Republic.[16] However, he did not trust Hitler and saw that Catholicism and National Socialism were in essence incompatible. On February 10, 1933, in preparation for the elections on March 5, Faulhaber issued a pastoral letter on "the rights and duties of the state and its citizens." While insisting that a government's authority stems from its respect for the authority of God, he refrained from advising Catholics how to vote. Nor did he comment on National Socialism. In private, he cautioned Cardinal Pacelli in early March to note the significant differences between Hitler and Mussolini. After the bishops' conferences reversed their position in late March, Faulhaber and the Bavarian bishops continued their wariness toward the new regime. They instructed that church bells were not to be rung for national celebrations and that Catholics were expected to speak out against the misconduct of government officials.[17]

By contrast, Archbishop Gröber believed that Catholicism and National Socialism were in principle reconcilable. He distinguished between the central, authentic values of Hitler's movement and its fringe attitudes and manifestations. In his judgment, the Catholic church could influence Nazism from within, supporting the nationalist movement's positive, primary thrust and trimming away its negative, secondary offshoots. Shortly after being consecrated the archbishop of Freiburg on June 20, 1932, Gröber instructed his priests to find points of agreement with the National Socialists and to take a more "prudent" approach when dealing with them.[18] Since he had close ties with Cardinal Pacelli and his associate Monsignor Ludwig Kaas, chairman of the Center party, his advice carried weight throughout Germany.[19] Gröber was linked to Kaas's view, expressed in a telegram to Hitler on his forty-fourth birthday, April 20, 1933: "For today's birthday sincere good wishes and the assurance of unflinching co-operation in the great enterprise of creating a Germany internally united, enjoying social peace and externally free."[20]

The bishops' statement of March 28 lifting their ban on the NSDAP resulted from the convergence of two differing assessments of this political party. According to one, held by Faulhaber,

National Socialism was fundamentally incompatible with Catholicism, but given the reality of Hitler's chancellorship it had to be dealt with and given a chance to succeed or fail. According to the other view, espoused by Gröber, National Socialism was reconcilable in principle with Catholicism and needed to be influenced by Catholic leaders.

1.2 CATHOLIC SCHOLARS' POLITICAL VIEWS

After the bishops had rescinded their ban against National Socialism, a number of Catholic scholarly leaders publicly expressed their views on the matter.[21] An immediate response came from those opposed to the bishops' announcement.[22] Konrad Algermissen at Hildesheim reported to Cardinal Bertram on March 31, 1933, that the bishops' announcement of March 28 had not lifted the widespread depression among priests and laity, "but in many cases had awakened the impression of a retreat by the Church."[23] A couple of weeks later, in *Stimmen der Zeit*, the Jesuits Jakob Overmans and Max Pribilla defended democracy and its rule of law, thereby implicitly taking issue with the bishops' reversal.[24] In April the Dominican Franziskus Stratmann, student chaplain in Berlin and leader of the Catholic Peace Union, wrote Cardinal Faulhaber: "The souls of the right-minded are upset by the despotism of National Socialism, and I am expressing nothing other than a fact when I say that the episcopal authority is reduced to inconsistency among countless Catholics and non-Catholics through the quasi-approval of the National Socialist movement."[25]

Another Catholic opponent of rapprochement with National Socialism was Dietrich von Hildebrand (1889–1977), a well-known phenomenologist at the University of Munich. Since the 1920s he had publicly denounced Hitler and was included, therefore, on the Nazi's list of "political dissidents" to be imprisoned.[26] In March 1933 he emigrated with his wife and son to Vienna, where he immediately established a weekly journal dedicated to telling the truth about Hitler and Nazism. In the summer of 1933 he opposed the Vatican's signing of a concordat with Berlin's National Socialist government. One year later Hildebrand's criticism of Hitler became inflamed after the "blood purge" of June 30, 1934. In an article entitled "The final mask falls!" Hildebrand described Hitler as "the gravedigger of German civilization" and added: "Whoever today still hopes for a reform or conversion of National Socialism refuses to see and hear."[27]

Ildefons Herwegen, the abbot of Maria Laach Abbey, voiced cautious support for National Socialist government in the spring of 1933.[28] He was wary of Hitler, for just prior to the bishops' ending of the ban against the NSDAP he gave refuge to Cologne's mayor Konrad Adenauer, whose life was threatened by the Nazis. (Adenauer had fled to the Abbey of Maria Laach and was sheltered there for over a year.) Nevertheless, as a political conservative, the abbot initially favored the bishops' accommodation to National Socialism. In late May, Herwegen expressed his view that Germany was undergoing a rebirth: "The people and the government were again being united through the activity of the leader Adolf Hitler." Therefore, Germans were rightly pledging their support to the new government. "The obedience of the people responds," said Herwegen, "to the faith of the leader in the people. True obedience of everyone to this one creates a new experience of community which allows our people to return to the ultimate roots of their commonality: to blood, earth and destiny."[29]

But Abbot Herwegen's endorsement of Hitler was conditional. Because of the importance of the tie between the people and their leader, the chancellor warranted the people's trust, declared Herwegen, only so long as Hitler acknowledged that his authority came from God. If the chancellor were to deny God's authority, then he would be opposed by the church, for a denial of God's absoluteness would eventually result in the government's oppression of the people. In the abbot's words:

> If the state were to deny that its authority is given by God and thus not submit to the divine laws, if the reason of the state itself were to be the ultimate guiding principle of the government's action and the ultimate source of its rule, then its self-divinization would finally lead to the servitude of the people and make the people into the illegitimate plaything of the state's institutions.

In early 1933 Herwegen wanted to give the legitimately elected chancellor a chance, but, as the abbot increasingly criticized Hitler and the Nazi regime, in 1935 he was forced to flee from Germany.

Some Catholic scholars, however, were not opposed to Hitler. They endorsed the new chancellor and gave theological rationales for their support. Karl Eschweiler (1886-1936), the respected neoscholastic theologian at the University of Braunsberg, insisted in June 1933 that National Socialism's emphasis upon the importance of the Germanic race for the renewal of Germany possessed similarities with Thomas Aquinas' acknowledgement that ethical decision making must respect the innate tendencies of human nature. History has shown, averred Eschweiler, that when philosophers have devalued the role of the natural order, including biology and race, in their fashioning of ethics, they have produced inadequate philosophies. Eschweiler judged: "In those cases when the opinion has prevailed that the so-called biological [factor] is something incidental and secondary for human thought, will and action, then a genuine philosophy, a true ethics and every good principle have become impossible."[30]

To make his case, Eschweiler appealed to the theological tenet that grace builds on nature:

> It is a Catholic truth that the grace of divine faith in the German people does not destroy their divinely created natural talents, but presupposes them. Indeed, the holiest obligation requires that we sustain and develop these natural talents against evil inclinations, for there are also racial consequences to original sin.

In Eschweiler's judgment, neoscholastic thought supported National Socialism's conviction that the rebuilding of German society could only come about by means of the renewal of the Germanic race. Based on this reasoning, Eschweiler spoke out in favor of the Nazi's sterilization law, which was enacted on July 14, 1933. As a consequence, he was censored by Rome.

Joseph Lortz (1887-1975), the famous historian of the Reformation who was also at the University of Braunsberg, took a stand in June 1933 similar to Eschweiler's. According to Lortz, Catholicism and National Socialism occupied the same ground in opposing the destructive forces within the Weimar Republic, namely, liberalism, immorality, relativism, atheism, and Bolshevism. Both cherished an organic view of life, a return to ethnic and racial origins, and the Christian faith as the basis of German society. This convergence of convictions meant that the Catholic church had much to gain by working with the National Socialist government. The church needed to respect Nazi rule, too, for it was more than just another government. The national elections in

March had demonstrated that Hitler and his party manifested the will of the people. In Lortz's words:

> National Socialism is today not only the legitimate possessor of governmental authority in Germany, it is—a few short months after its takeover of power—the German state itself. This state stands in a genuine, decisive struggle to rescue the entire people in all aspects of their lives. It has made its peace with the church through its public clarifications and its concordat with the Vatican. With an impetus unknown until now in Germany, this government is moving toward the attainment of the inner unity of all Germans. Therefore, German Catholicism should urgently pursue the task of reaching an agreement [concordat], based on internal similarities, with this government regarding the different arenas of Catholic life. This task is decisive for the future of the church in Germany as well as for the future of National Socialism.[31]

Michael Schmaus (1897–), then professor of dogma at the University of Münster, gave a lecture in July 1933 on the points of agreement between Catholicism and National Socialism. In his judgment, National Socialism represented "the sharpest and most serious protest against the mentality of the nineteenth and twentieth centuries." It correctly questioned the mechanistic, individualistic, and liberal attitudes of the Enlightenment, and it replaced these with a more "organic" view of reality. It valued "community, the people, connectedness, authority." Given this orientation, National Socialism was an ally of the Catholic church with its emphasis upon the common life, the natural bond among all people, and the place of authority. National Socialism and Catholicism could work together so that the German people would realize their mission in world history. "Since the divine will stands in the background of all history," said Schmaus, "we can read from history—without fear of deceiving ourselves—that God destined the German people for one of the greatest duties [in history]."[32] Finally, in accord with the theological principle of the continuity between grace and nature, the Catholic church should cooperate with the new government so that the church's work complements National Socialism's efforts for the social and economic rebuilding of Germany.

In sum, in the spring and early summer of 1933 Catholic leaders held a spectrum of views regarding the way that the Catholic

church needed to respond to the National Socialist regime. Algermissen, Overmans, Pribilla, Stratmann, and Hildebrand opposed
the lifting of the bishops' prohibition against membership in the
NSDAP. Voicing caution, Herwegen initially recommended that
Hitler be given a chance to put Germany's house in order. Eschweiler, Lortz, and Schmaus urged that the Catholic church not
retreat into a ghetto mentality but acknowledge the positive qualities in Hitler's movement.

It was within this context that Karl Adam published his article "Deutsches Volkstum und katholisches Christentum" (German
nationality and Catholic Christianity). Appearing in the summer
of 1933, this essay followed the public statements by Eschweiler,
Lortz, and Schmaus. Like these theologians, Adam based his support for Hitler in large part upon the axiom that "grace presupposes nature and completes it."[33] As noted in the previous
chapter, in the summer of 1933 Adam was being assisted by both
Faulhaber and Gröber in resolving his differences with the Holy
Office regarding his books. In "Deutsches Volkstum und katholisches Christentum" he took a position on National Socialism that
was closer to Gröber's than to Faulhaber's, for he argued that
Catholicism and National Socialism are reconcilable in principle.

Prior to reviewing Adam's essay, it is important to note that
Adam had already made public statements critical of the NSDAP. In
March 1932 Nazi students at the University of Tübingen had forced
the university senate to approve changes in voting procedures that
would favor the National Socialist students. Adam had participated
in these deliberations and had observed that "it is a scandal the
way the student body has been knuckled down by the National
Socialists."[34] One year later, when Adam wrote in favor of working
with the new government, he was already on record as having
criticized some of the National Socialists' actions.

1.3 TEXT: "DEUTSCHES VOLKSTUM UND KATHOLISCHES CHRISTENTUM"

The theme of Adam's essay "Deutsches Volkstum und katholisches Christentum" (July 1933) is specified in its title. In the
1930s the expression "*deutsches Volkstum*," literally meaning the
"German people," had nationalistic, cultural, and racial connotations.[35] The phrase "*katholisches Christentum*," "Catholic Christianity," conveyed the inclusive sense that Catholicism and

Protestantism are forms of one faith, i.e., "*Christentum.*" Thus, the title "Deutsches Volkstum und katholisches Christentum" pinpoints the issue, namely, the relationship between German nationalism and Christian belief. This question is explicitly posed at the start of the essay: "What does the German race give to Catholicism, and what does Catholicism give to the German race, so that each develops and fulfills itself?"[36] This twofold query is answered—after an encomium for Hitler as the leader who embodied Germany's rebirth—in two steps.

First, what does a people's race and culture bring to their Christian faith? According to Adam, the answer to this question depends on how one views the relationship between grace and nature. In the Protestant perspectives of Martin Luther and John Calvin, grace and nature are opposed, and thus religion and politics are discontinuous. In contrast, the Catholic position is grounded on the principle that grace presupposes nature. As a result of original sin, human nature is "wounded" but not "ruined," and thus it possesses a point of contact for God's supernatural activity. The inherent good qualities of human nature serve as the starting point for divine grace. Our honesty, purity, courage, and high-mindedness are "awakened" by grace and directed toward God. In the Catholic view, grace and nature collaborate in bringing about God's salvation. "Thus redemption in its full sense is," says Adam, "God's act and at the same time the work of humankind, a divine and human act—blood and spirit in one."[37]

The distinct theological anthropologies of Protestantism and Catholicism manifest themselves in ecclesiology. According to Luther and Calvin, the church is primarily concerned about Christians' relationship with God, and, as a result, pastoral care is limited to the ministry of "word and sacrament." In Catholic teaching the church directs its attention to Christians' life in the world as well as before God, and, as a consequence, for Catholics pastoral care includes education. This outlook is evident, observes Adam, in the German Catholic bishops' announcement of March 28, 1933, in which, after withdrawing their ban against National Socialism, the bishops claim primary responsibility for their schools, youth groups, and organizations for adults. Through these associations the church assumes its duty of educating the "whole living man." It presumes the good order, maintained by the government, and it contributes to this order through its programs. But the church's concerns go beyond those of the state. Thus, the church and the state are "organically linked." Adam states: "Without the church's work of formation the state's formation remains fragmentary. Conversely, it is on the basis of the state's formation that the church's education starts. The state's formation produces the natural material and basis for the church's supernatural effects."[38] This view of the interdependence of state and church answers the first question: Race, culture, and the state, all of which are aspects of human nature, are presupposed by the church and its educational programs, which are expressions of God's grace.

Second, what does the Catholic church contribute to national-racial ("*völkische*") identity? Catholicism respects a people's nation, race, and culture. "The sacramental and educational activity of the church can only be fruitful," holds Adam, "when the church carefully observes the blood-given determinations of a race or people." Specific instances of Catholicism adopting cultural forms can be cited. Pius XI encouraged Catholic missionaries to build up the local clergy in Africa and Asia. Over the centuries Catholicism has adapted, too, to the various cultures and races within Europe. German Catholicism is quite distinct from Italian Catholicism, each of which has its own saints, pilgrimages, and customs. German spirituality is characterized by its philosophical interest, whereas Italian Catholicism values more aesthetic, imaginative forms of faith. These examples show that the Catholic church is "the true mother of all national-racial identity." The answer to the second question is, says Adam, that "Catholicism needs a national-racial heritage in order to be a living Catholicism. Therefore, nationalism and Catholicism have no inner opposition. They belong together as the natural and supernatural orders."

Adam concludes the essay by answering a question about the Jewish people in Germany: "How do we as Catholic Germans stand in relation to Judaism?"[39] On the one hand, it is valid to have laws which restrict the involvement of Jews in German society. Germans have an obligation to cherish their racial identity, their "blood purity," and Jews are obliged to value their racial identity. This obligation for each people to esteem its race is based in the Old Testament's laws concerning Jews' interaction (e.g., in marriage) with their neighbors. Thus, Adam maintains, it is appropriate for the German government to set limits on the involvements of Jews in German society.

On the other hand, Germans have a duty to respect the Jewish women and men, indeed to treat them with "justice and love." There are at least two reasons for this respect. First, Catholics must remember that their faith prompts them to offer help to all people, regardless of religious belief and race. "As a trans-national community, embracing all races and heritages, the Catholic church is no less obligated to the *natura individua* of the Jews than to the racial character of other races." Second, Catholicism's respect for Judaism in particular is strengthened by the fact that Jesus was a Jew. To be sure, some Germans have tried to deny Jesus' Jewish lineage. But Jesus was surely a Jew, and, therefore, Catholics acknowledge their bond with all Jews.

The essay ends at this point, with the parenthetical note: "To be continued." In fact, Adam never completed the essay. Events in late 1933 and early 1934 dampened Adam's optimism regarding Hitler and prompted him to speak out against National Socialism.

2.1 CONTEXT: AUTUMN 1933

Immediately after the bishops' lifting of their ban against membership in the NSDAP on March 28, the Vatican and the German government initiated formal negotiations toward a concordat.[40] These meetings led to the signing of a tentative agreement by Cardinal Pacelli in Berlin on July 20. Into the late summer and early autumn, the German episcopacy was aware that Nazis were interfering in church life, for example, by disrupting Catholic newspapers and arresting priests who had spoken out against National Socialism. When the bishops mentioned these abuses to Vice Chancellor Franz von Papen, they were told that these acts were not condoned by the government but were the work of extremists who would eventually be arrested and prosecuted by the government. On September 10, Cardinal Bertram and representatives of the German bishops' conferences met with Pius XI, who expressed doubts about the concordat because of the continued harassment of Catholics in Germany. However, the pontiff ratified the concordat when the ecclesiastical delegation assured him that this agreement would provide the legal basis for safeguarding the rights of Catholics, their church, and its organizations.

By the late autumn of 1933 the German bishops found themselves increasingly at odds with the NSDAP. Hitler imposed his synchronization of German society with little respect for the Catholic church's institutions and activities. For example, the government and the NSDAP put increasing pressure on the thirty-three organizations of the German Catholic Youth to disband so that their 1.5 million members would join the Hitler Youth Organization. In many regions Catholic groups were forbidden to wear their traditional attire, display banners, and form processions. The Bavarian police banned all forms of public gatherings other than for worship. This prohibition outlawed such activities as a parish's socials, excursions, and sports events. As a result, Dachau's concentration camp was quickly filled with "political dissidents," many of whom were Catholics. When Dr. Emil Mühler, the former head of Munich's Catholic Action Association, publicly revealed that Dachau's prisoners were being tortured, he himself was arrested and imprisoned on November 29, 1933.[41]

Of course, Catholics were not the only group affected by Hitler's synchronization of German society. Jewish store owners had their shops boycotted, and Jewish doctors and lawyers were not allowed to renew their professional licenses. Protestant leaders took steps toward forming a *Reichskirche*, and those officials who questioned this form of *Gleichschaltung* were coerced into voicing support for it. On the evening of November 13, 1933, approximately 20,000 "German Christians" assembled for a rally at Berlin's *Sportspalast* and heard Reinhold Krause, a church leader and Nazi official, urge that the Protestant churches be "Nazified." He demanded the church's rejection of "all things not German in its services and confession, especially [beliefs and customs] from the Old Testament with its Jewish system of quid pro quo morality."[42] At the end of his speech, the rally voted in favor of Krause's "Nazification" of the churches. This assembly instantly became a scandal that compelled many Protestant officials to distance themselves from Krause and talk of a Nazi church.

The incident brought national prominence to the religious group called the "German Faith Movement."[43] Omission of "Christian" from this name was deliberate. Led by General Erich Ludendorff and Count Ernst von Reventlow, this circle broke with Christianity and worshipped Wotan and the other Teutonic gods. Members of the German Faith Movement were even married in ceremonies designed according to pagan rituals. By means of its worship and rituals the German Faith Movement attempted to supplant Christian practices with ancient Teutonic symbols, customs, and a mythos that were indigenous to the German people. This return to the past would ensure the rebirth of the German people, insisted the Movement's leaders. When Alfred Rosenberg learned that Reichsbischof Ludwig Müller had forced Krause to resign from his ecclesiastical position after the *Sportspalast* episode, Rosenberg declared that he could no longer be both a Christian and a National Socialist. He renounced his church affiliation and extolled membership in the German Faith Movement.

By December 1933 the Catholic bishops' dealings with the NSDAP had reached a crossroads. There could be no rapprochement between the Catholic church and the National Socialist regime, if Nazi leaders were intent on eradicating Judeo-Christian belief and its institutions from Germany. Therefore, in his four Advent sermons Cardinal Faulhaber spoke against the Nazification of Christian belief and defended the bond of the Christian faith with its Jewish origins. He courageously proclaimed that Christianity cannot be separated from Judaism. He opposed the German Faith Movement's claim that the churches should free themselves from the Hebrew Bible, with its ethics of "reward," which "encourages and consecrates an un-German spirit of self-seeking."[44] The prelate rhetorically asked, "Are the opponents of the Old Testament promises in reality so remote from all desire of reward that in return for their services they never expect any recognition, any rise in salary, any promotion—in short, any reward?" The New Testament, he insisted, can only be understood when set in relation to the Old Testament, for the younger covenant builds on the older one. "The God of the New Testament is not a different God from the God of the Old Testament."[45] With statements like these, Faulhaber sounded the alarm regarding National Socialism in general and the German Faith Movement in particular. As a result, he had threats made upon his life, and on January 27 and 28, 1934, shots were fired at the cardinal's residence.

Faulhaber's skepticism about National Socialism was shared by other members of the German episcopacy. On December 28, 1933, Bishop Johannes Sproll of the Diocese of Rottenburg-Stuttgart wrote a letter to Cardinal Bertram in which he observed: "The concordat will not put the government on notice, not even contain it. This is obvious."[46] (In March 1938, when Sproll refused to vote in favor of Germany's *Anschluss* of Austria, he was forced to flee his diocese until the end of the Second World War.)[47] In February 1934, at the insistence of Faulhaber and other bishops, the Vatican placed Rosenberg's *Der Mythus des 20. Jahrhunderts* (The myth of the twentieth century) (1930) on its Index of Forbidden Books. On April 8, 1934, Archbishop Gröber remonstrated against the "new heathenism" of the German Faith Movement. In a pastoral letter to the Archdiocese of Freiburg, he wrote: "As bishop, I say to you, the German *Volk* will not attain its future greatness by forgetting its Christian past but, instead, only by continuing to build upon the foundations of Christianity."[48]

In making this point, Gröber presented an idea that Karl Adam had publicly declared two months previously at an assembly of Catholic youth groups. On Sunday January 21, 1934, more than 10,000 young men and women gathered at Stuttgart's *Stadthalle* for the Catholic Conference's celebration of the nineteen-hundredth anniversary of "the world's redemption through Jesus Christ."[49] Bishop Sproll, who had just returned from his *ad limina* visit with Pius XI, briefly addressed the assembly, saying that he brought greetings from the Bishop of Rome. When Sproll finished, Karl Adam gave the main address, "Vom gottmenschlichen Erlöser" (On the divine-human savior), which I will briefly summarize.

2.2 TEXT: "VOM GOTTMENSCHLICHEN ERLÖSER"

A celebration of the suffering, death, and resurrection of Jesus Christ is not an anniversary in the usual sense of that word, Adam reflected. An anniversary ordinarily recalls something or someone in the past. But Christians' commemoration of the world's redemption in Jesus Christ celebrates someone in the present—the living Christ, whose "eternal, present life is no longer merely the life of a single [person], the life of Jesus Christ, but the life of the many, the life of millions of Christians, who jubilantly acknowledge Jesus Christ and are united through their flesh and blood in community with him."[50] To shed light on this mystery, one must first understand what Christ accomplished and then consider the renewal of the German people.

Jesus Christ has accomplished something "trans-historical." Through his birth to the Virgin Mary, the Son of God became a human being. He took on human feelings and will, indeed all that constitutes human existence, and he united humanity with

God. This 'event' occurred within history, for Jesus lived and died in Palestine more than nineteen hundred years ago, and yet it stands outside of time, for it has eternal significance. "Because Jesus' humanity is taken up into the eternity of God's Son, it is and remains the proper organ, the means, the instrument through which the eternal salvific will of God *per saecula saeculorum* redeems people of all times and regions."[51] God's grace enters into human affairs through Jesus Christ, specifically through his humanity, bringing divine forgiveness to humankind.

This is surely good news, for it brings us assurance and hope amid the turmoil of the world's history. In the historian's perspective, the death of Jesus was simply one among many tragedies. Caesar Augustus died, as did the other Caesars, and the Roman Empire collapsed. Eventually, the German race gained ascendancy and formed a new Reich. But this empire, too, was eventually destroyed by Napoleon and then by capitalism. In the believer's perspective, there has been one stable point in all of history's highs and lows. This point is Jesus Christ. He is not a past figure, but the person who meets people in every era, especially through the church's sacraments. When Christians gather for the Lord's Supper, they do not go to him, rather he comes to them: "Jesus, the God-man, the crucified, the risen one steps into your time, steps into your life, steps into your being. You are his, and he is yours."[52]

Union with Christ entails more than adoration, it also involves action. As we are united with Christ through our humanity, we become his disciples: "We follow him, we form his image in us." This image is not, however, a fixed form, but a cultural expression of Christ as he is known by a specific people. For the ancient desert fathers, Christ was the "divine athlete" who subdued Satan. For the Byzantine church, Christ was the *Pantocrator*. For the Gothic church, he was the "crucified Christ." For Francis of Assisi, Christ was the babe in the crib of poverty. For Germans, Christ is the "heroic, knightly" figure as is portrayed in Albrecht Dürer's etchings of the "manly Christ, the Christ of inner power, of inner superiority over need and death."[53]

If there is to occur a genuine national renewal, then, all Germans must be united in Jesus Christ and form his image in their lives. Germans need to look anew "for this heroic Christ, for the Christ of heroic self-giving." Can anyone doubt that new life is now

flowing into the German race, into "the German oak"? "Is there
not a new person, a new race in process, whose breath is hot and
damp, . . . a race, which has . . . returned to the inherited blood, to
the home earth and to that origin and holy source, from which
this race draws its best powers, namely, from the Christian faith?"

New energy is stirring among the people. That is definite,
says Adam. The issue is whether Germans will recognize the true
source of this renewal and then express this life in appropriate
forms. Unsuitable expressions have already occurred, and "we
have to deplore [these] misrepresentations and wild forms." Christians must affirm the "essence" of Germany's new life, along with
"its ideal powers and forces," but at the same time they must speak
out against its aberrations.

What is this essence? It is "a heroic spirit. It is the spirit
of spontaneous giving for the community of race, of the resolute
brotherhood." Its center point is Jesus Christ, whom Christians
honor because of his "heroic" life and death for all people, including the Jewish people. As Pope Pius XI and the German bishops
have made clear, Jesus lived and died as a Jew, and his race cannot
be denied, nor should it be. "It is exactly this [race] that our
ancestors above all saw and loved in the human figure of Christ."[54]
A "national-heroic ethic" must have Jesus Christ as its norm, and
it must also have him as its source. "The German oak cannot
otherwise wish to grow and to prosper," declares Adam, "than
by sinking the roots of its power into the wellspring of the Christian mystery, into the mother earth of our existential unity with
Christ." Despite the historical separation between Protestantism
and Catholicism, all Germans are united with one another in Jesus
Christ. He is their authentic source of national unity.

The "German blood" will be rejuvenated only by a return
to the ancient Nordic-Teutonic worship, say the leaders of the
German Faith Movement. But Christians cannot tolerate such talk.
"If the so-called German Faith Movement would like to establish a
different foundation for us Germans than that which is [already]
laid, namely, Jesus Christ, if the Movement perceives this foundation only in the realm of biology or only in the enigmatic rule of the
German will, then we point out that the true God, the infinite one,
is neither bound to blood nor to the will of blood."[55] The nation's
renewal depends upon a transcendent source which is "infinitely
richer than all racial-national life." This divine source possesses

truths that "tower above all purely earthly, racial yearnings and drives." This transcendent source holds truths that bestow on a people the "highest values of the divine will," truths that "create in a people a drive to heroic greatness, to the height and breadth of the supernatural, divine life."

The true God is the triune God who stands above creation and, out of love, freely chooses to enter into creation and history. Once we recall this genuine understanding of God, then we see the superficiality of the German Faith Movement's ideology. Adam states:

> If the German Faith Movement fundamentally denies this revelation of God, manifest in Christ, in its particularity and uniqueness, then this denial can only occur because the movement's god is a god enslaved to the world, a mutilated god, not that living, personal, infinite God who created heaven and earth. Because this movement denies the absoluteness of God, it rejects absolutely also the absoluteness of Christ and of Christianity.[56]

In conclusion, Adam urges that all Germans discover and affirm the true center of their race. "May all of us again seek and find that one and only one who, as he is the cornerstone for the entire world, determines its destiny and remains for us Germans the single source of life, out of which true German life blossoms." Everyone must pray for a strengthening of the nation's Christian faith. "Lord, Jesus Christ, you are the redeemer of the world, remain with us, among the German race, . . . so that we may become a race full of purity, courage, and cultivation, a race full of trust in God and piety, full of brotherly love and sacrifice, a free, a brave, a heroic race. Amen."[57]

3. RECEPTION: NAZISM AGAINST MODERATION

"Deutsches Volkstum und katholisches Christentum" and "Vom gottmenschlichen Erlöser" are representative of Adam's efforts to build a bridge between Catholicism and National Socialism. The first statement (July 1933) endorsed Hitler's regime and its potential compatibility with Catholicism. The second statement (January 1934) criticized the German Faith Movement as an extremist element within National Socialism. Both statements were motivated by the desire to safeguard the Christian and national values at the heart of German life—values which in the theologian's judgment National Socialism in its best moments also wanted to protect. Adam saw his task, therefore, as one of affirming the genuine values of the movement surrounding Hitler and rejecting the distortions.[58] However, this attempt to separate aberrations like the German Faith Movement from essential elements in German society such as community met immediate resistance.

Adam's speech of Sunday January 21 was well received by those assembled for the *Katholikentag* in Stuttgart.[59] The youth groups broke into strong applause and cheering when Adam finished speaking. Then, when the ceremony ended, the young men and women, still wearing their Catholic insignia, gathered outside the hall and processed through the streets until they were dispersed by the police for violating the government's prohibition against non-Nazi marches.

On Monday, Stuttgart's NSDAP newspaper, the *N.S. Kurier*, depicted the *Katholikentag* as a political provocation. It ran the headline, "Mobs against the German Christians: Agitating Conduct by Uniformed, Catholic Organizations" and said that Adam spoke with "unrestrained animosity" against the German Christians.[60] This report distorted the speech in two ways. First, it reported that the speaker had criticized the German Christians, when in fact he spoke against the German Faith Movement. Second, it described the speech's tone as one of hate, when Adam's words were conciliatory toward German nationalism.

In the next edition of the *N.S. Kurier* another article appeared with the headline "Blunders of a Professor—the Glorification of the History of the Jewish People." After giving a twisted review of Adam's speech, it declared: "We must sharply object that the history of the Jewish people is valued higher here than that of our own German people, although this speaker should know from his historical studies that Catholicism, as it conquered Germany, extirpated all symbols of German culture, or changed them into Christian values."[61] The report also disagreed with Adam's comment that German history has not displayed prophetic figures comparable to Moses, Isaiah, and Jeremiah. In placing the Jewish prophets above great German leaders, Adam had betrayed the German people, the *N.S. Kurier* charged.

On Tuesday January 23 Adam learned that Storm Troopers might disrupt his class on the doctrine of God at the University of Tübingen. Accompanied by the university's deputy rector, Professor H. W. Geiger, Adam arrived at the lecture hall to find strangers, some wearing "brown shirts," among his students. One Storm Trooper was reading aloud from the *N.S. Kurier* regarding the professor's speech in Stuttgart. As statements were read, hoots and whistles filled the hall. The room quieted down, however, as Adam entered. When he reached the podium, he greeted the assembly. In response, he received both applause and boos. Then, a Storm Trooper approached Adam and ordered him to leave the dais. At this point, Geiger came forward, asserted that he, not the Storm Trooper, was in charge, and he dismissed the class. As people stood to leave, a Storm Trooper began the Nazi anthem, and all in the room sang with their hands in salute—either because they chose to or because they felt coerced. Later that day groups of Storm Troopers loitered in Adam's neighborhood and pistols were fired at his home.

On Wednesday January 24 the rector's office posted this notice: "The course of Professor Adam has been dropped until further notice, according to the decision of the minister of culture [for the State of Württemberg]." This ban against Adam's courses so offended the faculty of Catholic theology that, in support of their colleague, these professors went on strike and stopped lecturing.[62]

Bishop Sproll immediately wrote to the minister of culture protesting the minister's decision and his allegations that in the address on January 21 Adam "had incited the youth to rebellion against the state's authority." Sproll reminded the minister of culture that Adam had written in support of Hitler and National Socialism in his article "Deutsches Volkstum und katholisches Christentum." Finally, the bishop urged that the state immediately reinstate Adam's courses in the university's curriculum and take steps to maintain order in Tübingen. Sproll sent Cardinal Bertram in Berlin a copy of his letter to the minister of culture, adding the note: "The struggle between faith and unbelief appears to be beginning."[63]

On Friday January 26 the minister of culture met with Adam. He pointed out that the professor had been censured by the government because his address "Vom gottmenschlichen Erlöser" contained statements divergent from the "official political point of view" and included remarks "degrading the German essence," because of the "emphasis on the weakness and depravity of our ancestors." The minister said that he would restore Adam's teaching license on the condition that the professor refrain from making political statements.[64]

Adam returned to the lecture hall on Monday January 29 and again found strangers, including five uniformed Storm Troopers, among the students. He said nothing about his address in Stuttgart and the incidents on the previous Tuesday but lectured on the doctrine of God. After a few minutes, two of the Storm Troopers stood up and noisily left the hall. The other three talked among themselves, disturbing the lecture. When they persisted, Adam invited them to leave the room, but they insisted upon remaining until the lecture's end.

While there were no further public incidents, Adam's case was pursued in official circles. It came to the attention of Vice Chancellor Franz von Papen and Freiherr von Rassler, Württemberg's head of the Arbeitsgemeinschaft Katholischer Deutscher (AKD). (Papen had founded the AKD in October 1933 to serve as a mediation board when conflicts arose between the Catholic church and the government.)[65] On January 31, 1934, Papen brought the case to the attention of Joseph Goebbels, the Third Reich's minister of propaganda, by presenting a formal complaint against Stuttgart's *N.S. Kurier*. He demanded that the government reprimand the Nazi reporter for writing a distorted account of Adam's speech. It was necessary, insisted Papen, not only to take action "on the one hand against such Catholic leaders and organizations whose conduct is subversive," but also "on the other hand not to refuse the protection of the state to those who—as here—were injured in a completely unjustified manner in their national respect."[66]

Papen's complaint went nowhere. The government would not punish the Nazi reporter, declared Goebbels, but it would review the censure against Adam. By saying that the central issue concerned religious and academic freedom, Goebbels pushed the case from his desk to that of the Reich's minister of the interior, Rudolf Buttmann. It sat on Buttmann's desk for three months. In April, when Papen saw that Buttmann would not act on the matter, he withdrew his complaint against the *N.S. Kurier* and the entire case was dropped. By its inaction, the Reich approved of the way in which Adam had been treated by the Nazi press, the Storm Troopers, and Württemberg's minister of culture.

4. Pursuing a Moderate Nationalism, 1934–1939

In "Deutsches Volkstum und katholisches Christentum" and "Vom gottmenschlichen Erlöser" Adam affirmed what he perceived to be the best aspects of German nationalism and grounded this nationalism in Christian belief. This conciliatory approach is further evident in Adam's statements of February 1935 and December 1939.

The conflict between the Nazi regime and the Catholic church broke into the open from 1935 through 1937, when Pius XI wrote his encyclical *Mit brennender Sorge*, condemning Nazism.[67] In early June 1934 the German bishops issued a pastoral letter protesting against the neopaganism of the German Faith Movement, the ideology of Alfred Rosenberg, the Reich's efforts for a national church, and the suppression of Catholic organizations and press. The Gestapo immediately seized the undistributed copies of this statement and forbad the publication of new copies. On June 30, 1934, the "Night of the Long Knives," Nazis murdered over one hundred of their "political" opponents, including such respected Catholics as Professor Friedrich Beck, newspaper editor Fritz Gerlich, Center party leader and head of Catholic Action Erich Klausener, and the leader of Catholic sports, Adalbert Probst. Three weeks later, on July 25, Austrian Nazis assassinated Austria's Chancellor Engelbert Dollfuss. Shocked by the violence of Hitler's movement, the Vatican rejected a proposed agreement regarding the implementation of its concordat with Germany. In October a group of Catholic scholars published criticisms of Nazi ideology, to which Rosenberg retaliated by writing *An die Dunkelmänner unserer Zeit* (To the obscurantists of our age). On January 24, 1935, Hitler appointed Rosenberg to the position of Plenipotentiary for the German Worldview, thereby giving official backing to Rosenberg's views and those of the German Faith Movement. The strife between the state and the church then expanded into the Nazi's "show trials" against Catholic lay leaders, nuns, brothers, and priests who were publicly accused of fraud, subversive activity, and the sexual abuse of children.

Speaking on February 5, 1935, in Tübingen to the St. Boniface Society, Adam delivered his lecture "Jesus Christus und der Geist unserer Zeit" (entitled in English "Jesus Christ and the Spirit of Our Age") in which he highlighted a point of convergence between Catholicism and modern thought. At the outset he noted that some eras and cultures are more conducive to the life of faith than others: "The spirit of the age makes discipleship of Jesus easier or more difficult, according as it is akin or alien to his spirit."[68]

The spirit or mentality of the twentieth century is more compatible with Christian faith, said Adam, than was the mentality of the late nineteenth century. In the second half of the 1800s, neo-Kantianism, in continuation of the Enlightenment, eliminated all features of Jesus Christ which did not fit within its narrowly "rational" scheme of reality. It described religion as an "idealistic monism" in which divine reality is merely a reflection of the human personality.[69] The German Faith Movement, with its psychological and anthropological view of Teutonic myths, embraced this monism. But, said Adam, this movement is waning, as is the Enlightenment mentality in general.

According to Adam, the "spirit of the [present] age" is a romantic one that values the body and soul as well as the intellect. Representatives of the neoromantic *Lebensphilosophie*, writers like Goethe, Nietzsche, Bergson, Ludwig Klages, and Stefan George, have promoted a "wholistic" view of personal existence. "Not the man who has renounced sensuous life, who has been divided and torn asunder by the disastrous opposition of body and spirit, of Bios and Logos, but the man who has been restored to inner unity and wholeness . . . he is the man of the future."[70]

In Adam's judgment, Christian belief is well served by neoromanticism, and, simultaneously, it transforms this outlook on life. On the one hand, the romantic thought illuminates "the character of Jesus," namely, "the incredible unity and wholeness of his personality." The vocabulary of the philosophy of life permits talk about the lack of an inner dichotomy in Jesus. It provides categories in which to see that Jesus enjoyed human pleasures when appropriate and also set them aside when his mission required this. In short, neoromantic language permits the awareness that Jesus attained "the sanctification of the whole man."[71]

On the other hand, Christian faith is changing the secular *Lebensphilosophie*, for it has established a new standard as to

what counts as "wholeness" and "heroism." Belief in Jesus Christ
overturns Nietzsche's ideas. The man or woman who wants to
become a full human being, a genuine *Übermensch*, patterns his or
her life after the example of Christ, as the ancient Christian martyrs
did. This person seeks what is "noble and great on this earth" as
seen in relation to "its final infinite fulfillment and completion by
God." The *Übermensch*, "striving naturally after moral loftiness,
[is] now laid hold of by the grace of the Holy Spirit in the depths
of his being, at the point where his natural moral capacities and
powers rise from his inmost soul."[72] In sum, according to Adam,
the true "hero" is "the saint."

This lecture was soon published in German as a short book.
One year later it was translated into French. In 1937 it appeared
in English in *Germany's New Religion*, along with essays by two
other professors at the University of Tübingen.[73] This book
includes three essays by Jakob Wilhelm Hauer (1881-1962), professor of Indology and the scientific study of religion, who collab-
orated with Alfred Rosenberg in the German Faith Movement. His
essays are "The Origin of the German Faith Movement," "An Alien
or a German Faith," and "The Semitic Character of Christianity."[74]
Germany's New Religion contains, too, the essay "Responsibility
and Destiny: The Difference Between Hauer's View and the Message of the Bible and the Reformers" by the Protestant theologian
Karl Heim, who, like Adam, opposed the German Faith Movement.

Catholic journals praised Adam. *Stimmen der Zeit* lauded the
German publication of Adam's essay because he took issue with
the neo-Kantian reductionism of Jesus Christ and presented an
understanding of the "whole Christ."[75] The *Clergy Review* judged
that of the three authors in *Germany's New Religion* only Adam
sufficiently upheld the supernatural character of God's revelation.
"Dr. Karl Adam's essay . . . shows that in the Christian religion
alone is to be found the divinely predestined perfection of human
nature, and that true heroism consists in the practice of Christian
virtue."[76] According to the *Tablet*'s review, Adam correctly refuted
Nietzsche's view of Christianity and also explained the Catholic
principle that "grace builds on nature."[77] Further, it pointed out
two shortcomings. First, Adam minimized the consequences of
original sin in human life and, second, he was too severe in his
criticism of the church.

"Jesus Christ and the Spirit of the Age" was another effort at bridge-building. Adam affirmed the *Lebensphilosophie* with its wholistic view of life, and at the same time he criticized Nietzsche's atheism and the German Faith Movement's claim to be Germany's true religion. The essay manifested, therefore, Adam's desire to wed Christian faith and German culture—an intention that surfaced again in late 1939.

Germany's Catholic bishops faced a new dilemma after the *Wehrmacht* invaded Poland on September 1, 1939.[78] How could they support their people and at the same time keep their distance from Hitler's belligerent policies and actions? How could they maintain their credibility and simultaneously communicate their misgivings about the aggression of the *Führer*? Shortly after the invasion, in an official statement, the bishops urged Catholics to fulfill their respective duties to the *Vaterland* and to extend compassion toward all people, including their enemies. On September 7, 1939, the Archdiocese of Munich's *Amtsblatt* stated that "in such hard times, where all become one, it is imperative that each one in the place where he is stationed fulfill his religious, patriotic and civil duty and that each one stand at the side of the other in a spirit of close Christian brotherly love and true solidarity."[79] Both the German bishops' statement and the Archdiocese of Munich's statement exhibited no enthusiasm for war.

Among the bishops' worries was their concern that Hitler would use the war as an excuse for violating the concordat with the Vatican. Included in this agreement was a secret appendix to the effect that in the event of war the government would not conscript Catholic priests and seminarians.[80] In the autumn of 1939, as young men were drafted to the *Wehrmacht*, the bishops labored to ensure the government's adherence to this clause.

At the same time Karl Adam publicly expressed a view contrary to the bishops' position. On December 10, 1939, he gave a lecture entitled "Die geistige Lage des deutschen Katholizismus" (The spiritual situation of German Catholicism) to an audience of a thousand Catholics in Aachen.[81] His theme concerned the compatibility of Catholicism and German culture. According to Adam, since Catholicism respects every particular culture and expresses its universal truths in local forms, German Catholics should enter more fully into their nation's "worldview."

The Catholic church could foster this cultural adaptation, noted Adam, in three concrete ways. First, the bishops should permit the government to conscript seminarians, so that these young men would get out of the seminary's sheltered environment and participate in their nation's cause. After this service for their country, the seminarians would be more effective as priests. Second, the Vatican should allow the Mass to be celebrated in the vernacular. If Germans could worship in their native tongue, they would have a more profound experience of the liturgy, and Catholic worship would have a stronger impact upon the German ethos. Third, the church should promote the veneration of German saints, the men and women who embodied Christian convictions and German values. According to Adam, steps like these three would make Catholicism more of a leaven in the nation's life. They would permit Catholics to be more fully German and simultaneously enable them to lead the German culture more deeply into the Christian faith. In Adam's words: "We must be Catholic in the very fibers of our hearts, but we must also—in order to promote Catholicism—be German to the core."[82]

This lecture had painful consequences for the theologian. Some nationalistic Catholics appealed to the lecture in their efforts to pressure the German bishops into changing their stance on the conscription of seminarians. On June 4, 1940, Baron Leopold von Nagel wrote an open letter to the episcopacy in which he quoted Adam on the value of military service for seminarians. As a result, Bishop Josef Kumpfmüller of the Diocese of Augsburg issued a pastoral letter reminding Catholics of the bishops' position on the drafting of seminarians. He specifically pointed out that Adam's views were not in agreement with those of the German bishops. Then, in a private meeting with Adam, Bishop Kumpfmüller insisted that the professor was "objectively incorrect" in calling for the conscription of seminarians and the use of German in the celebration of the Eucharist.[83] By his lecture, said the bishop, Adam had not helped either the Catholic church in Germany or his theological profession. Afterwards, in a report to Cardinal Faulhaber, Kumpfmüller wrote that Adam had come under the sway of Catholics who were very critical of the church. He also noted that it was difficult to communicate with the theologian for he was hard of hearing. Finally, Adam's lecture in Aachen had another consequence. The dioceses of Aachen, Augsburg, and

Cologne prohibited their seminarians at Tübingen from enrolling in Adam's classes.[84]

Karl Adam favored German nationalism, but he was not a National Socialist. Hitler's despotism tolerated no partial allegiance to the Third Reich, however; either a person publicly supported the *Führer*, or one was deemed a traitor. Nevertheless, Adam attempted to be a nationalist without being a Nazi. He tried to reconcile the Catholic church and National Socialism without any loss to the integrity of Christian faith. In hindsight we can see that Adam's vision of a new religious and cultural synthesis in Germany under Hitler was unattainable. Cardinal Faulhaber had properly assessed the situation in 1933: Catholicism and National Socialism were in principle incompatible.

Adam was beguiled by Nazi rhetoric and he made too little of numerous tragic incidents: Hitler's condoning of the Potempa murders, the NSDAP's boycotts against Germany's Jewish citizens, the harassment of Cardinal Faulhaber, the government's tacit approval of the Storm Troopers' abuse of Adam himself, the Night of the Long Knives, the Nazis' expulsion of Bishop Sproll from the Diocese of Rottenburg-Stuttgart, and the nationwide pogrom of the *Kristallnacht*.[85] For Adam, these events were not disclosures of the character of Hitler and the NSDAP, but aberrations within Germany's rebirth.

How could Adam's nationalism have been so uncritical? Commentators have rightly attributed his myopia to the *Lebensphilosophie*.[86] The Dutch theologian Mark Schoof has pointed to it: "Even a man who was as little concerned with politics as Karl Adam, following his predecessors at Tübingen and influenced, as they were, by Romanticism, believed that the 'spirit of the people' was a pillar of the Church and hoped together with many others, that the Nazis would be able to exert a healthy influence."[87] Walter Kasper has observed that Adam's "unbroken affirmation of the natural values of the national-racial community initially led him to commit himself to a deeply penetrating renewal of National Socialism."[88] According to Hans Kreidler, Adam's "romantic, organic" notion of life prompted him to endorse communal forms of life wherever they were struggling into existence, and, as a result, Adam did not sufficiently distinguish between the church's vision of community and the state's.[89]

After 1939 Adam limited his publications to such topics as our knowledge of God, ecclesiology, and Jesus Christ. And, in the aftermath of the war he did not comment on his prewar efforts to reconcile Catholicism and National Socialism. But his statements from 1933 to 1939 raise the question of the influence of the *Lebensphilosophie* not only on his political views but also on his theology. In what ways did neoromanticism contribute for the better to *The Spirit of Catholicism*, *Christ Our Brother*, and *The Son of God*? In what ways did it detract from his presentations on the church and Jesus Christ? This is the issue that we must take up in chapter 7, after in chapter 6 we review Adam's postwar writings and his last years.

6
Standing Aside (1946–1966)

In the 1950s the Catholic church experienced a fermentation that eventually produced the Second Vatican Council. Yves Congar, Alois Grillmeier, Henri de Lubac, Karl Rahner, Edward Schillebeeckx, and many other scholars were opening new paths in the doctrine of grace, ecclesiology, and christology. The church was clearly undergoing a "momentous theological breakthrough," said Grillmeier in 1957. And, he added: "The course of theological pursuits in recent years gives us occasion to hope that the foundations of a *Christological Age* have finally been laid."[1]

Karl Adam stood aside as these postwar developments took place. During the autumn semester of 1949–1950 he lectured on the doctrine of creation and grace, and he led a doctoral seminar on Mariology. Then, in March 1950, at the age of seventy-three, he retired with the academic rank of professor emeritus. As he ended his teaching career, he wrote two more books: *One and Holy* and *The Christ of Faith*. By 1953, for reasons of health, the Tübingen professor had given up his scholarly work and withdrawn from the public eye.[2] He lived in retirement for fifteen years before his death in 1966 at the age of eighty-nine.

Adam was not forgotten during his last years. His books were still read. In the United States they appeared in bookstores until the mid-1960s. Also, many of his colleagues publicly acknowledged Adam's help in laying the foundations of the new christological age. Their testimonials to the theologian will be reviewed after we consider his last two books.

1. TEXT: "ONE AND HOLY"

Karl Adam's theological interest in ecumenism began in the 1920s.[3] Since Adam held that we must view the mystery of the

church in relation to the mystery of Christ, he was both devoted
to the church and ready to question it. This orientation disposed
Adam to weigh Protestant critiques of the Catholic church. As
already noted, his critical distance on the church can be seen in the
last chapter of *The Spirit of Catholicism*, where he acknowledges
that the church has not consistently lived up to its ideal. He
showed his ecumenical commitment, too, in his appreciation of
the University of Tübingen's Catholic and Protestant faculties in
theology, for he stayed abreast of the writings of Barth, Bultmann,
and his colleague Karl Heim.

German Catholics in general became engaged in ecumenism
after the First World War. As they reflected on the war's horror,
the experience of fighting and dying with non-Catholics, and the
rise of atheism in the Weimar Republic, they searched for ways
to overcome their long-standing differences with Protestants.[4] In
the early 1930s Robert Grosche edited the ecumenical journal
Catholica. In 1938 Max Metzger founded the Una Sancta Brotherhood in Meitingen, Bavaria, and traveled throughout Germany
promoting discussion groups, lectures, and sermons on Catholic-
Protestant issues, including national politics. Metzger's efforts bore
fruit in Germany's Una Sancta movement. In 1939 the church historian Joseph Lortz undergirded the work of Grosche and Metzger
with his book *The Reformation in Germany*. Lortz described the
late medieval conditions and ecclesiastical abuses that led to the
Reformation and clarified that Martin Luther initially intended to
reform the church from within, not to establish a church. This
study gave Catholics a historical frame of reference within which
they could carry on discussions with Protestants.

Metzger and Adam became friends during the 1930s, and
Metzger increased Adam's awareness of ecumenism's possibilities.
In the Third Reich, as Hitler's synchronization of German life
increasingly threatened the autonomy of the churches, Metzger
campaigned even more vigorously for the uniting of Catholics and
Protestants against the totalitarian state. When the *Wehrmacht*'s
invasion of Poland began the Second World War, Metzger publicly
declared that Germany should stop fighting and end the war. At
this point, Adam urged Metzger to be cautious, for the Reich would
not tolerate dissension. But Metzger persisted in calling for church
unity and a cease fire. As a result, he was arrested by the Gestapo
and executed in June 1944.[5]

After the war Adam contributed to the Una Sancta movement by offering lectures and sermons on the theological causes of the Reformation and also on the theological basis of unity among the Christian churches. Of these talks, the most famous were the sermons given on the evenings of April 27, 28, and 29, 1947, to a large congregation in the Protestant Marcuskirche in Stuttgart.[6] Shortly afterwards, Adam gave these same sermons to large assemblies in Karlsruhe, and in 1948 they were published as the book *Una Sancta in katholischer Sicht*, entitled in English *One and Holy*.

One and Holy builds on Lortz's *The Reformation in Germany*. The first chapter argues that Martin Luther and the other Reformers were not denying the central truths of Catholicism but were challenging ecclesiastical abuses. The second characterizes Luther as an original thinker whose perceptions were valid but whose means of realizing these ideas were flawed. The third chapter offers concrete proposals for knitting together what was torn apart. Christian unity will come about as Catholics and Protestants understand better their respective doctrines, strengthen their bonds with Christ, and respect one another. "We must each take our own Confession seriously," said Adam; "we must each give ourselves unconditionally to Christ and His holy will; and, inspired by this love of Christ, we must each root out of ourselves all loveless prejudice against those of the other faith."[7]

The language of *One and Holy* is noteworthy, especially when compared with its author's prewar writings. The terms are descriptive but not romantic. The chapters' titles speak of the "roots of the Reformation," "Luther's turning away from the church," and "church unity." These titles create strong images without the rhetoric found in *The Son of God* and "Jesus Christ and the Spirit of Our Age." Nothing is said about Christian "heroism" and the "organic" quality of life. To be sure, the *Lebensphilosophie* is operative in comments about life's depths, the movement of history, the bonds of community, and the solidarity of all people. Yet, these ideas are expressed in modest terms: "But we do know that we ourselves, though we cannot create any final unity in Christendom, must do everything possible to prepare the way for *dynamic* unity, a unity of hearts and minds. If there cannot immediately be unity of faith, let there at least be unity of love."[8] Here is Adam's life-long vision of all people united in Christ, but now the vision is conveyed with a linguistic simplicity not found in his writings of the 1920s and 30s.

One and Holy was so well received in Germany that in 1949 it was translated into French, and one year later into Dutch.[9] It was published in England in 1951, and, simultaneously, its first chapter appeared in the United States as the pamphlet *The Roots of the Reformation*. The book received little comment in German periodicals, but it was praised in English-speaking journals. *Theological Studies* concluded its laudatory review by stating: "Whatever success attends Adam's endeavor, all must applaud the spirit of charity and understanding that animates it, just as all must share his conviction that it is high time for all Christians to be a *unanimous* witness to Christ."[10] The *Tablet* declared that the Tübingen theologian "draws out principles [for Christian unity], the knowledge and application of which are primary necessities for the soul of England and the world at large."[11] Dr. Eva-Maria Jung of Mainz's Institute for European Studies, a center for ecumenism, observed in 1955 that *One and Holy* brought international recognition to the Una Sancta movement.[12]

Commentators agree that Adam aided the rise of Protestant-Catholic dialogue in the mid-twentieth century. Heinrich Fries, who has given a great deal to ecumenism, has written that *One and Holy* anticipated theological developments in the 1960s: "The ecumenical ideas and issues which we face today would not exist without Karl Adam's contribution, not only in the text *One and Holy*, but also in his whole life's work, which turns around the central truths of Christ and the church."[13] In Fries's judgment, Adam prepared the way for the Second Vatican Council's Decree on Ecumenism (1964), for he located ecclesiology in relation to the person of Christ and Christ's mission in the world. This appraisal of Adam's work has been supported by Walter Kasper, who has said: "Karl Adam became one of the most important pioneer's of the ecumenical movement because of his renewed vision of the church."[14]

2. TEXT: "THE CHRIST OF FAITH"

In the 1920s and 30s Karl Adam wrote *Christ Our Brother* and *The Son of God* with the aim of producing a christology that combined historical research and the church's dogmatic teachings.

To accomplish this synthesis, he depended, as we have seen in earlier chapters, on three sources: Scripture and tradition, historical-critical study, and contemporary thought, especially the *Lebensphilosophie*. After the war Adam exhibited this same commitment to a theological synthesis in criticizing Rudolf Bultmann's program of "demythologizing" and in his last book *The Christ of Faith*.

In "Das Problem der Entmythologisierung und die Auferstehung des Christus" (The problem of demythologizing and the resurrection of Christ) (1952), Adam challenges Bultmann's effort to separate the truth of the gospels from their "mythology."[15] According to Adam, the attempt to demythologize the Scriptures, as spelled out in the Marburg theologian's essay "The New Testament and Mythology" (1941), waters down the mystery of Jesus Christ by means of historical-critical methods.[16] Similar to the liberal quest of the historical Jesus, the endeavor of discriminating between the gospels' content and their form results in an invention— namely, a historical reconstruction bearing little resemblance to Jesus Christ. Adam understands Bultmann to be saying that nothing extraordinary occurred within time and space during Jesus' ministry and after his death. What was extraordinary took place in the hearts and minds of Jesus' followers, who then presented their new, inner awareness of God and Jesus in terms of events in the outer world. These "mythological" ways of talking about God's action in people's lives must be recast in subjective, existential language so that genuine inner faith, similar to that of the first believers, might be awakened and nurtured.

Adam asserts that Bultmann's view of the accounts of the New Testament rests upon a number of erroneous convictions, namely, that God's grace does not change ordinary events but only the mentality of the viewer, that events in the natural world must conform to mechanistic laws of causality, and that Scripture alone is the source of Christian belief. These assumptions are overturned, though, when one takes seriously the Christian tradition. Study of the genesis of 1 Corinthians 15:3-5 shows that Jesus' followers were convinced that something objective had taken place in Jesus after his death. They handed on their good news initially by means of their oral living tradition, which attested to something outside of themselves. "The faith of the early witnesses of Christianity exists therefore," declares Adam, "primarily in the truth of an objective state of affairs. Since the early apostles acknowledged this state of affairs with all [their] being, they engaged in an existential decision [regarding it]."[17] If this faith is to be passed on to the next generation and if it is to nurture a rich theology, the gospels' accounts of Jesus' miracles and resurrection must be presented in all of their detail. Adam writes:

> A merely existential interpretation of salvation history misconstrues the enormous force and urgency, the integrity and conviction of the self-understanding and experience of the original witnesses. As a result, it empties faith in the resurrection of its concrete, vital, bright impulse and pushes it into the controllable realm of rootless mysticism. Obviously, no healthy theology can build on this foundation.[18]

Adam did not end his scholarly career with this criticism of Bultmann's work. Rather, he assembled his notes from twenty years' lectures on Jesus Christ and edited them into his last book *Der Christus des Glaubens*, entitled in English *The Christ of Faith* (1954). In this text, Adam makes an assumption that also shapes his earlier books. He assumes that if we want to delve into the mystery of "the living Christ," then we must do more than rely on the historian's reconstruction of Jesus' life and message. We must bring together three "images" of Christ: the Bible's "reflected image," Christian doctrine's "dogmatic image," and the contemporary church's "living image" of Christ.[19] Adam undertakes this synthesis by reviewing scriptural and doctrinal views of the "person of Christ" and then discussing the "work of Christ."

Instead of presenting a concise, imaginative representation of Christ of the sort produced in *Christ Our Brother* and *The Son of God*, *The Christ of Faith* provides a review of the church's testimony to Christ arranged according to the headings "son of man" and the "Son of God." As son of man, Jesus Christ is one with us in all things but sin, and as Son of God, he is the divine "person" who has reconciled humankind with God by assuming human nature in the incarnation and then dying on the cross. Within this perspective the book develops the same themes that are expressed in *Christ Our Brother* and *The Son of God*: Christ is the mediator between God and creation; Christ's humanity has redemptive significance; and all people are united with God and one another in the body of Christ. One new, controversial element is the discussion of Jesus' consciousness of himself as the Christ and of his destiny.[20] The overall effect of *The Christ of Faith* is that of a coherent mosaic of Christ—a mosaic shaped by the conviction that "we have to go to the living Church if we wish to know the living Christ."[21]

The Christ of Faith lacks the neoromantic language of *Christ Our Brother* and *The Son of God*. Like these earlier works, it speaks of Christ as the transcendent reality at the heart of human existence. However, it does so without employing the imagery of Christ as "hero." It relies on technical terms and distinctions— something rarely evident in the earlier texts—as it highlights a variety of images of Christ, for example, the son of man, the Son of God, and the new Adam. It insists that Christ unites in himself a truly divine nature and a truly human nature. But there is no analysis of how this unity is realized. As in *The Son of God*, *The Christ of Faith* presents Chalcedon's doctrine of two "natures" and one "person" in the image of two lines originating from a common point:

> The two opposing tendencies of his majesty and his lowliness that we observed at the beginning, and which can be traced through all his utterances, come together in the expression "Son of Man." It has two aspects, heavenly and earthly, divine and human. Thus he gave the most striking expression for his time and world of what was nearest to his soul: the consciousness of being a Saviour come down from heaven, a Saviour and judge in the simple garb of a man.[22]

The Christ of Faith was warmly, though not enthusiastically received by its readers. In 1957 it was translated into Spanish and English. Michael Schmaus, Munich's leading Catholic theologian in the 1950s, praised the text for its "elucidation and enrichment." Noting that the book meets "the demands of scholarly theology," he summed up his remarks by stating: "Thus there is produced an integrated, Catholic image of Christ which points contemporary men and women to a trustworthy foundation [for understanding] what the man willed by God looks like."[23] The same point was made in the *Zeitschrift für katholische Theologie*: "It is to be wished that this book ends up in the hands of many theology students, for it will give them not only a comprehensive knowledge of christology but will also convey to them a wonderment and enthusiasm for the center of theology, Christ."[24] *Theological Studies* observed that while the biblical scholarship is at points out of date, the book itself is a solid contribution to christology: "It would be a mistake, however, to allow the dated character of the book . . . to overshadow the enduring qualities which made Adam so revered a figure. The same blend of sober scholarship and passionate witness to the faith which made *The Spirit of Catholicism* a near-classic apology is still alive in his latest work."[25]

Reviewers spoke of two shortcomings to *The Christ of Faith*. First, the biblical research was out of date. Second, the book lacked an adequate account of the unity of Christ—the same criticism directed toward *Christ Our Brother* and *The Son of God*. This weakness in *The Christ of Faith* was evident to readers in part because the book appeared at the same time as Karl Rahner's essay, "Chalcedon—End or Beginning?" with its dialectical under-standing of the unity of Christ.[26] The inadequate discussion of the hypostatic union and the dated biblical exegesis indicated that *The Christ of Faith* belonged to a theological period that was ending in the 1950s.[27]

The Christ of Faith is still mentioned, though, whenever the history of contemporary christology is told. John Macquarrie refers to the text when he discusses modern efforts in dogmatic theol-ogy: "Even as late as 1954, Karl Adam's excellent book, *The Christ of Faith*, still reflected the traditional christology, though one must add that it showed the continuing strength of that christology."[28] Monika Hellwig, too, has mentioned Adam's work as a prototype of today's christology "from below": "In systematic theology early attempts included such works as Karl Adam's *The Christ of Faith*, in which a serious effort was made to bring the ascending Chris-tology suggested by New Testament scholarship into partnership with the post-Chalcedonian descending Christology that was the established norm."[29]

The Christ of Faith was published at the end of one theo-logical period and the beginning of another. It represented some of the finest elements of traditional theology. It was rooted in the church's testimony to Jesus Christ as "truly God" and "truly man," and it spoke to the readers of its day. At the same time, *The Christ of Faith* anticipated today's emphasis on the humanity of Jesus Christ and historical-critical study of the Bible. But, because the book lacked an adequate analysis of the hypostatic union and depended on out-of-date exegesis, it was eclipsed by the work of a new generation of theologians.

3. LATE RECOGNITION

When Alois Grillmeier said in 1957 that "the foundations of a *Christological Age* have finally been laid," he simultaneously mentioned Karl Adam as one of the theologians who had helped to build this foundation. According to Grillmeier, Adam and France's Paul Galtier—independent of each other—had produced books and articles that had contributed to a renewed appreciation of Christ's humanity in the twentieth century. "There is genuine value," stated Grillmeier, "in stressing the autonomy of Christ's humanity, as is to be seen in that type of Christology which is represented today by such theologians as Galtier and Adam."[30] As we noted previously, the patrologist judged that within the contemporary Scotist-Tiphanic school the book *The Christ of Faith* was "[t]he most significant presentation of this Christology in German."[31]

At the same time that Grillmeier commented on Adam's place within twentieth-century theology, other scholars were also acknowledging the work of the Tübingen theologian. Two festschrifts were dedicated to Adam during his years of retirement.[32] For Adam's seventy-fifth birthday in 1952, fourteen scholars wrote essays in his honor and had these published in the book *Abhandlungen über Theologie und Kirche*.[33] The authors included Roger Aubert, Johannes Betz, Yves Congar, Jean Leclercq, Karl Rahner, and Gottlieb Söhngen. To honor Karl Adam on his eightieth birthday, professors at the University of Munich and the University of Tübingen published essays in the book *Vitae et Veritati*.[34]

In 1956 Karl Rahner wrote an essay entitled "Theologie in der Welt" (Theology in the world) on Karl Adam's contribution to Catholic theology. The Tübingen professor, noted Rahner, was always proud of his roots in Bavaria: "Throughout his life he never denied his Bavarian nature, expressed in his powerful, down-to-earth quality and his unbroken 'naive' unity of spirit and life."[35] Rahner observed that Adam's "spirit and life" overflowed in a theological creativity that produced writings belonging under four headings: the history of dogma (e.g., *Der Kirchenbegriff Tertullians*), dogmatic theology (e.g., *The Spirit of Catholicism*), "religious" literature (e.g. *Christ Our Brother*), and contemporary issues (e.g., "Die Theologie der Krisis"). In Rahner's judgment, this literary corpus manifests Adam's profound, vibrant faith: "The eighteen books and almost three dozen articles are more than

merely learned, printed pages. They are the living testimony of a
Christian with a large heart."

What is Adam's place in the history of Catholic theology?
According to Rahner, Adam led the way in doing "theology in the
world." He labored during the upheaval that took place in Catholic
thought after the First World War, and he helped to bring about
the shift from the neoscholasticism of the nineteenth century to
the twentieth century's theological pluralism. In Rahner's words:

> This transition began between the two world wars. Karl Adam
> belongs to the theologians who contributed to it. He did so coura-
> geously, enthusiastically, without any programmatic jargon and sim-
> ply through a genuine, original theological effort. To be sure, Adam
> did not accomplish this transition on his own. But he was one of
> its foremost theologians.[36]

In 1958, to celebrate the golden anniversary of Adam's teaching career, Johannes Stelzenberger, professor at the University of
Tübingen, published a complete bibliography of Adam's works.
The list cites eighteen books, sixty-two articles, six essays in collec-
tions, and one hundred and seventy-eight book reviews. Not only
is the quantity and quality of Adam's writings impressive, noted
Stelzenberger, so too is the international reach of these texts: "An
entire generation of theology students sat inspired at the feet of
their beloved master and happily listened to his lectures. In the
farthest lands his literary works have found hungry and receptive
readers. . . . Karl Adam counts among the great missionaries in the
service of Jesus' teaching."[37]

From October 1959 until March 1960 Bayerische Rundfunk
aired a series of twelve radio programs on major, German-speaking
Protestant and Catholic theologians. The presentations treated Karl
Adam, Paul Althaus, Hans Urs von Balthasar, Karl Barth, Emil Brunner, Rudolph Bultmann, Yves Congar, Romano Guardini, Reinhold
Niebuhr, Karl Rahner, Heinrich Schlier, and Paul Tillich. To be
included on this list was itself a honor. Moreover, the text on
Adam gave this tribute: " 'The most successful theologian of our
age,' is what Karl Adam has been called. While success is no proof
of genuine merit, it is a fact that Karl Adam has shaped the view of
Christ and Church held by a generation of German Catholics; his
works have been translated into nearly every Western language,
and are being read around the world."[38]

The two festschrifts and the comments by Grillmeier, Rahner, and others show that Catholic scholars of the mid-twentieth century have viewed Adam as a theological pioneer between the wars.[39] He was, as Grillmeier pointed out, one of the theologians whose writings built the base for a new christological age. However, having prepared the way for this era, the Tübingen professor stepped aside. In Mark Schoof's words, Adam "worked in a different sphere, simply laying a broad foundation for the future. His greatness was that he recognized this possibility; his sorrow, that he could do no more."[40]

4. KARL ADAM AND AMERICAN CATHOLICISM

Catholics continued to be attracted to Adam's writings even while the theologian was receiving scholars' tributes at the end of his career. Throughout the 1950s they read his books and articles in ecclesiology, christology, and ecumenism. The longstanding appeal of Adam's work is evidenced in the impact of his writings in the United States.[41]

Adam's books were found on the shelves of many American Catholics in the years preceding the Second Vatican Council. *The Spirit of Catholicism* went through at least eleven printings in English, the last in the late 1960s. *Christ Our Brother* was a best-seller through the 1940s, and *The Son of God* was printed numerous times until the early 1960s. *One and Holy* and its first chapter *The Roots of the Reformation* served as standard texts for ecumenical discussions in the United States in the 1960s. When *The Spirit of Catholicism*, *The Son of God*, and *One and Holy* were printed in paperback, they were discussed at Catholic colleges and retreat houses until after Vatican II.

One of the earliest articles in English on Karl Adam appeared in 1931.[42] The *Fortnightly Review* carried a brief biographical sketch of Adam in order, it said, to correct mistaken impressions of the theologian. Many readers thought that Adam was a layman, for there had appeared a photograph of him in "secular garb" in a newsletter from Sheed and Ward Publishers. But, the article said, Adam was in fact a priest on the faculty of the University of Tübingen. He had written texts other than *The Spirit of Catholicism*. He had also authored scholarly studies on Tertullian and Augustine: "It is only of late that Dr. Adam has turned his facile pen to the more or less popular and apologetical treatment of such subjects as faith and the essence of Catholicism."[43]

Three years later, English-speaking Catholics learned about Adam's criticism of the Nazi's German Faith Movement. Soon after Adam spoke to the Catholic youth assembled in Stuttgart's *Stadthalle* on January 21, 1934, *Commonweal* published an abridged, English translation of the address. It prefaced Adam's text with this statement:

> No religious writer of today combines in a more remarkable way profound religious learning and understanding than does the German writer, Dr. Karl Adam. We present with deep satisfaction his present message to the world—the digest of a sermon delivered at a Catholic Youth meeting in Stuttgart, Germany—at a time when the utter collapse of non-religious systems of government, of education, of economics, of social reforms leave humanity, save for the Church, bewildered.[44]

St. John's Abbey, Collegeville, Minnesota, made some of Adam's essays available in English through its journal *Orate Fratres*, later named *Worship*.[45] *Orate Fratres* published "Sanctification of Marriage" in 1935 and "Dogmatic Bases of the Liturgy" in 1937.[46] "The Mystery of Christ's Incarnation," appearing in 1939, included an editor's note: "Once again, the third time within five years, *Orate Fratres* has the honor and privilege of presenting to its readers a series of articles by the greatest of living theologians, Dr. Karl Adam."[47] Only two parts of this article were published, presumably because of the Second World War. After the war, *Worship* published three more articles by the Tübingen professor: "Easter Sermon" in 1953, "Pentecost and Baptism" in 1954, and "An Act of Faith" in 1957.[48]

It was not only St. John's publication that spread Adam's ideas, so too did its liturgist Virgil Michel (1890–1938).[49] In his seminal work *The Liturgy of the Church* (1937), Michel discussed worship and the sacraments within the view of the church as the body of Christ. He credited Johann Adam Möhler with rejuvenating this ecclesiology in the nineteenth century, but he also recognized Karl Adam's role in keeping this ecclesiology alive in the twentieth century. Michel quoted *The Spirit of Catholicism* five times and referred to it at other points.[50] Michel's text as well as his other writings were instrumental in bringing about the liturgical renewal in the United States, and as a result, they indirectly disseminated Adam's ideas.

In the 1950s, after the appearance of *One and Holy* and *The Roots of the Reformation*, numerous Catholic journals carried texts by Adam and also articles about him. *Commonweal* published an essay by Adam on Protestant-Catholic dialogue in 1951.[51] In 1956 *Jubilee* featured an article about Adam that begins with a photograph of him dressed in a bow tie and a Bavarian smoking jacket and holding his book *One and Holy*, and it ends with a full page of quotations from this text. The author, Adolf Schalk, writes: "Dr. Adam's name is synonymous in the minds of Americans with the Una Sancta movement, which seeks an ultimate union in one Faith, . . . I questioned Adam about this movement, of which he has become a major symbol. One cannot find unity, he said to me, until the great wound between Catholicism and Protestantism is healed."[52]

In 1958 *Jubilee* published a lyrical reflection by Adam on the figure of Christ in John's Gospel. Representative of this text are its opening lines:

> St. John spent his youth on the quiet shores of the Lake of Gennesaret. . . . More than anyone else, he saw deep into the innermost life of the God-man. He heard words so delicate, so profound and gentle that his tongue stumbled when he tried to reproduce them, and he had to begin afresh to recapture all these nuances. Not one of the Apostles or the Evangelists traced the spiritual life of our Lord with such tenderness and such self surrender, or described it with such sympathy as he.[53]

Many influential American Catholics were devoted to the writings of Karl Adam.[54] Dorothy Day spoke highly of Adam's work, especially *The Spirit of Catholicism*. In her autobiography, *The Long Loneliness* (1952), she notes that she read *The Spirit of Catholicism* in the summer of 1929, when she was working as a cook at the Marist novitiate on Staten Island.[55] She had been a Catholic for only a year and a half and gladly accepted the literature on faith and prayer that Father McKenna gave her. "He brought me books to read," says Day, "and introduced me to such writers as Karl Adam and showed me how to say the Little Office of the Blessed Virgin."[56] Three years later, Peter Maurin urged Day to read even more of Adam's writings.[57] She did this and, as a result, the works of the Tübingen theologian assisted in the formation of Day's nascent Catholic spirituality.

Flannery O'Connor, the great American writer, was an avid reader of Karl Adam.[58] In a letter to Cecil Dawkins in 1957 she criticizes the superficial understanding that some Catholics have of their faith and calls for investigating Christian belief on one's own. She insists that "to discover the Church you have to set out by yourself." Then, recalling how she herself did this, she mentions her reliance on Adam: "The French Catholic novelists were a help to me in this—Bloy, Bernanos, Mauriac. In philosophy, Gilson, Maritain and Gabriel Marcel, an Existentialist. They all seemed to be French for a while and then I discovered the Germans—Max Picard, Romano Guardini and Karl Adam."[59]

In a book review in 1958 O'Connor declares that *The Christ of Faith* is an instance of "a proper Christology."[60] It is "a Christology of the living Church, based on tradition and dogma rather than on a reconstruction of Christ's times as in Daniel-Rops' *Jesus and His times* or on spiritual intuition as in Monsignor Guardini's *The Lord*." The christology of the Tübingen professor possesses such a wealth of Christian wisdom that, in O'Connor's judgment, it should be widely read and studied: "*The Christ of Faith* is a master work by one of the Church's greatest living theologians."

Prior to studying *The Christ of Faith*, O'Connor already prized *The Spirit of Catholicism*. She mentions the book in her review of Adam's "excellent" pamphlet, *The Roots of the Reformation*.[61] Also, she alludes to Adam's ecclesiology in her letters. Writing to "A" in 1955, O'Connor stresses the theme that the church is the visible expression of the Mystical Body of Christ in which individuals receive God's love and forgiveness: "However, the individual in the Church is, no matter how worthless himself, a part of the body of Christ and a particular in the Redemption."[62] This statement bears a family resemblance to Adam's comments on the communal character of salvation. In *The Spirit of Catholicism* Adam states:

> Communion of Saints—what a glad and blessed light illumines it! It is the hidden treasure, the secret joy of the Catholic. When he thinks on the Communion of Saints his heart is enlarged. He passes out of the solitariness of here and of there, or yesterday and tomorrow, of "I" and "thou," and he is enfolded in an unspeakably intimate communion of spirit and life. . . . [63]

O'Connor's view of the church shows Adam's influence. In a letter to Dr. T. R. Spivey in 1959 O'Connor emphasizes that the church is not just a human association but God's community in the world: "For us the Church is the body of Christ, Christ continuing in time, and as such a divine institution. The Protestant considers this idolatry. If the church is not a divine institution, it will turn into an Elks Club."[64] In these sentences we can hear Adam's voice in *The Spirit of Catholicism*: "When we define the Church as essentially the Kingdom of God and the Body of Christ, it follows as her first particular attribute that she is supernatural and heavenly."[65] At the same time O'Connor, like Adam, was honest about the church's shortcomings. In a letter of 1958 to Cecil Dawkins, she acknowledges that during its long history the church has made mistakes: "Christ never said that the Church would be operated in a sinless or intelligent way, but that it would not teach error . . . that the whole Church speaking through the Pope will not teach error in matters of faith."[66] O'Connor's realism about the church resembles the frank account of church history given in *The Spirit of Catholicism*. In fact, her comments seem to paraphrase Adam's statement that: "The Church has from God the guarantee that she will not fall into error regarding faith or morals; but she has no guarantee whatever that every act and decision of ecclesiastical authority will be excellent and perfect."[67]

Finally, it should be noted that Adam's *The Spirit of Catholicism* made a deep impression on American theologians. Robert McAfee Brown, the well-known Protestant theologian, has noted that one of his books was inspired by *The Spirit of Catholicism*. In the foreword to his book *The Spirit of Protestantism* (1961) he points out: "This book was originally conceived because there appeared to be no comparable Protestant counterpart to Karl Adam's *The Spirit of Catholicism*; namely, a book that tried to describe the faith unashamedly from the *inside* in such a way that it might also communicate to those on the *outside*."[68] In the book itself, Brown observes that Catholicism lends itself to being written about in a "definitive way," and he praises Adam's account of Catholicism: "There is no excuse for a Roman Catholic author to misrepresent the Roman Catholic faith, although few of them can represent it as magnificently as Karl Adam has done."[69] Brown makes it clear that he has high regard, too, for some of Adam's other works, especially *One and Holy*. Urging his readers to go

to Roman Catholic sources in order to understand what Roman
Catholicism is, he insists: "For Protestants, the best place to start
is surely Adam, *The Spirit of Catholicism*."[70]

The Jesuit theologian Avery Dulles has much respect for *The
Spirit of Catholicism*. In *The Catholicity of the Church* Dulles
appeals to Adam's work in support of the idea that Catholicism
includes a deep reverence for human nature: "In his masterful
work, *The Spirit of Catholicism* (1924), Karl Adam identified as
one of the elements of the Church's catholicity 'that she loves
and understands man's nature, his bodily and sensitive structure,
as well as his mental powers.' He goes on to say: 'Art is native
to Catholicism, since reverence for the body and for nature is
native to it.' "[71] Dulles' appreciation for *The Spirit of Catholicism*
is evident, too, in his book *The Reshaping of Catholicism*. In an
attempt to grasp the meaning of "Catholicism," Dulles reviews
Adam's answer to Friedrich Heiler's criticism of Roman Catholicism for being a complex of opposites.

> In his justly famed work, *The Spirit of Catholicism*, the German
> Catholic theologian Karl Adam responded to Heiler in 1924. Heiler,
> he conceded, had said many true things but had missed the essence
> of Catholicism, which is discernible only to those who live within
> the community of faith. Seen from within, Catholicism may be
> called the religion of affirmation rather than denial, of wholeness
> rather than of selectivity. The church, in its inmost reality, is a
> communion of persons in the life that was brought into the world
> through Jesus Christ. The life of grace, moreover, is expressed
> and communicated through tangible institutions, such as hierarchy,
> dogmas, and sacraments, which are not to be written off as merely
> human contrivances, still less as unchristian distortions. Adam thus
> rejected the charge made by Harnack and others that Catholicism
> set divine value on merely human institutions.[72]

Karl Adam withdrew from the public eye in the early 1950s,
but his writings did not. They continued to act like leaven within
the church, shaping Catholics' reflections upon their faith and
life in the modern world. *The Spirit of Catholicism*, *Christ Our
Brother*, *The Son of God*, *One and Holy*, and *The Christ of Faith*
belong among the books that prepared American Catholics for
Vatican II.

5. THE DEATH OF A FORERUNNER

Karl Adam died on Friday April 1, 1966, at the age of eighty-nine. On Tuesday April 5 his family, friends, and associates gathered for the funeral Mass at Tübingen's St. Johann Kirche.[73] Dr. Carl Joseph Leiprecht, bishop of Rottenburg-Stuttgart, presided at the liturgy, and Dr. Wilhelm Sedlmeier, the auxiliary bishop, preached the funeral homily. Along with the faculty of the University of Tübingen there were present Dr. Hugo Lang, the former abbot of St. Boniface Abbey in Munich, who had received his doctorate under Adam's direction in 1925; Abbot Damascus Zahringer of the Abbey of Beuron; Dr. Max Miller, the director of the national archives in Stuttgart; Dr. Birn, president of Baden-Württemberg; and Professor Millenstedt, the rector of the University of Tübingen. After the Mass a burial service was held at the grave in the *Stadtfriedhof*, where eulogies were given by Dr. Johannes Stelzenberger, dean of the Catholic faculty; Dr. Max Miller; and Dr. Sommer, the director of the Wilhelmsstift. Reflections upon Adam's life did not, however, end at his grave. In the subsequent weeks and months, others appeared in print.

Tübingen's *Schwäbisches Tagblatt* described Adam as "a researcher and teacher of great significance." After reviewing his career and publications, it quoted Adam's reflections regarding the nature of theology, which he gave on his seventieth birthday:

> I am a theologian and have felt myself never to be anything other than a theologian. To be a theologian is to trouble oneself in a scholarly manner about the Word of God. And because this Word of God has appeared corporeally in Jesus Christ, our theology is therefore christocentric. Since it pushes forward through the printed word of Scripture and tradition to the ultimate and to the depth, to the original, to the Spirit of Christ and of Christianity, it itself becomes pneumatological theology. This is a theology which is directed not [only] toward philological observations but knows from these that the Word of God is life and spirit. It clearly cannot be anything other than pneumatological theology, other than entirely human, completely human, time and again, [though] for centuries there has accumulated [much] to block and to erode the way to Christ. Therefore, it is at the same time critical theology. Its criticism is not however destructive but affirmative. It does not build the way to Christ, but makes it clear. Theology is always on the way to Christ.[74]

According to the *Schwäbisches Tagblatt*, just as Adam's theology was "dynamic," so too was the man himself. The newspaper reported that on the occasion of Adam's seventieth birthday Professor Theodor Steinbüchel had commented on the professor's "humanness": "Your name is an omen: Adam, you are a human being." Steinbüchel added: "You are the teacher who with a youthful heart can inspire young people for high scholarship and intelligent, generous ministry."[75] According to the newspaper, Adam was well-known for his humorous anecdotes about growing up in rural Pursruck, tutoring the sons of Crown Prince Rupprecht, and teaching religion to the Bavarian Cadet Corps. These stories were inspired by *"hilaritas christiana"* and a spirit of simplicity. In light of this reminiscence, the article concluded: "Whoever may be bound in friendship to this noble man and genuine Christian will always remember him in true love."

Among the testimonials were those written by Adam's former students who had become theologians. In a letter of condolence to Tübingen's faculty, the Protestant theologian Friedrich Heiler stated that he felt close to Adam for fifty-five years.[76] As a young Catholic, he had listened to Adam's lectures at the University of Munich from 1911 to 1915 and had stood by him during the time when his teacher was being investigated by the Holy Office. In their walks they had discussed Adam's options of turning to a career in medicine or joining the Old Catholics. When Heiler chose to join the Swedish Lutheran church, he did so without his teacher's approval. Nevertheless, they continued to correspond. In a book review Adam criticized Heiler's *Das Wesen des Katholizismus*. A few years later, he was angered when Heiler compared Adam's understanding of the act of faith with George Tyrrell's. It took an exchange of letters before this incident was behind them. Visiting Adam in the 1930s, Heiler again experienced his "fatherly affection." In 1962 he was filled with joy when he lectured for the first time at the University of Munich in the hall where, as a student, he had listened to Adam. Since the age of nineteen, Heiler had respected the theologian as his lifelong "teacher and friend."

Bernard Häring, now professor emeritus of the Alphonsianum in Rome, wrote a testimonial about his former teacher.[77] Adam's lectures, said Häring, were thoroughly grounded in historical research and philosophical rigor, and simultaneously they were alive and engaging: "Not seldom we could see tears in his eyes when he spoke on the true humanity of Christ, the Living Word of God." In the judgment of Häring, Adam's effort in the 1930s to build a bridge between the Catholic church and National Socialism was motivated by "love and a spirit of responsibility." Adam corrected his views and accepted the decision of the bishops to withdraw seminarians from his classes. In the late 1940s some students became upset because Adam's lectures on ecumenism seemed to them to devalue Mariology. After Adam learned of these students' concern, he changed his lectures, omitting comments on the study of Mary. Finally, Häring observed that Adam prepared the way to Vatican II: "No doubt he is one of the theologians who contributed in an outstanding way to the preparation of the Second Vatican Council. . . . Among the influential theologians of the Council some were his alumni. Had not almost all the bishops and theologians of the Council read his books?"

Fritz Hofmann honored his teacher in a major address to the faculty of the University of Tübingen at a memorial service held on June 6, 1966. According to Hofmann, Adam undertook "theology within the spirit of the Tübingen School."[78] His thought was guided by a threefold commitment to the appreciation of "the vital powers of [divine] revelation within history," the pursuit of "the inner 'synthesis of speculative [theology] with historical theology,'" and the value of theology inspired by "the spirit of piety." In his teaching and writing Adam drew on his devout daily prayer: the celebration of the Eucharist, the recitation of the Divine Office and the rosary, and meditation, especially as he walked in silence to the lecture hall. Inspired by the Catholic School of Tübingen, he pursued three themes: our knowledge of God as ultimately grounded in the community of faith, the church as the body of Christ, and Jesus Christ as the living reality at the center of life. According to Hofmann, the professor's discussion of these topics was striking because it spoke to his contemporaries. Adam's lasting contribution is, therefore, not only what he said but also the manner in which he said it. He did theology for his day. In Hofmann's words: "In this way, because Adam ventured to do theology for his time—a theology arising from faith and serving faith—[and] in spite of the fact that many of his expressions are out of date, he is a model for theologians who are prepared to serve their time out of the same spirit."[79]

Finally, Heinrich Fries described Adam as a "forerunner" of Vatican II's *aggiornamento*.[80] In Fries's judgment, Adam did not allow his scholarship to interfere with his humanness. He retained his Bavarian accent and his imaginative speech, and he conveyed a personal warmth and positive regard for all whom he met. Over the front door to his home was engraved Augustine of Hippo's statement: "Whoever wants to slander his neighbor should know that to such a person this house is closed." Adam lived what he taught, and what he taught sprang from his Christian faith. As a result, his lectures inspired his students' prayer. Fries recalled that "as seminarians in Tübingen we often took the theme of our meditations not from the obligatory meditation books but from Adam's hour lectures." In conclusion, Fries observed that *The Spirit of Catholicism*, *The Son of God*, and *One and Holy* influenced Vatican II's themes regarding the church and its mission in the world. In particular, Adam's work bore fruit in the council's Decree on Ecumenism. In Fries's words:

> His theology and the concerns therein were present in Rome and were confirmed in a unique manner: The holistic, theological and biblical view of the church, the dialogue of faith with humankind and the spirit of the time, the courage for openness and freedom, the disposition of acceptance and brotherhood, the ecumenical responsibility, the christocentric view as the way to unity for those who believe in Christ, the renewal of theology through the Sacred Scripture, the understanding of Catholicism not as a quantity but as an inner dimension, as the category of the inclusive affirmation of the Christian.[81]

Along with theologians' testimonials to Adam, British and American journals published moving obituaries. The *Tablet* began its statement with this laudatory comment:

> The recent death, at the age of ninety, of Karl Adam has passed almost unnoticed both in his own country and abroad, where between the two world wars he was widely and justly regarded as one of the few original thinkers of his time. The best known of his books, *The Spirit of Catholicism* and *The Son of God* now rank among the classics of the new theological emphasis on Christ

and the history of redemption which found fullest expression in the Second Vatican Council.[82]

The major periods in Adam's life, reported The *Tablet*, included his studies in Munich during the modernist crisis, his courageous steps toward a new kind of ecclesiology and christology after the First World War, and his contributions to ecumenism after the Second World War. "But times have changed in the way Karl Adam anticipated." Unfortunately, Adam did not actively participate in this new era, and so a generation of Catholics "has grown up which hardly knows his name but has come to accept as common currency much that the Tübingen professor minted."

The journal *America* succinctly summed up the theologian's life and work:

> As we listen to the advanced speculations of post-conciliar theologians, we are apt to forget that, in Horace's words, "there were many brave men before Agamemnon." Bavarian-born Father Karl Adam was one of the eminent European theologians who, perhaps more than they or anyone dreamed, prepared the field of theology for its present exuberant productivity.
>
> Karl Adam's writings—*The Spirit of Catholicism, Christ Our Brother, One and Holy, The Son of God, The Christ of Faith*—not only commanded professional respect, but ministered most fruitfully to the spirituality of plain folk who simply wanted to know more about Christ for personal and non-controversial reasons. Father Adam possessed an extraordinary theological gift: he was clear.
>
> On April 1, Karl Adam died at the age of 89, after 66 years of priesthood and 30 as a professional theologian. Many will miss him; but the Christ of whom he so lovingly and luminously wrote will welcome him.[83]

On March 24, 1966, eight days before Karl Adam's death, a historic event occurred. Paul VI and Michael Ramsey, Anglican Primate of All England, met in the Vatican's Sistine Chapel in order to establish a joint permanent theological commission for Anglican-Roman Catholic dialogue. In the course of the initial, formal gathering, Ramsey stated the reason for their common endeavor: "It is only as the world sees us Christians growing visibly in unity that it will accept through us the divine message of peace."

Paul VI affirmed this aim when he spoke of rebuilding "a bridge that for centuries had lain fallen between the Church of Rome and Canterbury: a bridge of respect, of esteem and charity."[84] In conclusion, the two church leaders symbolized their commitment to ecclesial reconciliation by embracing in the Kiss of Peace.

Though Adam had no knowledge of this momentous occasion because of his illness, he had indeed influenced the event through his writings. *The Spirit of Catholicism* presented the church not primarily as a juridical institution but as the community of people united in Christ. *Christ Our Brother* and *The Son of God* illuminated the person and work of Jesus Christ and affirmed that Christian faith is oriented toward Christ. *One and Holy* called for Protestant-Catholic dialogue, springing from union with Christ and shaped by mutual respect. *The Christ of Faith* reviewed the church's teachings on Jesus Christ as the "son of man" and the "Son of God." The theological convictions communicated in these books were clearly at work when Paul VI and Ramsey exchanged their Kiss of Peace.

Karl Adam had shaped the meeting of Paul VI and Michael Ramsey even more directly, too. As noted in chapter 2, Paul VI had studied *The Spirit of Catholicism* in the 1930s and expressed its vision of church in his first encyclical, *Ecclesiam Suam*, in 1964.[85] He had taken seriously Adam's insight that the church is "the unity of redeemed humanity, a unity made possible by the Incarnation of the Son of God; she is the cosmos of men, mankind as a whole, the many as one."[86] This understanding of the church as "the unity of redeemed humanity" was proclaimed to the entire world when, in the Sistine Chapel, Paul VI embraced the archbishop of Canterbury beneath Michelangelo's painting, *Creation*.

7

Catholic Theology
and Neoromanticism

Theology cannot be adequately done apart from culture. A believing community and its theologians live within a context larger than the church. They participate in what Bernard Lonergan has described as a society's "set of meanings and values that informs a way of life."[1] A local church's worship and service are shaped in part by a culture. Theology, too, is determined not only by God's revelation, as known within Scripture and tradition, but also by a society's meanings and values. "Theology consists," as Karl Rahner has said, "in conscious reflection upon the message of the gospel in a quite specific situation in terms of the history of the human spirit."[2] Thus, if theology is to be meaningful, it must take seriously its "specific situation." It must express the wisdom of the Christian faith in relation to a particular culture.[3]

Since its founding in 1817 the Catholic School of Tübingen has deliberately attempted to restate Christian truths within the culture of the day.[4] In the early 1800s, Drey and Möhler chose to do theology within the German romanticism of Schlegel and Schleiermacher. Later, Kuhn adopted the Idealism of Hegel and Schelling. At the end of the century, Paul Schanz (1841-1905) developed his apologetic theology in dialogue with the natural sciences and neo-Kantianism. And, as we have seen, in the 1900s Karl Adam tapped the *Lebensphilosophie* of Nietzsche, Bergson, and Scheler. All generations of the school's scholars have recognized that they learn and labor in commerce with their society's ideas and values. In Walter Kasper's words: "A prominent feature of the Tübingen theology of the last century was the courage to enter into an open encounter with the intellectual currents of the time."[5] This faculty has crafted its theology within the "triad of ecclesial-mindedness, scientific thoroughness and openness to the times."[6]

According to Yves Congar, the Catholic School at Tübingen has produced a trajectory of rich theology because of its attentiveness to culture.[7] In their interaction with German romanticism and neoromanticism the Tübingen theologians, holds Congar, have made fruitful use of three seminal ideas: a developmental view of history, an organic sense of life, and a regard for life as a divine gift. Möhler in the 1800s and Adam in the 1900s stressed, in their respective ways, that history unfolds in response to God's revelation, that all human beings as well as all aspects of human life are interconnected, and that grace encounters us within our everyday worlds. In short, Tübingen's Catholic scholars have rightly conveyed, in Congar's words, this imperative: "Let theology be called to the gift, made by God to man, of a new, supernatural life, let it pursue its work in an ambiance of faith and piety and, in its turn, let it inspire life."[8]

In Congar's judgment, the Catholic Tübingen School on occasion has not sufficiently questioned the culture of its day, however. It has at times lost its critical distance on romanticism and neoromanticism. In these instances the school did not serve Christian faith and theology as well as it could have, for it permitted romantic thought to blur the distinction between the subjective dimensions of Christian experience and the objective reality of God's self-disclosure. There have been moments, states Congar, when the school's theology "appears as too concretely concerned with faith as lived in the Church," as "too much a science of faith and not enough a science of Revelation."[9]

Congar's assessment of the Catholic Tübingen School provides a balanced perspective in which we can appraise the theology of Karl Adam.[10] When we apply Congar's comments on the school in general to the work of Adam in particular, we see that this theology's merit was its inclusion of contemporary ideas and values in order to express the church's vitality and wisdom. But we perceive, too, that this work's liability was its need for a greater recognition of the limits of its culture. To be more specific, Adam used the thought of his day to give his theology three strengths: (1) an emphasis on the humanity of Jesus Christ, (2) an understanding of the church as community, and (3) a figurative, nontechnical language. But this employment of the *Lebensphiloso-pbie* also resulted in three weaknesses: (1) the need for further consideration of the significance of Jesus' suffering and death, (2) room for greater conceptual clarity, and (3) the necessity of distinguishing more sharply between Christian discourse and the rhetoric of nationalism—in particular, of National Socialism. Each of these six points will be briefly discussed.

1. THREE STRENGTHS OF ADAM'S THEOLOGY

1.1 The Humanity of Jesus Christ

Adam took seriously Chalcedon's tenet that Jesus Christ is "truly man." He conceived of the Son of God as a human being, as an individual of flesh and blood who interacted with men and women in the synagogue, on the road, and at weddings. "What lay closest to Adam's heart," observed Fritz Hofmann, "was a description of the authentic humanity of Jesus. . . . "[11] Hans Kreidler has reiterated this point: "The strong emphasis on the humanity of Jesus and its significance for the salvation of humankind is the characteristic of Adam's incarnational christology."[12] While these comments are correct, something more can be said: This success in portraying Jesus Christ as a human being depends upon the neo-romantic ideas of development, organic unity, and life as a gift.

First, *Christ Our Brother* and *The Son of God* express development in Jesus' life. Jesus' preaching and healing, and his passion, death, and resurrection are manifestations of his abiding dedication to his Father's gracious will.[13] It is God's intention that all people might have life in abundance, and, therefore, each of Jesus' sayings and cures is a deliberate affirmation of life. Each expresses Jesus' love of everything human. Even his passion and death reveal his final yes to life's goodness, for Jesus' death is not the last word. His resurrection is his affirmation of life, as it is also God's. All that Jesus says, does, and endures is connected in the one, coherent drama of Jesus embracing life in all of its forms.

Second, an awareness of organic unity is also operating here. According to Adam, Jesus unites mind and heart and will.[14] He demonstrates a lucid intellect, as when he debates with the Pharisees. He feels things deeply, as when he is moved by the sight of the sick. And, he does what is right, regardless of the consequences. He heals on the Sabbath, though this infuriates the religious officials, and in the face of an absurd death he maintains his belief in God. Jesus' life is a tightly woven tapestry of thinking, feeling, and acting. Adam's Jesus is "the complete man."[15]

Third, there is the conviction that life is God's gift. According to Adam, divine grace meets a person not only in sacred places but also in the give-and-take of ordinary life. Jesus is a robust figure who hauls in fishing nets and savors bread, fish, and wine in the company of his followers. He delights in using images of wheat, coins, and sheep, and in telling parables about a father, a widow, and a marriage banquet. Jesus is not fearful about the future; he does not waver when faced with choices. He confidently makes decisions, so that "yes" means yes, "no" means no, and "maybe" is not uttered. Jesus is bursting with a vitality which is so forceful that it must originate in the source of all life, God.[16]

This portrait of Jesus as a human being stood out in the first half of the twentieth century. At the time, neoscholastic theology spoke of Jesus Christ in static metaphysical terms and thus implicitly presented Jesus Christ as an abstract entity uniting a "divine nature" and a "human nature." Liberal Protestantism worked within a neo-Kantian view of reality and reduced Christianity's founder to the status of an exemplary teacher of moral conduct. Neither of these views, judged Adam, offered an adequate account of Jesus Christ. Therefore, Adam employed key ideas from the neoromantic philosophy of life to depict Jesus as a man who was overflowing with so much vitality that he could have originated only out of the source of all life, God. "The Christian gospel announces primarily not an ascent of humanity to the heights of the divine in a transfiguration," contended Adam, " . . . but a descent of the Godhead, of the divine Word, to the state of bondage of the purely human."[17]

1.2 The Community of Christ

In *The Spirit of Catholicism* Adam insisted that the church is not primarily an institution but a community. Indeed, this community manifests the solidarity of the entire human family. As Hofmann noted, "For Adam, humanity is no conglomerate of discrete individuals, randomly tossed together, but the 'historical unfolding man,' an organic unity and totality, a single 'we.' Human beings abide in the divine plan of salvation not as isolated individual beings, but as members of one whole."[18] This statement has been reiterated by Kreidler: "In light of the incarnation, the church is [for Adam] an organism of a higher kind, the 'body of Christ.' All members of the church are living bearers of the body of Christ and should cooperate with one another in the living community of the 'communio sanctorum.' "[19]

Adam's ecclesiology rests upon three ideas from neoromanticism. First, development is inherent in the church. The church requires time to reach maturity. In Adam's view, it is like the oak tree whose growth, though slow, is solid and lasting.[20] The continuity of the community of Christ extends from the dawn of creation, through the history of Israel and the history of the church, to the Second Coming. The church's teachings too undergo maturation. Since change is a sign of vitality, it is to be expected that the church will continually find new ways to articulate its beliefs. According to Adam, the humanity of Jesus Christ is manifest not only in the historicity of his life but also in the unfolding of the church's life and teachings.

Second, this ecclesiology depends on the idea of organic unity. According to Adam, all lives are linked in their mutual relationships. What happens in one life affects all lives. In particular, what has occurred in Jesus Christ touches all of humankind. In fact, Christ has changed the basis of our common humanity because of what he has realized in his humanity.[21] Society need no longer be characterized by distrust and alienation, for Jesus Christ has strengthened the ties of all men and women with God, one another, and themselves. Now all people can acknowledge their membership in the one body of Christ. Indeed, because of the incarnation, this membership is based on one's humanity. People ought not disregard their race, culture, and emotions. They should respect these as the media in which they meet the incarnate Christ. The union of Christ's humanity with God means that our access to God is "through Christ," especially through Christ's humanity.

Third, in Adam's view the church, including its institutional aspects, is a gift from God, for all manifestations of life spring from the mystery of life itself.[22] The church and the sacraments make sense when one acknowledges that there is more to these realities than meets the eye. According to Adam, the church and the sacraments are symbols of God's activity in human affairs. They direct Christians to find and support new forms of life wherever they emerge, both within the church and within society at large. Recognition of the vitality released into creation by Christ means a readiness to consider new ideas, even those of Christianity's critics, such as Nietzsche.

Adam insisted that, contrary to Nietzsche's claim, Christians do not shy away from reality. Rather, they embrace everything in life, both joy and sorrow, good and bad, so that their discipleship to Christ leads to their own Christian "heroism."[23] Even the so-called passive virtues like humility and gentleness direct a person into the world, for they dispose the person to welcome the unknown and thus to follow Christ in ultimately courageous ways. The true body of Christ, the authentic church, is comprised of women and men who are filled with enthusiasm for the things of the earth and for their fulfillment in God's new creation.

Adam constructed his ecclesiology in dialogue with the *Lebensphilosophie*. He judged that development, organic unity, and attentiveness to the goodness of life are essential properties of the community united in Christ. Neoscholasticism emphasized that the church is an institution, albeit an institution founded by God, and liberal Protestantism perceived the church as an assembly of individual believers. But for Adam these views did not reach to the heart of the matter. The church is, said Adam, "the actual inner unity of redeemed humanity united with Christ. In the Catholic conception of the Church the decisive element is not this or that person, but all mankind."[24]

1.3 Figurative Language in Theology

Along with the stress upon the humanity of Christ and the church as the community of Christ, a third strength of Adam's theology was its figurative language. Karl Barth spoke of Adam's "warm, modern rhetoric."[25] Adam was, observed Hofmann, "the master of description," whose love of life gave him an eye for "the artistic form of the apprehended truth."[26] According to Kreidler, Adam's language is noteworthy for its descriptive character, its "realism":

> Splendid color and imagination characterize his speech. Sparkling with life, frothing over, magnificent and enthusiastic, it stands completely connected with the great emergence of the language of expressionism in the literature of his time; it breathes strong, religious

pathos, it gives evidence of rich experience, and it displays a life-filled power.[27]

Adam's kind of language was produced in part by the era. In the aftermath of the Great War, Germans turned away from rationalism, technology, and individualism and turned toward literature that incorporated human feelings, a return to nature, and the sense of community.[28] The writings of Stefan George, Hugo von Hofmannsthal, and Rainer Maria Rilke were widely read, as were the works of Dostoevsky, Tolstoy, Ibsen, and Zola with their "literary naturalism."[29] This literature nurtured the lyrical language of *The Spirit of Catholicism*, *Christ Our Brother*, and *The Son of God*. Dostoevsky's view of Jesus even appears on the first page of *The Son of God*.

Adam's imaginative discourse also originated out of the ideas of development, organic unity, and life as a gift. First, the idea of development is dependent on the category of narrative. Adam relied on the Old and New Testaments for their literary representations of God and Jesus.[30] Guided by his insight that the mystery of Christ concerns the descent of God into human life, he looked to the Bible to provide accounts of God's activity in history. This biblical hermeneutics was not as sophisticated as today's postcritical interpretation. Nevertheless, it aimed at illuminating the verbal sense of the Scriptures in order to focus on the 'person' who is disclosed in the Bible, the person who continues to be present to people and to invite their faith and love. "Adam has not presented a life of Jesus," observed Fries, "but has sought to delineate the form of Jesus Christ, as it rises up out of the New Testament and is articulated in the faith of the church."[31]

Second, neoromanticism's notion of organic unity directed Adam's attention to the role of images in theology. Adam wrote in such a way as to stimulate the reader's imagination so that the reader could see connections that, while not obvious, are part of the whole reality of Jesus Christ. Adam crafted statements on Jesus Christ that are filled with allusions to biblical testimony about Jesus' words and deeds. As a result, he evoked the reader's images of Jesus preaching on the shore of the Sea of Galilee, walking with Peter, James, and John, and suffering in the Garden of Gethsemane. What emerged, therefore, was the connectedness of Jesus' person and activities. Adam accomplished this presentation by appealing not only to the "dogmatic images" of doctrine but also to the "reflected images" of the Bible and the "living images" of contemporary believers.[32]

Third, the understanding of life as a gift resulted in an appreciation for the richness of personal existence. Adam avoided talk about Jesus' "human nature" and "divine nature"; he allowed for no implication that Jesus' humanity was an abstract entity. The theologian identified Jesus as we would single out any person, namely, by means of images and stories. To recall biblical accounts of Jesus eating with scribes, tax collectors, and his disciples is to provide a glimpse of his life, at once mundane and sublime, human and divine. For Adam, faith and theology entail, first, a relationship with Jesus Christ, and only secondarily do they involve theoretical discourse. As Fries has put it, Adam made it clear "that the Christian faith is not a relation to objects and propositions, but a relation to a person, and only afterwards an acceptance of assertions and truths about this person."[33]

The figurative language of this theology was not accidental. Adam opted for descriptive discourse in order to give a wholistic view of Jesus Christ, the church, and human life. Such an account was impossible in neoscholastic theology with its a highly conceptual form of discourse. Nor was it possible in Rudolf Bultmann's program of demythologizing, which pushed Christian belief in Jesus' resurrection "into the uncontrollable reaches of rootless mysticism," thereby neglecting Christian faith's "concrete, vital, burning impulse."[34] While Adam was capable of conceptual discourse and mystical thought, he was intent on fashioning a language that would display God's grace concretely at work within human life, especially in Jesus' life. To realize this intention he wrote his theology in imaginative, descriptive words. As Kasper has said, "Karl Adam was intent on describing the humanity of Jesus in gripping, indeed dramatic [terms]," and, as a result, he produced a "concrete christology."[35]

2. THREE SHORTCOMINGS OF ADAM'S THEOLOGY

2.1 Exploring the Paschal Mystery

The paschal mystery—the reality of the suffering, death, and resurrection of the "lamb of God"—is inexhaustible. There is always more for us to participate in and to understand. Hence, to say that Adam should have reflected further upon the mystery of the crucifixion can seem to be a criticism appropriate to every Christian theology. This recommendation is particularly relevant to Adam's work, however, for the Tübingen theologian has stressed the wholistic and meaningful aspects of the person and work of Jesus Christ at the expense of the tragic and absurd aspects of this mystery. As Kasper has stated, "Our question regarding Karl Adam's theology is whether it has sufficiently considered the experience of suffering in the history of humanity and has probed fully the paschal mystery."[36] I will pursue this observation in relation to Adam's views on the church's prophetic mission, the atonement, and theological anthropology.

The church is called by God to preach repentance, to summon all people to turn their hearts and minds to God. Curiously, however, *The Spirit of Catholicism* says little about this aspect of the church's mission. The text focuses on the church as community, centered in the risen Christ, but it hardly mentions the church as the bearer of the message that all people must die to self so that they might be raised to new life in Christ. How could Adam have overlooked such a central theme in Christian faith? Neoromantic views of development and life rely on the metaphor of growth in which change involves continuity. In this perspective there is little room for talk about personal limitations, poor judgment, and the misuse of one's time and energy.

The cross of Jesus Christ stands at the center of the Christian faith. It symbolizes such a complex reality that time and again we must ask, What does the cross mean? And, why does Jesus' death have "saving" significance for all people? In *Christ Our Brother* and *The Son of God* Adam said that someone had to take our place before the justice of God. Jesus' death on the cross manifests his self-emptying, out of obedience to God (Phil 2:3-11). In giving himself completely to God, Jesus Christ overcame our disobedience and satisfied the requirements of God's righteousness. These are rich ideas, but Adam did not expound on them. He simply repeated them.[37] Why? The philosophy of life stressed community and vitality, and it neglected an adequate discussion of alienation, human indifference, and the ways some human beings make other women and men into victims. Relying on neoromanticism's optimistic notion of human development,

Adam did not reflect sufficiently on the cross as a symbol of history's discontinuities and the presence of evil in human affairs.

Finally, we must note that the neoromantic idea of life prevented Adam from examining closely enough the human condition in general. The *Lebensphilosophie* maintained that all elements of the human personality contribute to human well-being. In general, it believed that something good comes out of life's dark forces. This naive outlook is exhibited in Adam's thought. In "Jesus Christ and the Spirit of the Age" Adam observed that while humankind's relationship with God is flawed, it has remained intact so that the "supernatural" order and the natural world are contiguous. For Adam, human nature is basically untouched by original sin.[38] But in holding this view, the theologian has overlooked the fact that many people live like Job; they find their lives seemingly cursed. Adam tended to make too little of the disharmony that has severed relationships within the human family, within the human heart, and between the human community and God. He adopted a theological anthropology colored by the roseate views of the philosophy of life.

Adam failed to inquire as fully as he could have into the church's prophetic mission, the suffering and death of Jesus Christ, and the brokenness of the human condition. The *Lebensphilosophie* directed the Tübingen theologian to understate the ways in which human life apparently stands apart from the reality of God. As Kreidler has pointed out, Adam's theology "comes to speak about the cross of Christ, but it cannot delve into it to its full depth and significance." Why? "The crisis-character of the cross is weakened," observed Kreidler, "through [Adam's view of] the a priori union of humankind with Christ—a union that is grounded in the incarnation."[39]

2.2 Conceptual Clarity in Theology

While Adam's writings were imaginative and descriptive, they were also at times conceptually fuzzy. In the late 1920s and early 1930s the Holy Office demanded that the professor revise some of the statements in his books. This judgment sprang in part from the Vatican's suspicion of any theological discourse other than that of neoscholasticism. But Rome's evaluation possessed a valid basis, too, in Adam's texts. Roger Aubert, who valued the efforts of the Tübingen theologian, acknowledged: "It is true that some of Adam's expressions lack precision."[40] Walter Kasper has agreed with Aubert: "Given his engaging, living language, Adam placed no great value on conceptual precision," and, therefore, "it is no wonder that Adam was faced with frequent misunderstandings."[41]

Ambiguity is evident in two of Adam's key concepts. First, in Adam's writings the notion of nature overlaps with the notion of grace. Adam wanted to shed light on the complementarity between God's acts and humankind's. He sought to recover the scholastic view that grace does not displace our natural abilities but strengthens them and brings them to fulfillment. He frequently cited the theological axiom that "grace presupposes nature and completes it."[42] But Adam failed to provide a nuanced interpretation of this principle. As a result, he implied an identity between grace and nature, and thus between God and humankind.[43] With this implicit confusion, it is no wonder that Adam's nationalism became problematic in the 1930s. Having closely linked German culture and divine grace, he could not sharply differentiate between them.

Second, Adam needed to clarify further the salvific significance of the incarnation. He held that the union of divinity and humanity in Jesus Christ has redemptive value for all people. The incarnation sanctified not just the humanity of Jesus Christ but also human nature in general so that it is the point of access to God for all who are born into the human family. Because God assumed flesh and blood in Jesus Christ, human nature is now sacramental. To accept one's humanity is to affirm God in Jesus Christ. This understanding of the incarnation is fundamentally correct, and yet it demands refinement. (This view of the incarnation was, in fact, refined by Karl Rahner.)[44] Without more precise qualification, Adam's emphasis on the incarnation can be pushed toward a secular humanism, in which there is no talk of Jesus Christ but only of a person's self-realization.

Why did Adam's writings exhibit conceptual ambiguities? The reason is that the philosophy of life placed more value on images than on notions. Nietzsche, Bergson, and Scheler were intent on fashioning a discourse that brought together mind and heart, that engaged the whole self, even if this cost linguistic precision. In this same spirit, Adam was intent on crafting an inclusive, synthetic language and less interested in a language marked by exactness and differentiation. He used words in ways that united ideas and feelings within the category "life" without attempting to give a clear definition of "life."[45] He chose to forego delimiting the notion of life, probably in order to remain true to reality's variety and movement. Thus, Mark Schoof has said: "At this level, to be accused of using 'concepts inaccurately' was not so serious, and his inaccurate use of concepts meant, in brief, that he avoided the neoscholastic terminology and aimed at a direct 'theology of life.' "[46] In Kreidler's words: "Adam's concept of life is in the first place not metaphysical-ontological, but stamped by the *Lebensphilosophie*."[47]

2.3 Theology and Nationalism

Karl Adam tried unsuccessfully to mediate between the church and National Socialism. In 1933 he stood with the Vatican, the German bishops, and most German theologians in wanting to give Adolf Hitler a chance to bring order to German society.[48] In January 1934 he publicly criticized the Nazis' German Faith Movement, which he took to be unrepresentative of authentic German nationalism. As a result he was harassed by Storm Troopers and briefly suspended from teaching by the government. One year later he lectured on the potential compatibility between Catholicism and German nationalism—a compatibility directly at odds with the neopaganism of Alfred Rosenberg and Jakob Wilhelm Hauer. In December 1939 he proposed that seminarians be included in the draft and, as a consequence, he was censured by the bishop of Augsburg. This unfortunate story of one prominent theologian's misdirected good intentions calls attention to the detrimental influence of neoromanticism.

Throughout the nineteenth century and the early twentieth century, romantic thought generated the vague, though powerful idea of *das Volk*, of the national-racial community.[49] Rejecting the Enlightenment's view that the state is derived from a social contract among discrete individuals, romantics like Friedrich Schlegel and Goethe regarded the state as the outgrowth of humankind's communal nature, and Idealists like Fichte, Hegel, and Schelling saw the state as the total reality in which individual men and women find their identity. In the late 1800s and early 1900s neoromanticism and Idealism were combined with biological and evolutionary theories to yield the belief that humankind's social units are ethnic and racial. There emerged the racial (*volkische*) theories of Joseph Gobineau (1816–82) and Paul de Lagarde (1827–91), whose views were popularized in the early twentieth century by Theodore Fritsch, Dietrich Eckhart, and Artur Dinter.[50]

Nazi ideology exploited the *volkische* movement. It espoused an anthropological dualism which claimed that Germans possess a racial and moral superiority over all other peoples. In this view, the German people have the world mission of overcoming "degenerate races" and promoting a "pure" race of Germans for the good of creation.[51] This anthropological dualism was supported by a myth that can be put as follows: The German "people" receive their "life" from their "blood" and "earth." If the German "race" is to realize its bright "future" and fulfill its singular, lofty "destiny" in world history, it must be kept "racially pure." It must separate itself from other races, preventing them from contaminating German blood, and it must establish a world "empire" for the ultimate well-being of the earth and all peoples. In remaining true to their racial "spirit," the German people will become "heroic," "noble," and "self-sacrificing" in imitation of Wittekind, the leader of the pagan Saxons.

While German neoromanticism fueled this racist ideology, it also supported balanced views of social reality. It distinguished between the notion of society and the notion of community, and directed people to foster their "organic" ties. This concept of community shaped the thought of Scheler, Guardini, and Adam, none of whom advocated the German radicals' myth of racial dualism. However, since romantic thought eschews clear distinctions and precise definitions, it provided few points of reference by which to differentiate between, on the one hand, an understanding of community based on common values and, on the other, an ideology of race. The adjective "*völkische*" was ambiguous. It could function in the soft sense of "cultural" identity, or in the hard sense of "racial, national" identity. Moreover, terms like "life," "earth," "destiny," "spirit," "heroic," "noble," and "self-sacrificing" could be used either in a Christian context or within the racist ideology. It was often impossible to detect their exact connotation, especially in Germany's highly charged social and political situation of the 1920s and 30s.

The neoromantic understanding of community and its view
of life as a unity of feeling, thinking, and acting made Adam's
views appear at times similar to those of National Socialism. In
this regard, Hans Kreidler has observed: "It is his theology of
life which brought Karl Adam's thought into the neighborhood
of the worldview of National Socialism. The organic thought of
romanticism comes to bear on his notion of 'life'."[52] According
to Adam, human life is not so much an individual endeavor as it
is a communal one. It springs from the natural associations that
bind people into families, regions, and nations. Life flows into
the Christian assembly when the church is rooted in a people's
natural groupings. As Kreidler has noted, Adam "refers time and
again to the connection of the ecclesiastical community and the
Volk community, and he posits the unconditional, encompassing yes to community as the essential element of Catholicism."[53]
Given this orientation to support what nurtures organic connections among people, Adam was inclined to affirm his points of
agreement with National Socialism's language of *das Volk* without
stressing his differences.

Since Adam's discourse is that of community, it bears a family resemblance to National Socialism's talk about *das Volk*. For
instance, *The Spirit of Catholicism* depends on the same vocabulary from which Hitler drew his terms and images. The book
calls for a break with the Enlightenment mentality, insisting that
"[t]his bloodless, sterile man of mere negation cannot ultimately
live."[54] In its literary context, the word "blood" functions in a
figurative sense, but when quoted in the 1930s apart from the
book it could have been taken in a literal, hence racial, sense.
Adam could have seemed to be a proponent of the view that race
determines a person's moral quality. In a similar way, *Christ Our
Brother* and *The Son of God* were cast within the neoromantic language of heroism: "Jesus is in every respect an heroic, epic figure,
heroism incarnate."[55] Within these books, "heroic" is defined by
the gospels, as are such terms as "virility," "austere uprightness,"
and "self-sacrifice." But when Adam's statements were read apart
from the entire texts, they could easily be misconstrued to have
nationalistic and racial connotations.

Adam's language most closely resembled that of National
Socialism in his essay "Deutsches Volkstum und katholisches Christentum" (July 1933). The use of the word "nationality" ("*Volkstum*") in the title is telling; the National Socialists too emphasized

this term. The essay's opening paragraph indicates the tone of the entire piece. According to Adam, while the Enlightenment produced leaders who were "bloodless and sterile," Germany's poets and Idealists called for the "return to those primal powers which formed and created our people: blood and spirit, blood and religion, German blood and Christianity."[56] Therefore, if Germans wish to be renewed as a people, they must extend their roots into "the earth" of Christianity. And, if Catholics want to attain their full and proper stature on German soil, they must acknowledge that God's grace relies on sound human nature, on "the wholesome blood" of the people whom the church invites into the Catholic faith. For everyone's well-being, there must emerge a German Catholicism.

Six months after writing "Deutsches Volkstum und katholisches Christentum," Adam distinguished Christian-based nationalism from the Nazis' neopagan nationalism. His speech "Vom gottmenschlichen Erlöser" (January 1934) to Catholic youth in Stuttgart challenged the National Socialists' racism. The Nazis utilized the word "blood" literally when they said that people with Jewish blood were degenerate, and they concluded that if Jesus were born of Jewish blood, he could not be Germany's messiah. In this address Adam insisted that national rebirth did not depend on racial purity but on Christian faith. He declared that Jesus was Jewish and confronted Nazi racism by insisting: "Whoever seeks to uproot the German people from their life source [Jesus Christ] sins not only against the body and blood of Jesus Christ, but also commits an offense against the body and blood of the German people."[57] By employing "blood" here in a figurative manner, Adam drove home his point that all people regardless of their race can live in union with Christ. With this speech the theologian went on record as opposing the Nazis' anthropological dualism. As a consequence he had his course at the University of Tübingen disrupted and his teaching license revoked.

One year later, in his lecture "Jesus Christ and the Spirit of the Age," Adam again distanced his language of community from National Socialism's talk of *das Volk*, for he insisted that God's revelation transcends race and culture. Making an obvious reference to the German Faith Movement, he observed: "Natural revelation and theology are always conditioned by 'blood' and 'nation.' "[58] But divine revelation is "supraracial, supranational. . . . When it reaches men and races, it strikes them not as something native to them, but as something strangely alien, as something 'wholly other.' "[59] According to Adam, appropriate talk about "the people" and their "blood" uses these terms in a figurative way and allows their meaning to be determined by a transcendent point of reference, God and Jesus Christ, as known in the Jewish-Christian tradition. This discourse is not the Nazis' rhetoric with its literal usage of "people" and "blood."

In the early 1930s Karl Adam's language of community and the National Socialists' language of *das Volk* seemed to have much in common. But by 1934 and 1935 Adam deliberately employed "people," "earth," "blood," "destiny," and "hero" in ways that highlighted his differences with the views of Rosenberg and Hauer. At this point, however, the theologian's efforts were too late. Hitler's totalitarian rule controlled Germany's life and language. Since it was not clear at the outset that there were significant differences between Adam's talk about community and Hitler's talk about *das Volk*, Adam found himself compromised and trapped by National Socialism.[60]

The historian Donald Dietrich has offered an observation in general about German Catholic theologians in the 1930s that applies to Adam in particular: "With both conservatives and Nazi radicals using the same terms, the ultimate effect was an inability to clarify the political values upon which the state was thought to rest."[61] In 1933 Adam himself did not see that his efforts to construct a bridge between Catholicism and National Socialism were naive. Analysis has shown that this myopia was caused by neoromanticism.

3. "THEOLOGY FOR ITS TIME"

Neoromanticism contributed both strengths and weaknesses to the theology of Karl Adam. It equipped Adam (1) to shed new light on the humanity of Jesus Christ, (2) to view the church as the community of Christ, and (3) to cast his thought in a figurative language. However, it did not give the Tübingen theologian the categories (1) to explore the tragic dimensions of the paschal mystery, (2) to clarify key concepts, and (3) to distinguish sharply enough between his language of community and the Nazi ideology of *das Volk*. The notions of development, organic unity, and life as gift served Adam well, and yet they also placed limits on his thought which he did not overcome.

This assessment raises a question about the adequacy of Adam's theological method. The method of the Catholic Tübingen School is one of correlation, directed toward "the intimate, most intimate synthesis of speculative [theology] with historical theology."[62] It presupposes that theologians participate in the life of the church and tap three sources: Scripture and tradition, historical inquiry, and contemporary thought. This method produces a theology that is both "dogmatic and apologetic," a theology that investigates the Jewish-Christian tradition on its own terms and at the same time brings this wisdom into dialogue with one's culture.[63]

This method bore much fruit for Adam: five international bestsellers and over sixty articles on theological and pastoral issues. These texts prepared the way for the Second Vatican Council's understanding of the church, its mission, and its ecumenism, as they aided in the recovery of the humanity of Jesus Christ. They were taken seriously by continental theologians like Karl Barth, Heinrich Fries, Alois Grillmeier, Bernard Häring, Friedrich Heiler, Walter Kasper, Hans Küng, Pope Paul VI, Karl Rahner, and Edward Schillebeeckx, and by English-speaking theologians like Robert McAfee Brown, Avery Dulles, and Virgil Michel. They also influenced the thought of Dorothy Day, Flannery O'Connor, and Evelyn Underhill. In Adam's hands the school's method of correlation led to rich, seminal ideas in ecclesiology and christology.

Is this method responsible, however, for the shortcomings in Adam's thought, especially for his inability to be more clearheaded in his appraisal of National Socialism? No. The problem lay not with the method but with the theologian. Adam was not sufficiently critical of the thought his day, the *Lebensphilosophie*. He rightly perceived its merits—the notions of development, organic unity, and life as gift—which corrected the limitations of the neoscholasticism and neo-Kantian thought. But the professor did not adequately recognize neoromanticism's limits—its optimistic view of human nature and its avoidance of conceptual clarity and linguistic precision.[64] As a result, in his political comments Adam drew on one of his three sources, namely, the philosophy of life, without placing it under full scrutiny from the other sources, namely, the Jewish-Christian tradition and historical research. In short, Adam erred in not adhering closely enough to the Tübingen School's theological method.

The theological method of the Catholic Tübingen School is meant to bring together Christian faith and culture.[65] However, there may be situations in which this goal cannot be attained. One of these occurs when the Vatican permits only one kind of theology, as it did when, beginning in the late 1800s, it promoted only neoscholasticism. Such a policy stands at odds with a theological method attentive to a local church and the meanings and values of its situation.[66] To some degree, Adam's conflict with the Holy Office sprang not from his textual ambiguities but from Rome's disapproval of a theology that was not neoscholastic.[67] In this context a theologian could not realize the goal of creating a fruitful dialogue between Christianity and the thought of the day. When Rome opposes theological pluralism in principle, then the theological method of the Catholic Tübingen School cannot be properly executed without a conflict between the Vatican and the theologians who use Tübingen's method.

One cannot help but wonder what might have occurred if the Holy Office had communicated its concerns about Adam's texts to Adam himself in a different manner. Rome's concerns were valid. But they could not be fully heard because of the secretive, juridical way in which they were conveyed to Adam. They resulted only in minor linguistic changes in Adam's texts. Perhaps more substantial changes would have taken place in Adam's theology if the Vatican had taken a more dialogical, scholarly approach to the theologian—an approach that acknowledged at the outset the merits of Adam's work.

The aim of theological reconciliation is also not attainable within a totalitarian state. When a civil government is intent on strictly controlling a society's language and action, it must suppress an inquiry that evaluates a situation in relation to sources outside of the state. Adam's confrontation with Nazism in January 1934 was bound to take place, for the theologian was intent on remaining faithful to the Jewish-Christian tradition and historical research. He had committed himself to a truth greater than the Nazis' myth. A genuine exchange between Christian faith and a particular culture can only come about when a society and its government possess a readiness to revise their values and structures. When this is not the case, the Tübingen School's synthetic approach will not produce unity but tension. It will generate a theology that stands against the society, a theology that is, in Congar's words, "a science of Revelation."

Walter Kasper has rightly observed that Karl Adam wrote "a theology for his time and for the people of his time."[68] Adam deliberately adopted the ideas and language of his day in order to display the vitality of the truths of Christianity. Perhaps his lasting contribution is, therefore, not so much what he wrote but how he wrote it. Through his successes and failures, he has encouraged us to do theology for our day. More specifically, he has taught us three things. One lesson is the value of a method of correlation that is firmly anchored within the life of the church. Participating within a believing community, the theologian must tap all sources that nourish that church's worship and service. A second lesson is the necessity of entering into one's culture and simultaneously undertaking a critique of that system of meanings and values— a critique grounded in Scripture and tradition and also historical analysis. A third lesson is the importance of doing theology for one's local church and society, so that Christians might faithfully undertake the mission of Christ in the world. In Kasper's words, Adam has taught us that "[a] theology which does not have the courage to be limited [to its time] will in the end help no time."[69]

Karl Adam's life and work bridged the period from the late 1800s to the mid-1900s. Born while Bismarck was chancellor, Adam grew up under the reign of Kaiser Wilhelm II, and he served as a priest and professor during the Great War, the Weimar Republic, the Third Reich, the Second World War, and the founding of the Federal Republic of Germany. He spanned the period from the First Vatican Council to the Second Vatican Council, living during the pontificates of eight popes: Pius IX, Leo XIII, Pius X, Benedict XV, Pius XI, Pius XII, John XXIII, and Paul VI. When he began his formal education, the Vatican espoused only neoscholasticism. It prohibited historical-critical research in biblical studies and was suspicious of the application of critical methods to the history of dogma. When the Vatican showed a bit more toleration of new ideas during the 1920s and 30s, Adam produced his effective writings in ecclesiology and christology. After the Second World War, Adam stepped aside and watched the gradual flowering of theological pluralism in neo-Thomism, the *nouvelle théologie*, transcendental Thomism, the historical-critical research of the Bible, and scriptural-based systematic theology. To recollect this theologian's life and work is, therefore, to review one hundred years of drastic changes in governments, culture, church polity, and theology.

Theology is determined not only by its 'object', divine revelation, but also by its context. Knowing this, Karl Adam did theology for his time. He employed a language nurtured by German neoromanticism and sought to recover the wisdom contained within Scripture and tradition. In speaking fruitfully to his own age, he prepared the way for future theologians to speak to their day. As early as 1924 he gave an exciting vision of the future of Christian belief and theology—a vision that anticipated Karl Rahner's essay in 1979 on the coming of a "world church."[70] In *The Spirit of Catholicism* Adam envisioned the interplay between the church and the non-Western cultures, when he wrote:

> We Catholics acknowledge readily . . . that Catholicism cannot be identified simply and wholly with primitive Christianity, nor even with the Gospel of Christ, in the same way that the great oak cannot be identified with the tiny acorn. There is no mechanical identity, but an organic identity. . . . Thousands of years hence Catholicism will probably be even richer, more luxuriant, more manifold in dogma, morals, law and worship than the Catholicism of the present day. A religious historian of the fifth millennium A.D. will without difficulty discover in Catholicism conceptions and forms and practices which derive from India, China and Japan, and he will have to recognize a far more obvious "complex of opposites."[71]

Karl Adam's Life and Work:
A Chronology

1876   October 22. Born in Pursruck (Oberpfalz), Bavaria

1895   Graduation from the Gymnasium in Amberg (Oberpfalz)

1900   June 10. Ordained a priest for the Diocese of Regensburg

        August 1 - September 1, 1901. Parochial ministry in Riekofen near Regensburg

1901   September 1 - May 23, 1902. Parochial ministry in Neustadt an der Waldnaab

1902   May 23. Receives the bishop's permission to begin doctoral studies at the University of Munich

1904   December 10. Receives Ph.D. in theology. Dissertation: *Der Kirchenbegriff Tertullians*

1908   Completes his Habilitationsschrift, *Die Eucharistie des hl. Augustin*

        April 26. Privatdozent for dogmatic theology and the history of dogma at the University of Munich

1909   April 1 - August 31, 1912. Religion teacher at the Wilhelmsgymnasium, Munich

1910   "Der Antimodernisteneid und die theologische Fakultäten"

        The Holy Office investigates Adam's writings

1912   September 1 - October 31, 1917. Religion teacher at the Bavarian Cadet Corps in Munich

1915   December 31. Adjunct Professor at the University of Munich

1917   November 1. Professor of Moral Theology at the University of Strasbourg

1918   December 10. Withdraws from the University of Strasbourg in compliance with the postwar civil service laws in France

1919   January 1. Lecturer in dogmatic theology at the Hochschule for Philosophy and Theology in Regensburg

            October 1. Professor of Dogmatic Theology at the University of Tübingen

            "Glaube und Glaubenswissenschaft im Katholizismus"

1924   *Das Wesen des Katholizismus*

1925   March. Declines an invitation to join the faculty at the University of Bonn

1926   "Die Theologie des Krisis"

            Christus unser Bruder (four chapters)

1927   "Die katholische Tübinger Schule"

1928   *Christus und der Geist des Abendlandes*

1930   *Christus unser Bruder* (seven chapters)

1931   *Die geistige Entwicklung des heiligen Augustinus*

1932   August. The Holy Office requires the revision of *Das Wesen des Katholizismus*

1933   *Jesus Christus*

            June. The Holy Office requires the revision of *Christus unser Bruder*

            July. "Deutsches Volkstum und katholisches Christentum"

            August. The Holy Office requires the revision of *Jesus Christus*

1934   January 21. "Vom gottmenschlichen Erlöser"

            January 23. Storm Troopers disrupt Adam's lecture

1935   *Jesus Christus und der Geist unserer Zeit*

            November 6. Declines an invitation to join the faculty at the University of Würzburg

1939   December 10. "Die geistige Lage des deutschen Katholi-
        zismus"

1948   March 31. Retires from full-time duties at the University
        of Tübingen

        Una Sancta in katholischer Sicht

1952   "Das Problem der Entmythologisierung"

1954   *Der Christus des Glaubens*

1966   April 1. Adam dies in Tübingen and is buried in Tü-
        bingen's Stadtfriedhof

This chronology is derived in part from Johannes Stelzenberger, "Biographie Karl Adam," *TQ* 137 (1958): 330–47.

Abbreviations

BOOKS BY KARL ADAM

a*COB*	*Christ Our Brother* (1931)
a*CuB*2	*Christus unser Bruder* (1930)
a*CuB*3	*Christus unser Bruder* (1934)
a*JC*1	*Jesus Christus* (1933)
a*JC*3	*Jesus Christus* (1934)
a*SC*	*The Spirit of Catholicism* (1929)
a*SoG*	*The Son of God* (1934)

JOURNALS

StdZ	*Stimmen der Zeit*
ThQ	*Theologische Quartalschrift*
ThS	*Theological Studies*
ZkTh	*Zeitschrift für katholische Theologie*

OTHER WORKS

EPh	Paul Edwards, ed., *The Encyclopedia of Philosophy* (New York: Macmillan, 1967), 8 vols.
HK 6/1	Hubert Jedin, ed., *Handbuch der Kirchengeschichte* 6/1 (Freiburg: Herder, 1971).
HK 6/2	Hubert Jedin, ed., *Handbuch der Kirchengeschichte* 6/2 (Freiburg: Herder, 1973).
HK 7	Hubert Jedin and Konrad Repgen, eds., *Handbuch der Kirchengeschichte* 7 (Freiburg: Herder, 1979).

LThK   *Lexikon für Theologie und Kirche*, 2nd ed. (Freiburg: Herder, 1957–1967), 10 vols.

VCII   Austin Flannery, ed., *Vatican Council II* (Collegeville: Liturgical Press, 1975).

Notes

1. THE MAKING OF A THEOLOGIAN

1. Bernard Häring, "In Memory of Karl Adam," *Ave Maria* 13 (June 11, 1966): 6. In 1946 Karl Adam taught Häring, who was then a new doctoral student at the University of Tübingen. Häring has recalled that Adam went out of his way to initiate a conversation with him after class, and when he learned about Häring's academic background, he urged Häring to stop attending class and to work on his dissertation; see B. Häring, *Meine Erfahrung mit der Kirche* (Freiburg: Herder, 1989), p. 38.

2. See R. William Franklin, *Nineteenth-Century Churches* (New York: Garland Publishing, 1987), p. 213.

3. Walter Kasper, "Karl Adam," *ThQ* 156 (1976): 251-58. For some of these details, I am drawing on the rich recollections of Paschal Botz, O.S.B., St. John's Abbey, Collegeville, Minnesota. From 1931 through 1934, Botz studied with Karl Adam, who directed his doctoral dissertation on the biblical and patristic witness regarding the virginity of Mary.

4. See Johannes Stelzenberger, "Bibliographie Karl Adam," *ThQ* 137 (1958): 330-47. Throughout the book, the English titles are used for texts that originally appeared in German when these texts have been published in English.

5. Karl Adam is still mentioned today in discussions of Catholic theology in the twentieth century. See Walter Kern et al., eds., *Handbuch der Fundamentaltheologie* 4 (Freiburg: Herder, 1988): 223, 276, 363; Peter Eicher, ed., *Neues Handbuch theologischer Grundbegriffe* 2 (Munich: Kösel, 1984): 293.

6. See Hans Kreidler, "Karl Adam und Nationalsozialismus," in Geschichtsverein der Diözese Rottenburg-Stuttgart, ed., *Rottenburger Jahrbuch für Kirchengeschichte* 2 (Sigmaringen: Jan Thorbecke, 1983): 129-40. Edward Schillebeeckx, who was deeply influenced by Adam's theology, has conjectured that little has been said about Adam in recent decades "probably because he defended Nazi-ism during the war"; see

E. Schillebeeckx, *God Is New Each Moment*, trans. D. Smith (New York: Seabury, 1983), p. 12.

7. Kasper, "Karl Adam," p. 251.

8. See Robert Schreiter, *Constructing Local Theologies* (Maryknoll, N.Y.: Orbis, 1985).

9. A version of part of this chapter was presented to the Working Group on Roman Catholic Modernism at the annual meeting of the American Academy of Religion on November 20, 1989. I am indebted to the constructive criticisms of the participants, especially Paul Misner.

10. See Roger Aubert, "Die Theologie während der ersten Halfte des 20. Jahrhunderts," Herbert Vorgrimler, ed., *Bilanz der Theologie im 20. Jahrhundert* 2 (Freiburg: Herder, 1969): 7-70, 24 n. 25.

11. Throughout this chapter and the entire book, I am indebted to Hans Kreidler's fine systematic exposition of Adam's theology; see H. Kreidler, *Eine Theologie des Lebens* (Mainz: Matthias Grünewald, 1988).

12. See Joseph Heiler, "Karl Adam," *Die Schildgenossen* 8 (1928): 411-21, 524-35; Roger Aubert, "Karl Adam," in Hans J. Schultz, ed., *Tendenzen der Theologie im 20. Jahrhundert* (Stuttgart: Kreuz, 1966), pp. 156-62.

13. See Wolfgang Zorn, *Bayerns Geschichte im 20. Jahrhundert* (Munich: C. H. Beck, 1986); Andreas Kraus, *Geschichte Bayerns* (Munich: C. H. Beck, 1983).

14. See Zorn, *Bayerns Geschichte im 20. Jahrhundert*, p. 55.

15. Thomas Mann, "Gladius Dei" (1902), in *Gesammelte Werke* 8 (Oldenburg: S. Fischer, 1960): 197-215. This translated excerpt is taken from Richard Grunberger, *Red Rising in Bavaria* (New York: St. Martin's, 1973), p. 22.

16. See Heinz Hürten, *Kurze Geschichte des deutschen Katholizismus 1800-1900* (Mainz: Matthias Grünewald, 1986), pp. 136-59; Henry Littlefield, *History of Europe Since 1815* (New York: Barnes and Noble, 1963).

17. See Hajo Holborn, *A History of Modern Germany* 3 (New York: Alfred A. Knopf, 1969), pp. 390-413; Koppel Pinson, *Modern Germany* (New York: Macmillan, 1954), pp. 250-73, 454-66.

18. René Wellek, "Romanticism Re-examined," in S. G. Nichols, ed., *Concepts of Criticism* (New Haven, Conn.: Yale University Press, 1963), pp. 199-221, 221. On romanticism and German Catholicism, see Thomas F. O'Meara, *Romantic Idealism and Roman Catholicism* (Notre Dame, Ind.: University of Notre Dame Press, 1982); Crane Brinton, "Romanticism," in *EPb* 7: 206-9; Alexander Dru, *The Contribution of German Catholicism* (New York: Hawthorn, 1963), pp. 32-48; Edgar Alexander, "Church and Society in Germany," trans. Toni Stolper, in Joseph N.

Moody, ed., *Church and Society* (New York: Arts, 1953), pp. 329-581, esp. 366-406. For texts representative of romanticism, see Joseph Fitzer, *Romance and the Rock* (Philadelphia: Fortress, 1989).

19. Thomas Mann, *The Magic Mountain*, trans. H. T. Lowe-Porter (New York: Vintage, 1969), p. 694.

20. For a fuller account of German romanticism, see Marshall Dill, Jr., *Germany* (Ann Arbor: University of Michigan Press, 1970), pp. 95-100; Frederick Copleston, *A History of Philosophy* 7/1 (Garden City, N.Y.: Image Books, 1965), pp. 29-38.

21. Herbert Schnadelbach, *Philosophy in Germany, 1831-1933*, trans. E. Matthews (Cambridge: Cambridge University Press, 1984), p. 142.

22. See Holborn, *History of Germany*, pp. 398-99; Walter Kaufmann, "Nietzsche, Friedrich," in *EPh* 5: 504-14.

23. Friedrich Nietzsche, *Thus Spoke Zarathustra* (1883-91), in *The Portable Nietzsche*, trans. and ed. Walter Kaufmann (New York: Viking, 1954), p. 238.

24. Ibid., p. 125.

25. See Holborn, *History of Modern Germany*, p. 401; Pinson, *Modern Germany*, p. 460; die historische Kommission bei der bayerischen Akademie der Wissenschaften, ed., *Neue Deutsche Biographie* 6 (Berlin: Duncker and Humbolt, 1964): 236-41.

26. Because of George's criticism of democracy, Ernst Troeltsch included his writings among those "revolutionary books against the [Weimar] revolution." Quoted in Pinson, *Modern Germany*, p. 461.

27. Stefan George, *Poems*, trans. C. N. Valhope and E. Morwitz (New York: Pantheon, 1943), p. 195.

28. Ibid., p. 223.

29. Gordon Craig, *Germany, 1866-1945* (New York: Oxford University Press, 1978), p. 181.

30. See Roger Aubert and Rudolf Lill, "Die Auseinandersetzung zwischen Katholizismus und Liberalismus" and "Der Sieg des Ultramontanismus," in *HK* 6/1: 696-796.

31. See Oskar Köhler, "Der Weltplan Leos XIII," in *HK* 6/2: 3-27; O. Köhler and Bernhard Stasiewski, "Das Lehramt und die Theologie," ibid., pp. 316-40; Rudolf Lill, "Der deutsche Katholizismus zwischen Kulturkampf und 1. Weltkrieg," ibid., pp. 515-27.

32. The difference between Pius IX and Leo XIII has been noted by Karl Rahner, who has stated: "As strange as it sounds, in comparison to Pius IX, Leo XIII was a liberal and a man open to the world." See K. Rahner, "The Importance of Thomas Aquinas" (1982), in Paul Imhof and Hubert Biallowons, eds., *Faith in a Wintry Season*, trans. H. Egan et al. (New York: Crossroad, 1990), pp. 41-58, 57.

33. On German Catholic theology in the late 1800s, see Thomas F. O'Meara, *Church and Culture* (Notre Dame, Ind.: University of Notre Dame Press, 1991). On the Catholic church's efforts to address social and political issues at the end of the nineteenth century, see Paul Misner, *Social Catholicism in Europe* (New York: Crossroads, 1991).

34. On historicism, see John Macquarrie, *Jesus Christ in Modern Thought* (Philadelphia: Trinity, 1990), pp. 260-66; Alister McGrath, *The Making of German Christology* (New York: Basil Blackwell, 1986), pp. 53-68.

35. See Adolf Harnack, *What Is Christianity?* trans. T. B. Saunders (New York: Harper and Row, 1957), pp. 124-31.

36. See Ernst Troeltsch, "Historical and Dogmatic Method in Theology" (1898), in idem, *Religion in History*, trans. J. L. Adams and W. F. Bense (Minneapolis: Fortress Press, 1991), pp. 11-32; idem, *The Absoluteness of Christianity and the History of Religions*, trans. D. Reid (Richmond, Va.: John Knox Press, 1971); idem, *Der Historismus und seine Probleme*, in *Gesammelte Schriften* 3 (Tübingen: J. C. B. Mohr, 1922); idem, "Historiography," in James Hastings, ed., *Encyclopedia of Religion and Ethics* 6 (New York: Charles Scribner's Sons, 1955): 716-23. For a fuller exposition of Troeltsch's thought and its implications for theology, see Claude Welch, *Protestant Thought in the Nineteenth Century* 2 (New Haven, Conn.: Yale University Press, 1985), pp. 266-301; Van Harvey, *The Historian and the Believer* (New York: Macmillan, 1966), pp. 3-37.

37. Karl Adam, book review of A. Harnack, *Dogmengeschichte*, 6th ed. (Tübingen: J. C. B. Mohr, 1922), in *ThQ* 104 (1923): 102-3.

38. Karl Adam, *The Son of God*, trans. P. Hereford (New York: Sheed and Ward, 1934), p. 17. Hereafter, this text will be referred to as a*SoG*.

39. Karl Adam, *Christ and the Western Mind*, trans. E. Bullough (New York: Macmillan, 1930), p. 34. The original German text was *Christus und der Geist des Abendlandes* (1928).

40. See Francis Schüssler Fiorenza and John P. Galvin, eds., *Systematic Theology* 1 (Minneapolis: Fortress Press, 1991), pp. 27-34, 37; Emerich Coreth et al., eds., *Christliche Philosophie im katholischen Denken des 19. und 20. Jahrhunderts* 2 (Graz: Styria, 1988); Gerald McCool, *From Unity to Pluralism* (New York: Fordham University Press, 1989); idem, *Catholic Theology in the Nineteenth Century* (New York: Seabury, 1977), pp. 129-144; Gottlieb Söhngen, "Neuscholastik," *LThK* 7 (1962), col. 923-26.

41. See Avery Dulles, *Revelation Theology* (New York: Herder and Herder, 1969), p. 137. Protected from the Kulturkampf, the theologate at

Valkenburg had grown into a major center for Jesuit studies. Karl Rahner studied here from 1929 to 1933.

42. Karl Adam, book review of C. Pesch, *De Deo uno secundum naturam, de Deo trino secundum personas*, 5th and 6th eds. (Freiburg: Herder, 1925), in *ThQ* 106 (1925): 157-58. This translation and others from the German throughout the book are my own, unless otherwise noted.

43. Adam, *Christ and the Western Mind*, p. 28.

44. See Gabriel Daly, *Transcendence and Immanence* (Oxford: Clarendon, 1980); Peter Neuner, *Religion zwischen Kirche und Mystik* (Frankfurt am Main: Josef Knecht, 1977); Alec Vidler, *The Modernist Movement in the Roman Church* (Cambridge: Cambridge University Press, 1934), pp. 229-30.

45. Yves Congar, *Tradition and Traditions*, trans. M. Naseby and T. Rainborough (London: Burns and Oates, 1966), pp. 215. The original French edition appeared in 1960.

46. See Daniel Donovan, "Church and Theology in the Modernist Crisis," *The Proceedings of the Catholic Theological Society of America* 40 (1985): 145-59; Thomas Loome, *Liberal Catholicism, Reform Catholicism, Modernism* (Mainz: Matthias Grünewald, 1979); Köhler and Stasiewski, "Das Lehramt und die Theologie"; Roger Aubert, "Die modernistische Krise," in *HK* 6/2: 316-27, 435-46; August Hagen, *Der Reformkatholizismus in der Diözese Rottenburg* (Stuttgart: Schwaben, 1962).

47. See Loome, *Liberal Catholicism, Reform Catholicism, Modernism*; Aubert, "Die modernistische Krise," pp. 437-46; T. Mark Schoof, *A Survey of Catholic Theology, 1800-1970*, trans. N. D. Smith (New York: Paulist, 1970), pp. 72-76; Adolf Kolping, *Katholische Theologie* (Bremen: Carl Schüneman, 1965), pp. 46-48; August Hagen, "Reformkatholizismus," *LThK* 8, col. 1085; John Heaney, *The Modernist Crisis* (Washington, D.C.: Corpus Books, 1968), pp. 422-30.

48. See Josef Müller, *Der Reformkatholizismus: Die Religion der Zukunft* (Würzburg: Echter, 1898).

49. *Hochland* pursued its vision until 1971, when it took a new direction and was renamed *Neues Hochland*. See Wolfgang Frühwald, "Katholische Literatur im 19. und 20. Jahrhundert in deutschland," in Anton Rauscher, ed., *Religiös-kulturelle Bewegungen im Deutschen Katholizismus seit 1800* (Paderborn: Ferdinand Schöningh, 1986), pp. 9-26; Wilhelm Spael, *Das katholische Deutschland im 20. Jahrhundert* (Würzburg: Echter, 1964), pp. 148-75; Dru, *The Contribution of German Catholicism*, pp. 107-24.

50. See Norbert Trippen, *Theologie und Lehramt im Konflikt* (Freiburg: Herder, 1977), pp. 110-84.

51. Albert Ehrhard, *Der Katholizismus und das zwanzigste Jahrhundert im Licht der kirchlichen Entwicklung der Neuzeit* (Stuttgart: Joseph Roth, 1902), pp. 348, 349-50. See Donovan, "Church and Theology in the Modernist Crisis," p. 149.

52. Albert Ehrhard, "Die neue Lage der katholischen Theologie," *Internationale Wochenschrift für Wissenschaft, Kunst und Technik* 2 (1908): 65-84. This excerpt is taken from Donovan, "Church and Theology in the Modernist Crisis," p. 154.

53. Schoof, *Survey of Catholic Theology*, p. 76; Spael, *Das katholische Deutschland im 20. Jahrhundert*, pp. 163-68.

54. Karlheinz Dietz et al., *Regensburg zur Römerzeit*, 2nd ed. (Regensburg: Friedrich Pustet, 1979), pp. 13-28.

55. See J. Heiler, "Karl Adam," pp. 411-21.

56. Karl Adam, *Der Kirchenbegriff Tertullians* (Paderborn: Ferdinand Schöningh, 1907). The quality of this work is reflected in the fact that it was recently cited by Killian McDonnell, "Communion Ecclesiology and Baptism in the Spirit," *ThS* 49 (1988): 671-93, 681, passim.

57. Karl Adam, *Die Eucharistielehre der heiligen Augustin* (Paderborn: Ferdinand Schöningh, 1908), pp. iii-iv.

58. See Karl Adam, "Der Antimodernisteneid und die theologischen Fakultäten," *Katholische Kirchenzeitung für Deutschland* 1 (1910): 83-85.

59. See Alfons Auer, "Karl Adam, 1876-1966," *ThQ* 150 (1970): 131-43; Friedrich Heiler, "Zum Tod von Karl Adam," *ThQ* 146 (1966): 257-60.

60. See *Verzeichnis der Vorlesungen*, University of Munich, Winter-Spring Semester (1910-1911); Stelzenberger, "Bibliographie," p. 333.

61. See Trippen, *Theologie und Lehramt im Konflikt*, pp.268- 405; Joseph Schnitzer, *Der katholische Modernismus* (Berlin: Protestantische Schriftenvertrieb, 1912).

62. Crown Prince Rupprecht commanded Germany's Sixth Army in the First World War. He was regarded as one of Germany's most competent military commanders, especially noted for his role in the battle of Verdun. See Barbara Tuchman, *The Guns of August* (New York: Macmillan, 1962).

63. Beginning with the pontificate of Benedict XV in 1914, most German Catholic theologians discouraged the use of the phrase "Reform Catholicism." For instance, in 1938 Karl Adam and Karl Rahner spoke against a book calling for a revival of Reform Catholicism. See Schoof, *Survey of Catholic Theology*, p. 91.

64. See Rudolf Reinhardt, "Die katholische-theologische Fakultät Tübingen im 19. Jahrhundert," in Georg Schwaiger, ed., *Kirche und Theologie im 19. Jahrhundert* (Göttingen: Vandenhock and Ruprecht,

1975), pp. 55-87, 64, 80; Max Seckler, *Theologie vor Gericht* (Tübingen: J. C. B. Mohr [Paul Siebeck], 1972); Hagen, *Der Reformkatholizismus in der Diözese Rottenburg*, pp. 129-52. Also, see "Eine Liste der Tübinger," *ThQ* 150 (1970): 177-86.

65. See Romano Guardini, *Berichte über mein Leben* (Düsseldorf: Patmos, 1984), pp. 79-86, 124.

66. See Karl Adam, *Das sogenannte Bussedikt des Papstes Kallistus* (Munich: Kirchenhistorischen Seminar, 1917); idem, *Die kirchliche Sündenvergebung nach dem hl. Augustin* (Paderborn: Ferdinand Schöningh, 1917).

67. See *Verzeichnis der Vorlesungen*, University of Tübingen (1919-1920).

68. Karl Adam, "Theologischer Glaube und Theologie" in idem, *Glaube und Glaubenswissenschaft im Katholizismus*, 2nd rev. ed. (Rottenburg: Bader, 1923), pp. 17-43, 33. The original text appeared as "Glaube und Glaubenswissenschaft im Katholizismus," *ThQ* 101 (1920): 131-55.

69. See J. Heiler, "Karl Adam," pp. 524-35; Roger Aubert, *Le Probleme de L'Acte de Foi* (Louvain: E. Warny, 1945), pp. 522-47; Johannes Flury, *Um die Redlichkeit des Glaubens* (Fribourg: Universitätsverlag, 1979), pp. 149-64.

70. See note 68 above. Erich Przywara's critique of Adam's view appeared in *StdZ* 105 (1922-23): 128-31. Adam responded in his book review of Przywara's *Religionsbegrundung*, in *ThQ* 105 (1924): 133-37. See also E. Przywara, *Ringen der Gegenwart* 2 (Augsburg: B. Filser, 1929), pp. 710-12.

71. Karl Adam, "Die Theologie der Krisis," in Fritz Hofmann, ed., *Gesammelte Aufsätze zur Dogmengeschichte* (Augsburg: Haas & Cie, 1936), pp. 319-37, 325. The original text appeared in *Hochland* 23/2 (1926): 271-86.

72. Ibid., pp. 333-34.

73. Discussions in English of the Catholic Tübingen School include: Franklin, *Nineteenth-Century Churches*; James Burtchaell, "Drey, Möhler and the Catholic School of Tübingen," in Ninian Smart et al., eds., *Nineteenth-Century Religious Thought in the West* 2 (Cambridge: Cambridge University Press, 1985): 111-39; O'Meara, *Romantic Idealism and Roman Catholicism*, pp. 94-110, 138-60; McCool, *Catholic Theology in the Nineteenth Century*, passim; Wayne Fehr, *The Birth of the Catholic Tübingen School* (Chico, Calif.: Scholars Press, 1981); Elmar Klinger, "Tübingen School," in Karl Rahner et al., eds., *Sacramentum Mundi* 6 (New York: Herder, 1970): 318-20; Josef Rupert Geiselmann, *The Meaning of Tradition*, trans. W. J. O'Hara (New York: Herder and Herder, 1966); Dru, *The Contribution of German Catholicism*, passim.

A recent doctoral dissertation on the topic is Douglas McCready's "The Christology of the Catholic Tübingen School: Drey to Kasper" (Ph.D. diss., Temple University, 1987).

74. Karl Adam, "Die katholische Tübinger Schule," in Hofmann, ed., *Gesammelte Aufsätze*, pp. 389-412, 391. The original text appeared in *Hochland* 24/2 (1926-1927): 581-601.

75. Ibid., p. 392. This essay is one among many presentations in German on the Catholic Tübingen School: Paul Schanz, "Die katholische Tübinger Schule," *ThQ* 80 (1898): 1-49; Josef Rupert Geiselmann, *Die katholische Tübinger Schule* (Freiburg: Herder, 1964); Heinrich Fries, "Tübinger Schule," *LThK* 10: 390-92; Walter Kasper, "Verständnis der Theologie Damals und Heute," in Joseph Ratzinger and Johannes Neumann, eds., *Theologie im Wandel* 1 (Munich: Erich Wewel, 1967): 91-115; Rudolf Reinhardt, ed., *Tübinger Theologen und ihre Theologie* (Tübingen: J. C. B. Mohr [Paul Siebeck], 1977). Also, the school's theologians are discussed in Heinrich Fries and Georg Schwaiger, eds., *Katholische Theologen Deutschlands im 19. Jahrhundert* (Munich: Kösel, 1977), 3 vols.

76. Adam, "Die katholische Tübinger Schule," p. 392.

77. *Symbolik* led to a conflict between Möhler and his Protestant colleague Ferdinand Christian Baur. See Joseph Fitzer, *Möhler and Baur in Controversy, 1832-1838* (Tallahassee: American Academy of Religion, 1974).

78. These lectures were never published. Kuhn's major publication was his three-volume *Die Apologetik als wissenschaftliche Nachweisung* (Apologetics as a scholarly demonstration) (1838, 1843, 1847). Karl Adam neglected to mention Kuhn's book on Jesus Christ that bears similarities to the christology which Adam himself would develop. Kuhn wrote *Das Leben Jesu, wissenschaftlich bearbeitet* (1838) in order to refute David Friedrich Strauss's *Das Leben Jesu, kritisch bearbeitet* (1835-36). See William Madges, *The Core of the Christian Faith* (New York: Peter Lang, 1990); Norman Perrin, *Rediscovering the Teaching of Jesus* (New York: Harper and Row, 1976), pp. 212-13; Albert Schweitzer, *The Quest of the Historical Jesus*, trans. W. Montgomery (New York: Macmillan, 1968), p. 107.

79. Adam, "Die katholische Tübinger Schule," p. 395.

80. Ibid., p. 397.

2. In Search of Catholic Identity

1. Throughout this chapter and subsequent chapters I use the English titles of Adam's texts when these texts have been published in

English, and I take the quotations from the English versions so long as they correspond to the appropriate edition of the text in German.

2. Peter Hebblethwaite, "The Need for Reform," *Tablet* 241 (August 15, 1987): 863-64. See idem, "Understanding German Catholics—the Work of H. G. Barnes," *New Blackfriars* 68 (April 1987): 179-91; John Thiel, "Karl Adam and the Council," *Month* 17 (November 1984): 378-81.

3. See Schoof, *Survey of Catholic Theology*, pp. 76-81; Leo Scheffczyk, "Grundzüge der Entwicklung der Theologie zwischen dem Ersten Weltkrieg und dem Zweiten Vatikanischen Konzil," in *HK* 7: 263-301.

4. See Erich Przywara, "Der Ruf von heute" (1930), in *Katholische Krise*, ed. Bernhard Gertz (Düsseldorf: Patmos, 1967), pp. 89-105. See also idem, "Die funf Wenden" (1930), in *Katholische Krise*, pp. 106-22; idem, "Le mouvement théologique et reliqieux en Allemagne," *Nouvelle Revue Théologique* 56 (1929): 565-75; Roger Aubert, "Les grandes tendances théologiques entre les deux guerres," *Collectana Mechliniensia* 16 (1946): 17-36.

5. See Craig, *Germany, 1866-1945*, pp. 468-97; Peter Gay, *The Outsider as Insider* (New York: Harper and Row, 1968).

6. See Stephen Kern, *The Culture of Time and Space, 1880-1918* (Cambridge, Mass.: Harvard University Press, 1983).

7. See H. O. Pappé, "Philosophical Anthropology," in *EPh* 6: 159-66; Kolping, *Katholische Theologie*, pp. 64-70.

8. See Richard Schmitt, "Phenomenology," in *EPh* 6: 135-51 and Herbert Spiegelberg, *The Phenomenological Movement*, 3rd ed. (The Hague: Martin Nijhoff, 1982).

9. See Alois Baumgartner, *Sehnsucht nach Gemeinschaft* (Munich: Ferdinand Schöningh, 1977), pp. 18-86; Gay, *The Outsider as Insider*, p. 80.

10. Holborn, *History of Modern Germany*, pp. 411-13; Hürten, *Kurze Geschichte*, pp. 183-208.

11. See Friedrich Heer, "Weimar—Ein religiöser und weltanschaulicher Leerraum," in Hubert Cancik, ed., *Religions- und Geistesgeschichte der Weimarer Republik* (Düsseldorf: Patmos, 1982), pp. 31-48; Erwin Iserloh, "Innerkirchliche Bewegungen und ihre Spiritualität," in *HK* 7: 307-37.

12. To glimpse how Barth differed from Otto, see Robert Krieg, "Narrative as a Linguistic Rule: Fyodor Dostoevsky and Karl Barth," *International Journal for the Philosophy of Religion* 8 (1977): 190-205.

13. See F. Heiler, "Zum Tod von Karl Adam"; Wolfgang Philipp, "Friedrich Heiler," in Schultz, ed., *Tendenzen der Theologie im 20. Jahrhundert*, pp. 387-91; Paul Misner, ed., *Friedrich von Hügel, Nathan Soderblom, Friedrich Heiler* (Paderborn: Bonifacius, 1981), pp. 13-42,

passim; idem, "The Two Ecumenisms of Friedrich Heiler," *Andover Newton Quarterly* 16 (1975): 238-49. A doctoral dissertation comparing Heiler's *Der Katholizismus* and Adam's *The Spirit of Catholicism* is Thomas Skrabak Edwards's "Karl Adam and Friedrich Heiler on the Essence of Catholicism" (Ph.D. diss., The Catholic University of America, 1989).

14. See Kreidler, *Eine Theologie des Lebens*, pp. 223-26; Fritz Hofmann, "Theologie aus dem Geist der Tübinger Schule," *ThQ* 146 (1966): 262-84, 275; J. Heiler, "Karl Adam," pp. 411-12.

15. See Avery Dulles, "The Catholicity of the Augsburg Confession," *Journal of Religion* 63 (October 1983): 337-54, esp. 345-47; idem, *The Catholicity of the Church* (Oxford: Clarendon, 1985), passim.

16. Friedrich Heiler, *Der Katholizismus* (Munich: Ernst Reinhardt, 1923), p. 597.

17. Ibid., p. 12.

18. Ibid., pp. xxxiv, 622, 659.

19. Ibid., p. 643.

20. See Friedrich Heiler, *Evangelische Katholizität* (Munich: Ernst Reinhardt, 1926).

21. At Tübingen, the Protestant theologian Karl Heim joined in this discussion with his book *Das Wesen des evangelischen Christentums* (1926).

22. See Scheffczyk, "Grundzüge der Entwicklung der Theologie," pp. 266-67; Kolping, *Katholische Theologie*, pp. 105-13; George La Piana, "Recent Tendencies in Roman Catholic Theology," *Harvard Theological Review* 25 (1922): 233-92.

23. Peter Wust gave an insightful analysis of Catholic theology in Germany in his "Die Rückkehr des deutschen Katholizismus aus dem Exil," in Karl Hoeber, ed., *Die Rückkehr aus dem Exil* (Düsseldorf: L. Schwann, 1926), pp. 16-35.

24. Romano Guardini, *The Church and the Catholic, and the Spirit of the Liturgy*, trans. A. Lane (New York: Sheed and Ward, 1935), p. 14. This book consists of two distinct texts. The first text on ecclesiology is translated from the original German book *Vom Sinn der Kirche* (Mainz: Matthias Grünewald, 1922). The second text on the liturgy is translated from the original German book *Vom Geist der Liturgie* (Freiburg: Herder, 1918).

25. Guardini, *The Church and the Catholic*, p. 17.

26. Ibid., p. 19.

27. Ibid., p. 29.

28. Scheffczyk, "Grundzüge der Entwicklung der Theologie," p. 265.

29. Karl Adam, *The Spirit of Catholicism*, trans. J. McCann (New York: Macmillan, 1929), p. 9. Hereafter, this text is referred to as a*SC*. The original German text is idem, *Das Wesen des Katholizismus* (Augsburg: L. Schwann, 1924).

30. a*SC*, p. 2.

31. Ibid., p. 24.

32. Ibid., p. 32.

33. Ibid., p. 80.

34. Ibid., p. 99.

35. Ibid., p. 140.

36. Ibid., p. 158.

37. Ibid., p. 193.

38. Ibid., p. 229. Adam's frankness about the church is also evident in his "The Mystery of Christ's Incarnation and of His Mystical Body," *Orate Fratres* 13 (1939): 337–44, 392–99, 433–40. This article originally appeared as "Das Geheimnis der Inkarnation Christi und seines mystischen Leibes: Vom Ärgernis zum sieghaften Glauben" in Hermann Tüchle, ed., *Die Eine Kirche* (Paderborn: Bonafacius, 1939), pp. 33–54.

39. See Scheffczyk, "Grundzüge der Entwicklung der Theologie," p. 268; Aubert, "Die Theologie des 20. Jahrhunderts," pp. 34–35; Heinrich Fries, *Wegbereiter und Wege* (Olten-Freiburg: Walter, 1968), p. 30; Hofmann, "Theologie der Tübinger Schule," p. 269; J. Heiler, "Karl Adam," pp. 531–32.

40. a*SC*, p. 15.

41. Ibid., p. 31.

42. See Adam, *Die Eucharistielehre*; idem, "Notizen zur Echtheitsfrage der Augustin zugesprochen Schrift 'De unite ecclesia,'" *ThQ* 91 (1909): 86–115; idem, *Die kirchlichen Sündenvergebung nach dem heiligen Augustin*; idem, *Die geheime Kirchenbusse nach dem heiligen Augustin* (Kempten: Kösel, 1921); idem, *Die geistige Entwicklung des heiligen Augustinus* (Augsburg: Haas and Grabherr, 1931), which appeared in English as *St. Augustine: The Odyssey of His Soul*, trans. J. McCann (New York: Macmillan, 1932).

43. a*SC*, p. 15.

44. Ibid., p. 35.

45. Ibid., p. 214. While I have tried to use gender inclusive language throughout this book, I have not modified quotations.

46. a*SC*, p. 2.

47. Ibid., p. 213.

48. See Paul-Werner Scheele, "Johann Adam Möhler," in Fries and Schwaiger, *Katholische Theologen* 2: 70–98; Thomas O'Meara, "Revelation and History: Schelling, Möhler and Congar," *Irish Theological Quarterly* 53 (1987): 17–35; Hervé Savon, *Johann Adam Möhler*, trans.

Charles McGrath (Glen Rock, N.J.: Paulist, 1966). Also see chapter 1, n. 73 and n. 75.

49. Johann Adam Möhler, *Die Einheit in der Kirche oder das Prinzip der drei ersten Jahrhunderts* (Tübingen: Heinrich Laupp, 1825).

50. Johann Adam Möhler, *Symbolism*, trans. J. B. Robertson (London: Gibbings, 1894), p. 260. For the German, see idem, *Symbolik*, 5th ed. (Mainz: Florian Küpferberg, 1838), vol. 1, ch. 5, art. 36, p. 337.

51. a*SC*, p. 15.

52. Ibid., p. 49. On the notion of the "living tradition," see Geiselmann, *The Meaning of Tradition*.

53. a*SC*, pp. 40, 217.

54. See Peter Spader, "The Primacy of the Heart," *Philosophy Today* 29 (1985): 223-29; Edward Vacek, "Scheler's Phenomenology of Love," *Journal of Religion* 62 (1982): 156-77; Heinz Leonardy, *Liebe und Person* (The Hague: Martinus Nijhoff, 1976); Alois Dempf, "Schelers System der christlicher Geistphilosophie als Grundlage einer religiösen Erneuerung," in Paul Good, ed., *Max Scheler im Gegenwartsgeschehen der Philosophie* (Bern: Francke, 1975), pp. 39-45; Alexander von Schoenborn, "Max Scheler on Philosophy and Religion," *International Philosophy Quarterly* 14 (1974): 285-308; Wilfred Hartmann, "Max Scheler's Theory of Person," *Philosophy Today* 12 (1968): 246-61; Manfred Frings, *Max Scheler* (Pittsburgh: Duquesne University Press, 1965).

55. Max Scheler, *Formalism in Ethics and Non-Formal Ethics of Values*, trans. M. Frings and R. Funk (Evanston, Ill.: Northwestern University Press, 1973), p. 391.

56. Ibid., p. 523.

57. Max Scheler, "Soziologische Neuorientierung und die Aufgaben der deutschen Katholiken nach dem Krieg" (1915/1916), in *Gesammelte Werke* 4, ed. Manfred Frings (Bern: Franck, 1982): 373-472, 434.

58. Ibid., pp. 440, 442.

59. See Erich Przywara, "Corpus Christi Mysticum" (1940), in *Katholische Krise*, pp. 123-52, 123.

60. See Richard Schäffler, *Die Wechselbeziehungen zwischen Philosophie und katholischer Theologie* (Darmstadt: Wissenschaftliche Buchgesellschaft, 1980); Heinrich Fries, *Die katholische Religionsphilosophie der Gegenwart* (Heidelberg: F. H. Kerle, 1949), pp. 176-84.

61. a*SC*, p. 8.

62. Ibid., p. 33.

63. Adam, "Die katholische Tübinger Schule," p. 392.

64. See Hubert Jedin, "Die Päpste Benedikte XV., Pius XI. und Pius XII.," in *HK* 7:22-36.

65. Erich Przywara, "Wesen des Katholizismus," *StdZ* 108 (1924-1925): 47-62, 50. See also idem, *Ringen der Gegenwart* 2: 584-85.

66. Hermann Dieckmann, "Besprechung," *Scholastik* 5 (1930): 268-75, 272.

67. Karl Barth, "Roman Catholicism" (1928), in idem, *Theology and Church*, trans. L. P. Smith (New York: Harper and Row, 1962), pp. 307-33.

68. George Orwell, review of *The Spirit of Catholicism*, in *New English Weekly* (1932), reprinted in Sonia Orwell and Ian Augus, eds., *The Collected Essays, Journals and Letters of George Orwell* 1 (London: Seker and Warburg, 1968): 79-81.

69. See Kreidler, *Eine Theologie des Lebens*, pp. 296-318; Auer, "Karl Adam."

70. See Mario Bendiscioli and M. Marcocchi, "La censura del S. Ufficio a 'L'essenza del Cattolicesimo' de K. Adam: notizia di un carteggio (1929-1935)," *Studi e memorie* 7 (1979): 95-147.

71. According to Paschal Botz, when Adam learned of the Holy Office's tentative decision, he told Botz that he could withdraw from writing his doctoral dissertation under Adam's direction. Botz stayed with his professor, as did Fritz Hofmann, who was also a doctoral student at the time and later joined Tübingen's faculty. Ten months later, when Adam received word that *The Spirit of Catholicism* required only minor linguistic changes, he brought this letter to class and wept with relief as he read it to his students, who then broke into applause. Botz and Hofmann worked with Adam on revising the text to Rome's satisfaction.

72. See Kreidler, *Eine Theologie des Lebens*, pp. 302-6.

73. Paschal Botz has recalled that Adam never said anything derogatory about the Holy Office. If Adam knew the authors of the Vatican's report on *The Spirit of Catholicism*, he never mentioned their names.

74. Karl Adam, *Das Wesen des Katholizismus*, 4th printing (Augsburg: L. Schwann, 1927), p. 10. Book reviews not mentioned here include Bernhard Braubach, "Karl Adam und das Wesen des Katholizismus," *Hochland* 23/2 (1926): 488-95; D. Leonard Fendt, "Katholische Theologie der Gegenwart," *Zeitschrift für Theologie und Kirche* 34 (1926): 430-59.

75. See Kreidler, *Eine Theologie des Lebens*, pp. 310-13. The translations of the sixth and seventh printings of Adam's texts, as quoted in Kreidler, *Eine Theologie des Lebens*, are my own.

76. Stelzenberger, "Bibliographie," p. 333. The Dominican theologian Otto Pesch has recently noted that *The Spirit of Catholicism* was a "pioneering" work in Catholic ecclesiology; see O. Pesch, *Thomas von Aquin* (Mainz: Matthias Grünewald, 1989), p. 379 n. 130.

77. Joseph Bluett, "The Mystical Body of Christ: 1890-1940," *ThS* 3 (1942): 261-89, 262. Although Bluett does not cite *The Spirit of Catholicism*, he does refer to Adam's "Le Christ dans l'Eglise," *Revue*

Apologetique 52 (1931): 257-72, and his "The Mystery of Christ's Incarnation and of His Mystical Body" (1939). On the shift in ecclesiology from "body of Christ" to "people of God," see Kevin McNamara, "The Idea of the Church," *Irish Theological Quarterly* 33 (1966): 99-113.

78. See Avery Dulles, *Models of the Church* (Garden City, N.Y.: Doubleday, 1974), pp. 51-66; Jerome Hamer, *The Church Is a Communion*, trans. R. Matthews (New York: Sheed and Ward, 1964), pp. 13-23; Felix Malmberg, *Ein Leib—Ein Geist* (Freiburg: Herder, 1960), pp. 16-31.

79. Pius XII, *Mystici Corporis* (June 29, 1943), (Washington, D.C.: National Catholic Welfare Conference, 1943), art. 63, p. 28.

80. Aubert, "Les grandes tendances théologiques entre les deux guerres," p. 29.

81. Aubert, "Die Theologie des 20. Jahrhunderts," p. 35.

82. Louis Bouyer, "Où en est la théologie du Corps mystique," *Revue des Sciences religieuses* 22 (1948): 313-33, 316.

83. Gotthold Hasenhüttl, *Charisma* (Freiburg: Herder, 1969), pp. 321-27, 323.

84. Kasper, "Karl Adam," p. 254.

85. Yves Congar, *Jalons pour une Théologie du Laicat* (Paris: Cerf, 1953), pp. 183, 241, 258, 382, 395.

86. Congar, *Tradition and Traditions*, pp. 63, 187, 217, 218.

87. Scheffczyk, "Grundzüge der Entwicklung der Theologie," p. 268.

88. Hebblethwaite, "Understanding German Catholics—the Work of H. G. Barnes," p. 180.

89. Paul VI, *Ecclesiam Suam* (August 6, 1964), in *The Pope Speaks* 10 (1964-1965): 253-92; art. 10, p. 255.

90. a*SC*, p. 210.

91. Paul VI, *Ecclesiam Suam*, art. 10, p. 255.

92. Ibid., art. 26, p. 260.

93. Ibid., art. 35, p. 263.

94. Thiel, "Karl Adam and the Council."

95. *Lumen Gentium* (1964), chapter 1, art. 7, in *VCII*, p. 355.

96. Ibid., chapter 1, art. 7, and chapter 7.

97. Häring, "In Memory of Karl Adam."

98. Hofmann, "Theologie der Tübinger Schule," p. 277.

99. Fries, *Wegbereiter und Wege*, p. 30.

100. Hamer, *The Church Is a Communion*, pp. 13-18.

101. Hofmann, "Theologie der Tübinger Schule," p. 283.

3. Doing Christology "From Below"

1. Walter Kasper, *Jesus the Christ*, trans. V. Green (New York: Paulist, 1976), pp. 17-19.

2. See Robert Lachenschmid, "Christologie und Soteriologie," in Herbert Vorgrimler and Robert Vander Gucht, eds., *Bilanz der Theologie im 20. Jahrhundert* 3 (Freiburg: Herder, 1970): 82-120.

3. a*SoG*, p. 1. Cf. Karl Adam, *Christ Our Brother*, trans. J. McCann (New York: Macmillan, 1931), p. 60. Hereafter, this text is referred to as a*COB*.

4. a*SoG*, p. 152.

5. See Kreidler, *Eine Theologie des Lebens*, p. 148; Kasper, "Karl Adam," p. 256. On the limits of the metaphor "from below," see Nicholas Lash, "Up and Down in Christology," in Stephen Sykes and Derek Holmes, eds., *New Studies in Theology* 1 (London: Gerald Duckworth, 1980): 31-46.

6. See Craig, *Germany, 1866-1945*, pp. 469-97; Gay, *The Outsider as Insider*.

7. See Aidan Kavanagh, "Liturgical and Credal Studies," in Henry Bowden, ed., *A Century of Church History* (Carbondale: Southern Illinois University Press, 1988), pp. 216-44; Alois Baumgartner, "Die Auswirkungen der liturgischen Bewegung auf Kirche und Katholizismus," in Rauscher, ed., *Religiös-kulturelle Bewegungen im deutschen Katholizismus seit 1800*, pp. 121-36; Theodor Maas-Ewerd, *Die Krise der liturgischen Bewegung in Deutschland und Österreich* (Regensburg: Friedrich Pustet, 1981), pp. 41-55; Erwin Iserloh, "Innerkirchliche Bewegungen und ihre Spiritualität," *HK* 7: 301-11; E. Iserloh, "Die Geschichte der liturgischen Bewegung" (1959), in idem, *Kirche—Ereignis und Institution* 1 (Münster: Aschendorff, 1985): 436-51; R. William Franklin, "The Nineteenth-Century Liturgical Movement," *Worship* 53 (1979): 12-39; L. C. Sheppard, "Liturgical Movement, Catholic," in *The New Catholic Encyclopedia* 8 (New York: McGraw- Hill, 1967): 900-905. I am indebted to Mark Searle for his advice on this section of the chapter.

8. Guardini, *The Church and the Catholic, and The Spirit of the Liturgy*, pp. 156-57.

9. Josef Jungmann, *The Place of Christ in Liturgical Prayer*, 2nd ed., trans. A. Peeler (Staten Island, N.Y.: Alba House, 1965), p. 147. The statements quoted here appear in the original text, *Die Stellung Christi im liturgischen Gebet* (Münster: Aschendorff, 1925), and they are retained in the revised edition.

10. Jungman, *The Place of Christ*, p. 170.

11. Ibid., p. 246.

12. Ibid., p. 278.

13. Christian Pesch, *Compendium theologiae dogmaticae*, rev. ed. (Freiburg: Herder, 1921) 3:1-23. On neoscholastic christology, see Fiorenza and Galvin, *Systematic Theology* 1:252-53; Dulles, *Revelation Theology*, pp. 136-39.

14. One attempt to incorporate the conclusions of Jungmann's study into theology was the "theology of proclamation" undertaken by J. Jungmann, F. Dander, F. Lakner, and H. Rahner at the University of Innsbruck. See Hans B. Mayer, "Josef Andreas Jungmann, S.J.," *ZkTh* 97 (1975): 220-24; Balthasar Fischer and Hans B. Mayer, eds., *J. A. Jungmann* (Innsbruck: Tyrolia, 1975); Aubert, "Die Theologie des 20. Jahrhunderts," pp. 25-27.

15. Karl Adam, "Durch Christus, unsern Herrn," *Seele* 8 (1926): 321-29, 355-64.

16. Jungmann, *The Place of Christ in Liturgical Prayer*, p. xiv.

17. a*COB*, p. 131. The original German text of seven chapters is idem, *Christus unser Bruder*, 2nd rev. ed. (Regensburg: Joseph Happel, 1930). Hereafter, this second edition is referred to as a*CuB* 2.

18. a*COB*, p. 2.

19. Ibid., p. 14.

20. Ibid., p. 28.

21. Ibid., p. 59.

22. Ibid., pp. 60-61.

23. Ibid., pp. 75-76.

24. Ibid., p. 106.

25. Ibid., p. 142.

26. Ibid., p. 148.

27. Ibid., p. 180.

28. Ibid., p. 196.

29. See Kreidler, *Eine Theologie des Lebens*, pp. 28-33, 197-201.

30. a*COB*, pp. 59, 67, 68.

31. Ibid., p. 62.

32. See Kreidler, *Eine Theologie des Lebens*, p. 180.

33. a*COB*, p. 73.

34. Adam, *St. Augustine: The Odyssey of His Soul*, p. 36.

35. Ibid., p. 45.

36. a*COB*, pp. 21, 29, 85.

37. On the "new quest" for the historical Jesus, see Norman Perrin, *Rediscovering the Teaching of Jesus*, pp. 207-48.

38. a*COB*, pp. 7, 88.

39. Adam also refers to the works of Matthias Scheeben, Karl Barth, and Karl Heim. See a*COB*, pp. 129, 153, 164.

40. See Scheele, "Johann Adam Möhler," in Fries and Schwaiger,

Katholische Theologen 2:70-98; Savon, *Johann Adam Möhler*, pp. 80-99.

41. Möhler, *Symbolism*, pp. 46-54.

42. a*COB*, p. 190.

43. On Scheler's notion of person, see the literature cited in chapter 2, n. 54.

44. Scheler, *Formalism in Ethics*, pp. 496-97.

45. a*COB*, p. 74.

46. Hofmann, "Theologie der Tübinger Schule," p. 282; cf. Kreidler, *Eine Theologie des Lebens*, p. 180.

47. Stelzenberger, "Bibliographie," p. 334.

48. "Weihnachtsbücherschau," *Hochland* 25/1 (1927-1928): 326-29. This review treats the first edition of *Christus unser Bruder* (1926).

49. "Dogmatik, Dogmengeschichte, Mystik," *Theologie und Glaube* 23 (1931): 254-56. A similar assessment is offered by Ludwig Hertling, "Gegenwart," *ZkTh* 56 (1932): 307-8.

50. Evelyn Underhill, "The Swiss Prophet," *Spectator* 147 (August 1, 1931): 163.

51. A. N. Raybould, "In the Vanguard of Catholic Thought," *Catholic World* 137 (1933): 658-66, 662.

52. John Wise, "Christologists Three," *Thought* 11 (1936): 392-408, 401.

53. See Auer, "Karl Adam."

54. See Kreidler, *Eine Theologie des Lebens*, pp. 306-8.

55. a*CuB*2, p. 30; idem, *Christus unser Bruder*, 3rd rev. ed. (Regensburg: Joseph Happel, 1934), p. 35. Hereafter, the third edition is referred to as a*CuB*3. These quotations are translated from Kreidler, *Eine Theologie des Lebens*, pp. 311-12.

56. a*CuB*2, p. 56; a*CuB*3, p. 62.

57. See Yves Congar, *Christ, Our Lady and the Church*, trans. H. St. John (Westminster: Newman Press, 1957), p. 69.

58. *Gaudium et Spes* (1965), art. 22, in *VCII*, pp. 922-23.

59. See Kreidler, *Eine Theologie des Lebens*, p. 217.

60. a*COB*, p. 59.

61. Karl Rahner, "Chalkedon—Ende oder Anfang?" in Alois Grillmeier and Heinrich Bacht, eds., *Das Konzil von Chalkedon* 3 (Würzburg: Echter, 1954): pp. 3-49; Rahner, "Current Problems in Christology," *Theological Investigations* 1, trans. C. Ernst (Baltimore: Helicon, 1961): 149-200.

62. Francis Schüssler Fiorenza, "Christology after Vatican II," *Ecumenist* 18 (1980): 81-89; Kasper, *Jesus the Christ*, p. 17.

63. Rahner, "Current Problems in Christology," p. 149.

64. a*COB*, p. 45.

65. Hofmann, "Theologie der Tübinger Schule," p. 282. Adam's emphasis on the humanity of Jesus Christ was manifested not only in his books but also in articles such as his "Jesu menschliches Wesen im Licht der unchristlichen Verkündigung," *Wissenschaft und Weisheit* 6 (1939): 111-20.

66. Rahner, "Current Problems in Christology," p. 157.

67. Ibid., p. 158. The similarity between Adam and Rahner is also evident in Rahner's "The Eternal Significance of the Humanity of Jesus for Our Relationship with God" (1953), *Theological Investigations* 2, trans. C. Ernst (Baltimore: Helicon, 1967): 35-46; see Kreidler, *Eine Theologie des Lebens*, p. 160 n. 1.

68. Alois Grillmeier, "The Figure of Christ in Catholic Theology Today," in Johannes Feiner et al., eds., *Theology Today* 1: *The Renewal of Dogma*, trans. P. White and R. Kelly (Milwaukee: Bruce, 1965): 66-108, 82 n. 16. Original text: A. Grillmeier, "Zum Christusbild der heutigen katholischen Theologie," in J. Feiner et al., eds., *Fragen der Theologie heute* (Einsiedeln: Benziger, 1957), pp. 265-99. Grillmeier refers specifically to Karl Adam's *The Christ of Faith* (1954), in which Adam restates the christology of a*COB* and a*SoG*.

69. For an exposition of scholastic christologies, including those of Scotus and Tiphanus, see Philipp Kaiser, *Die Gott-menschliche Einigung in Christus als Problem der spekulativen Theologie seit der Scholastik* (Munich: Max Hueber, 1968).

70. See Karl Rahner, "Theologie in der Welt," *Frankfurter Allgemeine Zeitung* (October 26, 1956), p. 10.

71. Karl Rahner, *I Remember*, trans. H. Egan (New York: Crossroad, 1985), p. 38.

72. a*COB*, p. 60.

73. Grillmeier, "The Figure of Christ," p. 81.

74. Rahner, "Current Problems in Christology," pp. 162-63.

75. Grillmeier, "The Figure of Christ," pp. 85-95.

76. Ibid., p. 182.

77. Lachenschmid, "Christologie und Soteriologie," p. 96. A doctoral dissertation on Adam's christology is currently being written by Wolfram Schmidt at the University of Regensburg.

78. See Kasper, *Jesus the Christ*, pp. 243-45; Lachenschmid, "Christologie und Soteriologie," pp. 83, 95-96; Grillmeier, "The Figure of Christ," pp. 85-95; Rudolf Haubst, "Probleme der jüngsten Christologie," *Theologische Revue* 52 (1956): 145-62; Joseph Ternus, "Das Seelen- und Bewusstseinsleben Jesu," in Grillmeier and Bacht, eds., *Das Konzil von Chalkedon* 3:81-237.

79. See Pius XII, *Sempiternus Rex Christus* (October 8, 1951), in

Amanda Watlingen, ed., *Christ Our Lord* (Wilmington: McGrath, 1978), pp. 243-60.

80. Kreidler, *Eine Theologie des Lebens*, p. 180.

81. *Gaudium et Spes*, art. 22, in *VCII*, pp. 922-23; see Kreidler, *Eine Theologie des Lebens*, p. 217.

82. See Vidler, *The Modernist Movement in the Roman Catholic Church*, pp. 228-30.

83. Jungmann's student and colleague Balthasar Fischer claimed that Adam oversimplified the thesis of Jungmann's *Die Stellung Christi im liturgischen Gebet*; see B. Fischer, "Vom Beten zu Christus," in Josef G. Plocer, ed., *Gottfeiern* (Freiburg: Herder, 1980), pp. 94-99; Grillmeier, "The Figure of Christ," p. 106 n. 50. Hans Kreidler responded to Fischer, in *Eine Theologie des Lebens*, p. 161.

84. Vidler, *The Modernist Movement in the Roman Catholic Church*, p. 230 n. 1.

85. a*COB*, p. 60.

86. See Kreidler, *Eine Theologie des Lebens*, p. 180.

4. USING SCRIPTURE IN CHRISTOLOGY

1. Schillebeeckx, *God Is New Each Moment*, p. 12.

2. Ibid., pp. 12-13.

3. a*SoG*, p. 72. The original German text is idem, *Jesus Christus* (Augsburg: Haas & Grabheer, 1933). Hereafter this text is referred to as a*JC* 1.

4. On the "original quest," see Perrin, *Rediscovering the Teaching of Jesus*, pp. 207-48.

5. My previous discussions of Adam's biblical hermeneutics are Robert Krieg, "Karl Adam's Christology," *Heythrop Journal* 25 (1984): 456-74; idem, "Zur Aktualität der Christologie Karl Adam," *ThQ* 166 (1986): 92-107.

6. See Klaus Reinhardt, *Der dogmatische Schriftgebrauch* (Munich: Ferdinand Schöningh, 1970), pp. 331-37.

7. See Kreidler, *Eine Theologies des Lebens*, pp. 133, 147, 199; Kolping, *Katholische Theologie*, pp. 82-86, 89, 113-19.

8. See Raymond F. Collins, *Introduction to the New Testament* (Garden City, N.Y.: Doubleday, 1983), pp. 41-55.

9. See chapter 1, n. 36.

10. See Collins, *Introduction to the New Testament*, pp. 207-14.

11. The phrase "literary-hermeneutical approaches" is used by Sandra Schneiders in her article "Hermeneutics," in Raymond Brown et al., eds., *The New Jerome Biblical Commentary* (Englewood Cliffs, N.J.:

Prentice-Hall, 1990), pp. 1146-65, 1160. See also Edgar McKnight, *Post-Modern Use of the Bible* (Philadelphia: Fortress, 1988); William Placher, "Paul Ricoeur and Postliberal Theology," *Modern Theology* 4 (October 1987): 35-52; Collins, *Introduction to the New Testament*, pp. 231-271; Norman Petersen, *Literary Criticism for New Testament Critics* (Philadelphia: Fortress, 1978).

12. a*SoG*, p. 20.

13. Ibid.

14. See Pius XII, *Divino afflante Spiritu* (September 30, 1943), in *Rome and the Study of Scripture* (St. Meinrad: Grail Publications, 1962), pp. 80-107; Collins, *Introduction to the New Testament*, pp. 370-74.

15. See Hans Frei, *The Eclipse of Biblical Narrative* (New Haven, Conn.: Yale University Press, 1974), pp. 17-51; Edgar Krentz, *The Historical-Critical Method* (Philadelphia: Fortress, 1975).

16. See Raymond Brown, "What the Biblical Word Meant and What It Means," in his *The Critical Meaning of the Bible* (New York: Paulist, 1981), pp. 23-44; Krentz, *The Historical-Critical Method*; Krister Stendahl, "Biblical Theology, Contemporary," in *The Interpreter's Dictionary of the Bible, A-D* (Nashville: Abingdon, 1962), pp. 418-32. See also Raymond Brown's and George Lindbeck's essays in Richard Neuhaus, ed., *Biblical Interpretation in Crisis* (Grand Rapids, Mich.: Wm. B. Eerdmanns, 1989).

17. See Aubert, "Die Theologie des 20. Jahrhunderts," p. 16; Kopling, *Katholische Theologie*, pp. 113-19; Augustin Bea, "Biblische Kritik und neuere Forschung," *StdZ* 114 (1927-28): 401-12.

18. See Frei, *The Eclipse of Biblical Narrative*. On Frei's work, see essays by James Buckley, Coleman O'Neill, William Placher, and David Tracy, in *Thomist* 40 (1985); George Lindbeck, "The Bible as Realistic Narrative," in Leonard Swidler, ed., *Consensus in Theology?* (Philadelphia: Westminster, 1980), pp. 81-85.

19. For example, see Karl Barth, *Church Dogmatics* 4/2 (Edinburgh: T. & T. Clark, 1958), pp. 233-64; David Kelsey, *The Uses of Scripture in Recent Theology* (Philadelphia: Fortress, 1975), pp. 39-55.

20. Postcritical hermeneutics was creatively adopted by the late Hans W. Frei, a student of Barth. See Hans Frei, *The Identity of Jesus Christ* (Philadelphia: Fortress, 1975); idem, "Niebuhr's Theological Background," in Paul Ramsey, ed., *Faith and Ethics* (New York: Harper Torchbooks, 1957), pp. 9-64.

21. See Adam, "Die Theologie der Krisis." Adam's similarity to Barth has been noted by Aubert, "Karl Adam," p. 157.

22. a*SoG*, p. 1.

23. Ibid., p. 22.

24. Ibid., p. 36.

25. As mentioned in chapter 1, n. 78, Johannes Kuhn wrote his *Das Leben Jesu* (1838) in order to refute D. F. Strauss's *Das Leben Jesu*. Since Kuhn argued on the basis of the validity of oral tradition in the church, it may be that his work influenced Adam. In any case, Adam's emphasis upon tradition bears a family resemblance to Kuhn's. According to Norman Perrin, Kuhn's view of Scripture and tradition was "[a] hundred years ahead of its time in many ways"; see Perrin, *Rediscovering the Teaching of Jesus*, p. 213.

26. a*SoG*, p. 98.

27. Ibid., pp. 97, 109.

28. Ibid., p. 132.

29. Ibid., p. 143.

30. Ibid., p. 192.

31. Ibid., p. 251.

32. Ibid., p. 264.

33. Ibid., p. 282.

34. Ibid., p. 203-4.

35. Fries, *Wegbereiter und Wege*, p. 31.

36. This is one point of similarity between Adam's use of Scripture and Barth's, as noted by Reinhardt, *Der dogmatische Schriftgebrauch*, p. 335.

37. a*SoG*, pp. 203; for the German see a*CuB*3, pp. 228-29. Cf. Fries, *Wegbereiter und Wege*, p. 32.

38. a*SoG*, p. 132.

39. Lachenschmid, "Christologie und Soteriologie," p. 96.

40. a*SoG*, p. 291.

41. For literature on Scheler's ethics, see chapter 2, n. 54. Because of Scheler's concern for values, Ernst Troeltsch called Scheler "the Catholic Nietzsche." See E. Troeltsch, *Gesammelte Werke* 3:609.

42. Scheler, *Formalism in Ethics*, p. 574.

43. Max Scheler, "Vorbilder und Führer" (1921), *Schriften aus dem Nachlass* 1 in *Gesammelte Werke* 10, ed. Maria Scheler (Bern: A. Francke, 1957): 257-88, 280.

44. a*SoG*, p. 134.

45. Ibid., pp. 155, 203, 263.

46. Ibid., p. 97.

47. Kreidler, *Eine Theologie des Lebens*, p. 216.

48. Hofmann, "Theologie der Tübinger Schule," pp. 281-82.

49. Fries, *Wegbereiter und Wege*, pp. 27-28.

50. Ibid., p. 34. The recollections of Hofmann and Fries have been independently supported by Paschal Botz. According to Botz, during Adam's lectures everyone—students and professors, Catholics and Protestants, Germans and non-Germans—felt like the disciples on the road to

Emmaus, who afterwards asked, " 'Did not our hearts burn within us while he talked to us on the road, while he opened to us the scriptures?' " (Lk 24:32).

51. See Auer, "Karl Adam, 1876-1966."

52. Stelzenberger, "Bibliographie," p. 332.

53. Bernhard Jansen, "Die Christusvorträge von Karl Adam," *StdZ* 124 (1932): 193.

54. Anton Stonner, "Übersichten," *Der katholische Gedanke* 7 (July-September, 1933): 311.

55. Bernhard Bartmann, review of *Jesus Christus* in *Theologie und Glaube* 25 (1933): 761-62.

56. Review of *The Son of God, Tablet* 163 (June 23, 1934): 786.

57. Wise, "Christologists Three," p. 392.

58. Kreidler, *Eine Theologie des Lebens*, pp. 296-318.

59. a*JC* 1, p. 59; idem, *Jesus Christus*, 3rd printing (Augsburg: Haas & Grabheer, 1933), p. 56. Hereafter, the third printing is referred to as a*JC* 3. These quotations are translated from Kreidler, *Eine Theologie des Lebens*, pp. 310-15.

60. a*JC* 1, p. 49; a*JC* 3, p. 46.

61. a*JC* 1, p. 169; a*JC* 3, p. 158.

62. a*JC* 1, p. 193; a*JC* 3, p. 180. Cf. a*SoG*, p. 171.

63. For articles on this topic, see Josef Pfammatter, "Katholische Jesusforschung im deutschen Sprachraum," in idem, ed., *Theologische Berichte* 7 (Zurich: Benziger, 1978): 101-48; Hans Koch, "Neue Wege in der Christologie," *Herder Korrespondenz* 29 (1975): 412-18; Lachenschmid, "Christologie und Soteriologie"; Franz Mussner, "Die katholische Leben-Jesu-Forschung und ihre heutigen Aufgaben," *LThK* 6, cols. 859-64.

64. Hans Küng has listed Karl Adam among the theologians who stand out for work in christology; H. Küng, *On Being a Christian*, trans. E. Quinn (Garden City, N.Y.: Doubleday, 1976), p. 129. Küng has also cited Adam's contributions to theology in his book *The Church* (Garden City, N.Y.: Image Books, 1976), pp. 32, 74, 93, 383. While Küng is similar to Adam in directing attention to Jesus, he differs in his reliance on the "new historiography"; see Robert Krieg, "Is Jesus the Focus of Küng's Christology?" *Heythrop Journal* 22 (1981): 243-60.

65. Kasper, *Jesus the Christ*, p. 9.

66. Kasper, "Karl Adam," p. 258; Walter Kasper, *The God of Jesus Christ*, trans. M. J. O'Connell (New York: Crossroad, 1984), p. ix. See also idem, *Theology and Church*, trans. M. Kohl (New York: Crossroad, 1989), p. 5.

67. Kasper, "Karl Adam," p. 255.

68. See Robert Krieg, *Story-Shaped Christology* (New York: Paulist, 1988), pp. 34-64.

69. Edward Schillebeeckx, *Jesus*, trans. H. Hoskins (New York: Seabury, 1979), p. 33.

70. On Schillebeeckx's use of Scripture in *Jesus*, see Krieg, *Story-Shaped Christology*, pp. 65-87.

71. Schillebeeckx, *Jesus*, p. 571.

72. Ibid., p. 75.

73. Ibid., p. 77. See Krieg, *Story-Shaped Christology*, pp. 65-87.

5. CONFRONTED BY NAZISM

1. Kreidler, "Karl Adam und Nationalsozialismus, pp. 129-40, 132; cf. idem, *Eine Theologie des Lebens*, p. 33.

2. Hofmann, "Theologie des Tübinger Schule," p. 281.

3. Literature that comments on Karl Adam in the Third Reich includes Friedrich Heer, "Weimar—Ein religiöser und weltanschaulicher Leerraum," in Cancik, ed., *Religions- und Geistesgeschichte der Weimarer Republik*, pp. 31-48, 36-37; Uwe Dietrich Adam, *Hochschule und Nationalsozialismus* (Tübingen: J. C. B. Mohr [Paul Siebeck], 1977), pp. 21, 24, 39, 71; Baumgartner, *Sehnsucht nach Gemeinschaft*, p. 165; Walter Jens, *Eine deutsche Universität* (Munich: Kindler, 1977), p. 325; Paul Sauer, *Württemberg in der Zeit des Nationalsozialismus* (Ulm: Suddeutsche Verlagsgesellschaft, 1975), passim.

4. Throughout this chapter I am drawing extensively on Klaus Gotto and Konrad Repgen, eds., *Die Katholiken und das Dritte Reich*, 3rd rev. ed. (Mainz: Matthias Grünewald, 1990); Donald Dietrich, *Catholic Citizens in the Third Reich* (New Brunswick, N.J.: Transaction Books, 1988); Ernst Helmreich, *The German Churches under Hitler* (Detroit: Wayne State University Press, 1979); Klaus Scholder, *Die Kirchen und das Dritte Reich* 1: *Vorgeschichte und Zeit der Illusionen, 1918-1934* (Frankfurt: Ullstein, 1977, 1986); idem, *Die Kirchen und das Dritte Reich*, 2: *Das Jahr der Ernüchterung 1934, Barmen und Rom* (Frankfurt: Ullstein, 1985, 1988); Guenther Lewy, *The Catholic Church and Nazi Germany* (New York: McGraw Hill, 1964). I am indebted to Roger Brooks, Robert J. Wegs, and Albert K. Wimmer for their comments on an earlier version of this chapter.

5. Adam manifested his nationalism in some of his writings after 1939. See Karl Adam, "The Mystery of Christ's Incarnation and of His Mystical Body" (1939); "Jesus, der Christus, und wir Deutsche, I & II," *Wissenschaft und Weisheit* 10 (1943): 73-103; "Jesus, der Christus, und wir Deutsche, III," *Wissenschaft und Weisheit* 11 (1944): 10-23; "Das

Problem des Geschichtlichen im Leben der Kirche," *ThQ* 128 (1948): 257-300. As already noted, Edward Schillebeeckx has mentioned that Adam "defended Nazi-ism during the war"; E. Schillebeeckx, *God Is New Each Moment*, p. 12. According to John Bowden, in 1942 Schillebeeckx, a seminarian at the time, opposed Adam's "positive" approach to National Socialism by writing a 300-page response to a secretly circulated speech by Adam—a speech entitled "Christianity in the New Order"; J. Bowden, *Edward Schillebeeckx: In Search of the Kingdom of God* (New York: Crossroad, 1983), p. 28. The influence of nationalism upon Adam's thought has been noted by Alice Gallin, *Midwives to Nazism* (Macon, Georgia: Mercer University Press, 1986), p. 26.

6. On Protestant theologians in the Third Reich, see Robert Ericksen, *Theologians under Hitler* (New Haven, Conn.: Yale University Press, 1985); Helmreich, *The German Churches under Hitler*. Karl Adam's mediating stance toward National Socialism was similar to that of the Lutheran theologian Paul Althaus (1888-1966).

7. See Ludwig Volk, "Nationalsozialistischer Kirchenkampf und deutsche Episkopat," in Gotto and Repgen, eds., *Die Katholiken und das Dritte Reich*, pp. 49-92. Documentation representative of the bishops' quandary is assembled in Peter Matheson, *The Third Reich and the Christian Churches* (Grand Rapids: William B. Eerdmans, 1981).

8. Quoted in Lewy, *The Catholic Church and Nazi Germany*, p. 25.

9. See Alfred Rosenberg, *Der Mythus des 20. Jahrhunderts* (1930). On the Nazi program of 1920, see Lewy, *The Catholic Church and Nazi Germany*, p. 7.

10. See Alice Gallin, *German Resistance to Hitler* (Washington, D.C.: Catholic University of America Press, 1961), passim.

11. See Richard Grunberger, *A Social History of the Third Reich* (London: Weidenfeld and Nicolson, 1971), p. 17. Hitler's telegram was abhorrent to some Germans, for example, to Dietrich Bonhoeffer's father; see Eberhard Bethge, *Dietrich Bonhoeffer*, trans. E. Mosbacher et al. (New York: Harper and Row, 1970), p. 191.

12. See John Zeender, "The Genesis of the German Concordat of 1933," in Nelson Minnich et al., eds., *Studies in Catholic History* (Wilmington, Del.: Michael Glazier, 1985), pp. 617-665.

13. Grunberger, *A Social History of the Third Reich*, pp. 8-10, 29.

14. Quoted in Lewy, *The Catholic Church and Nazi Germany*, p. 39.

15. See Gordon Zahn, *German Catholics and Hitler's Wars* (New York: Sheed and Ward, 1963), passim. Zahn's book has been published anew by the University of Notre Dame Press, 1988. My references are to the earlier edition. See also Volk, "Nationalsozialistischer Kirchenkampf und deutsche Episkopat"; Heine Hürten, "Bischofamt im 'Dritten Reich,'" *Internationale katholische Zeitschrift* 14 (November 1985): 536-49.

16. For biographical sketches of Faulhaber, Herwegen, and other leading German figures, see Jürgen Aretz et al., eds., *Zeitgeschichte in Lebensbildern* (Mainz: Matthias Grünewald, 1973-1984), 6 vols.

17. See Lewy, *The Catholic Church and Nazi Germany*, p. 41.

18. Ibid., p. 22. See also Bruno Schwalbach, *Erzbischof Conrad Gröber und die nationalsozialistische Diktatur* (Karlsruhe: Badenia: 1985).

19. Zeender, "The Genesis of the German Concordat of 1933," p. 643.

20. Quoted in Lewy, *The Catholic Church and Nazi Germany*, p. 47.

21. See Lewy, *The Catholic Church and Nazi Germany*, pp. 107-9; Donald Dietrich, "Catholic Theologians in Hitler's Reich: Adaption and Critique," *Journal of Church and State* 29 (Winter 1987): 19-45.

22. See Dietrich, "Catholic Theologians in Hitler's Reich," passim.

23. See Scholder, *Die Kirchen und das Dritte Reich* 1:321.

24. Lewy, *The Catholic Church and Nazi Germany*, p. 43.

25. Scholder, *Die Kirchen and das Dritte Reich* 1:321.

26. See Werner Roder und Herbert Strauss, eds., *Biographisches Handbuch der deutschsprachigen Emigration nach 1933* 1 (Munich: K. G. Saur, 1980): 295.

27. Lewy, *The Catholic Church and Nazi Germany*, p. 171.

28. See Emmanuel von Severus, "Herwegen, Ildefons," in *Neue Deutsche Biographie* 8 (1968): 723.

29. This unpublished address, given by Herwegen on May 26, 1933, is summarized and quoted in Karl Dietrich Erdmann, *Deutschland unter der Herrschaft des Nationalsozialismus, 1933-1939* (Munich: Deutscher, 1987), p. 185. See also Spael, *Das katholische Deutschland im 20. Jahrhundert*, p. 309.

30. Karl Eschweiler, "Die Kirche im neuen Reich," *Deutsches Volkstum* (June 1933), quoted in Scholder, *Die Kirchen und das Dritte Reich* 1:541.

31. Josef Lortz, *Katholischer Zugang zum Nationalsozialismus kirchengeschichtlich gesehen* (Münster: Aschendorff, 1933), quoted in Scholder, *Die Kirchen und das Dritte Reich* 1:545. According to Erwin Iserloh, Lortz was convinced in general that the Catholic church needed to enter into each culture and change it from within; E. Iserloh, "Joseph Lortz (1887-1975)," in idem, *Kirche—Ereignis und Institution* 1:35-37.

32. Michael Schmaus, *Begegnungen zwischen katholischem Christentum und nationalsozialistischer Weltanschauung* (Münster: Aschendorff, 1933), quoted in Scholder, *Die Kirchen und das Dritte Reich* 1:544.

33. Regarding this axiom, see Kasper, *Jesus the Christ*, pp. 190, 195 n. 66; John Mahoney, *The Making of Moral Theology* (Oxford:

Clarendon, 1987), pp. 72-115; Joseph Ratzinger, "Gratia Praesupponit Naturam," in J. Ratzinger and H. Fries, eds., *Einsicht und Glaube* (Freiburg: Herder, 1962), pp. 151-65.

34. Adam, *Hochschule und Nationalsozialismus*, p. 24.

35. The expression *"das deutsches Volkstum"* was used by the German nationalist Friedrich Ludwig Jahn (1778-1852) as the title of his book *Deutsches Volkstum* (1830). Later, it served as the title for Wilhelm Stapel's conservative journal.

36. Karl Adam, "Deutsches Volkstum und katholisches Christentum," *ThQ* 114 (1933): 40-63, 48.

37. Ibid., p. 53.

38. Ibid., p. 56.

39. Ibid., p. 60. In 1933 there were ninety Jews who were permanent residents of Tübingen. See David Fiensey, "Relations between Jews and Christians in Tübingen, West Germany," *Explorations* 2 (Summer 1988): 2; Lilli Zapf, *Die Tübinger Juden* (Tübingen: Katzmann, 1974); Paul Sauer, *Die jüdischen Gemeinden in Württemberg und Hohenzollern* (Stuttgart: W. Kohlhammer, 1966).

40. See Lewy, *The Catholic Church and Nazi Germany*, pp. 57-93; Helmreich, *The German Churches under Hitler*, pp. 237-56; Zeender, "The Genesis of the German Concordat of 1933," pp. 617-65.

41. Lewy, *The Catholic Church and Nazi Germany*, p. 111.

42. See Helmreich, *The German Churches under Hitler*, pp. 133-56; see also Ericksen, *Theologians under Hitler*, passim.

43. See Scholder, *Die Kirchen und das Dritte Reich* 1 and 2; Mario Bendiscioli, *The New Racial Paganism*, trans. G. Smith (London: Burns, Oates and Washbourne, 1939). Bendiscioli was Adam's friend and translated his books into Italian; see Auer, "Karl Adam, 1876-1966," p. 133.

44. Michael von Faulhaber, *Judaism, Christianity and Germany*, trans. G. D. Smith (New York: Macmillan, 1935), pp. 35-37.

45. Ibid., p. 11.

46. See Volk, "Nationalsozialistischer Kirchenkampf und deutsche Episkopat," p. 58.

47. See Nathaniel Micklem, *National Socialism and the Roman Catholic Church* (London: Oxford University Press, 1939); August Hagen, *Geschichte der Diözese Rottenburg* 3:544-55; Helmreich, *The German Churches under Hitler*, p. 297; Paul Kopf, *Johannes Baptista Sproll* (Sigmaringen: Thorbecke, 1988).

48. See Zahn, *German Catholics and Hitler's Wars*, p. 123.

49. See Karl Adam, "Vom gottmenschlichen Erlöser," in *Glaubenstage und Glaubenswallfährten* (Paderborn: Bonifacius, 1934), pp. 111-45. This address was also published as "Christus gestern und heute, Christus allezeit," in *Katholik Sonntagszeitung*, Mainz (February 25,

1934), 9-11. An abridged version of the address appeared in English as "In the Jubilee Year," *Commonweal* 19 (August 10, 1934): 361-63; see chapter 6, n. 44. Cf. Kreidler, "Karl Adam und Nationalsozialismus"; Hagen, *Geschichte der Diözese Rottenburg* 3:522.

50. Adam, "Vom gottmenschlichen Erlöser," p. 11.

51. Ibid., p. 14.

52. Ibid., p. 18.

53. Ibid., p. 20.

54. Ibid., p. 21.

55. Ibid., p. 23.

56. Ibid., p. 24.

57. Ibid.

58. In taking this tack, Adam was basically following the dominant approach of the German bishops and the Vatican. In 1937 Pope Pius XI said that he had signed the concordat of 1933 with the Nazi government in a spirit of "moderation," so as "not to draw out the wheat with the cockle"; see Pius XI, *Mit brennender Sorge* (March 14, 1937), in the *Tablet* 170 (April 3, 1937): i-iv, i.

59. See Kreidler, "Karl Adam und Nationalsozialismus," pp. 134-36.

60. Scholder, *Die Kirchen und das Dritte Reich* 2:140.

61. See Kreidler, "Karl Adam und Nationalsozialismus." My account draws extensively on Kreidler's.

62. Pascal Botz has recalled the strike by the Catholic faculty.

63. Scholder, *Die Kirchen und das Dritte Reich* 2:142.

64. Kreidler, "Karl Adam und Nationalsozialismus," p. 136.

65. Lewy, *The Catholic Church and Nazi Germany*, p. 109.

66. Scholder, *Die Kirchen und das Dritte Reich* 2:141-42.

67. See Helmreich, *The German Churches under Hitler*, pp. 269-73; Lewy, *The Catholic Church and Nazi Germany*, pp. 151-55; Gallin, *German Resistance to Hitler*, pp. 171-72. See also n. 58 above.

68. Karl Adam, "Jesus Christ and the Spirit of the Age," in Wilhelm Hauer, Karl Heim, and Karl Adam, eds., *Germany's New Religion*, trans. T. S. K. Scott-Craig and R. E. Davies (New York: Abingdon, 1937), pp. 117-68, 117. For the German, see idem, *Jesus Christus und der Geist unserer Zeit* (Augsburg: Haas & Grabheer, 1935), p. 7.

69. Adam, "Jesus Christ and the Spirit of the Age," p. 129.

70. Ibid., p. 143.

71. Ibid., p. 145.

72. Ibid., p. 156.

73. See Adam, "Jesus Christ and the Spirit of the Age." Jakob Wilhelm Hauer wrote his first essay for publication in *Germany's New Religion*. He originally gave his second essay as a speech in Berlin's *Sportspalast* in April 1935 to a gathering of ten thousand Nazi supporters.

His third essay is an extract from his book *A German View of God* (1935). Karl Heim's essay originally appeared in *Evangelische Theologie* (July 1935).

74. Karl Adam's political naiveté is evident in an anecdote, told by Bernhard Hanssler, about Adam greeting Hauer, dressed in his SS uniform, in the mid-1930's: "One day I joined Adam at his home. On the way [to the university] we met Hauer, who lived in the same neighborhood as Adam. Adam, completely unmindful of the grave time and forgetting all national obligations greeted [Hauer], 'Servus, Herr Kollege!' This was countered with a deeply religious and obviously reproachful 'Heil Hitler.' " See B. Hanssler, *Bischof Johannes Baptista Sproll* (Sigmaringen: Thorbecke, 1984), pp. 94ff.; reprinted in Hermann Werner, *Tübingen 1945* (Stuttgart: Konrad Theiss, 1986), p. 201.

75. Anton Koch, "Der ganze Christus," *StdZ* 130 (1935-1936): 197-200.

76. *Clergy Review* 13 (1937): 314.

77. John Murray, "A New Paganism," *Tablet* 170 (July 24, 1937): 124-25.

78. See Helmreich, *The German Churches under Hitler*, pp. 347-50; Lewy, *The Catholic Church and Nazi Germany*, pp. 224-29; Zahn, *German Catholics and Hitler's Wars*, pp. 60-83.

79. Quoted in Gallin, *German Resistance to Hitler*, p. 223.

80. Helmreich, *The German Churches under Hitler*, p. 352-58.

81. See Kreidler, "Karl Adam und Nationalsozialismus," pp. 136-38. For a critical response to Adam's lecture, see Josef Joos, *Am Räderwerk der Zeit* (Augsburg: Winfried-Werk, 1951), pp. 155-57.

82. Quoted in Kreidler, "Karl Adam und Nationalsozialismus," p. 138.

83. Ibid.

84. From an interview with Hans Kreidler, July 2, 1988.

85. On November 9, 1938, nearly a hundred Jews were slain, 30,000 arrested, almost two hunderd synagogues burnt down, and at least 7000 Jewish businesses destroyed; see *New York Times*, October 3, 1988, p. 10. In Berlin, Father Bernhard Lichtenberg (1875-1943), pastor of St. Hedwig's Church, saw the significance of the *Kristallnacht*, condemned the Nazis from the pulpit, and was eventually arrested by the Gestapo. He died while being transported to a concentration camp. For a collection of essays on anti-Semitism, see Otto Dov Kulka and Paul Mendes-Flohr, eds., *Judaism and Christianity under the Impact of National Socialism* (Jerusalem: The Historical Society of Israel and The Zalman Shazar Center for Jewish History, 1987).

86. Vincent Berning has proposed that K. Eschweiler, J. Lortz, M. Schmaus, and K. Adam were uncritical of National Socialism because

they "envisioned the total state as the contemporary reincarnation of the medieval German empire"; cf. V. Berning, "Modernismus und Reformkatholizismus in ihrer prospektiven Tendenz," in Franz Pöggeler, ed., *Die Zukunft der Glaubensunterweisung* (Freiburg im Breisgau: Seelsorge, 1971), pp. 9-32, 22.

87. Schoof, *Survey of Catholic Theology*, p. 88.

88. Kasper, "Karl Adam," p. 256.

89. Kreidler, "Karl Adam und Nationalsozialismus," p. 138.

6. STANDING ASIDE

1. Grillmeier, "The Figure of Christ," p. 66.

2. Kreidler, "Karl Adam und Nationalsozialismus," p. 129.

3. See Leonard Swidler, *The Ecumenical Vanguard* (Pittsburgh: Duquesne University Press, 1966), p. 193.

4. See Erwin Iserloh, "Die Geschichte der ökumenischen Bewegung," in *HK* 7, pp. 458-73; Swidler, *The Ecumenical Vanguard*; Eva-Maria Jung, "A Modern Approach to Protestants: Una Sancta in Germany Today," *Catholic World* 180 (March 1955): 411-17.

5. See Adolph Schalk, "Karl Adam," *Jubilee* 4 (June 1956): 16-21.

6. Swidler, *The Ecumenical Vanguard*, pp. 177, 193-95.

7. Karl Adam, *One and Holy*, trans. C. Hastings (New York: Sheed and Ward, 1951), p. 111. Cf. idem, *Una Sancta in katholischer Sicht* (Düsseldorf: Patmos, 1948), p. 123.

8. Adam, *One and Holy*, p. 130.

9. See Stelzenberger, "Bibliographie," p. 335.

10. James Tyne, review of *One and Holy*, *ThS* 13 (1952): 255-57.

11. Henry St. John, "Problems of Reunion," *Tablet* 204 (July 10, 1954): 39-40.

12. Jung, "A Modern Approach to Protestants," p. 414.

13. Fries, *Wegbereiter und Wege*, p. 35.

14. Kasper, "Karl Adam," p. 255.

15. Karl Adam, "Das Problem der Entmythologisierung und die Auferstehung des Christus," *ThQ* 132 (1952): 385-410. This essay was reprinted in Hans Warner Bartsch, ed., *Kerygma und Mythos* 5 (Hamburg: Herbert Reich, 1955): 101-19.

16. See Rudolf Bultmann, "New Testament and Mythology," in Hans Werner Bartsch, ed., *Kerygma and Myth*, trans. R. Fuller (New York: Harper and Row, 1961), pp. 1-44.

17. Adam, "Das Problem der Entmythologisierung," p. 409.

18. Ibid., p. 410.

19. Karl Adam, *The Christ of Faith*, trans. J. Crick (New York:

Pantheon, 1954), pp. 50-53. Cf. idem, *Der Christus des Glaubens* (Düsseldorf: Patmos, 1954), pp. 62-65.

20. Adam, *Christ of Faith*, pp. 261-86.

21. Ibid., p. 6.

22. Ibid., p. 118. Cf. a*SoG*, p. 132.

23. Michael Schmaus, "Der Christus des Glaubens," *Münchener Theologische Zeitschrift* 7 (1955): 67. Adam's writings are frequently cited in Schmaus's texts; for example, see M. Schmaus, *Katholische Dogmatik*, 5th ed. (Munich: Hueber, 1953), 5 vols.

24. E. Gutwenger, "Karl Adam," *ZkTh* 77 (1955): 244.

25. Thomas E. Clarke, "The Christ of Faith," *ThS* 19 (1958): 236-64, 264.

26. See Grillmeier, "The Figure of Christ," pp. 81, 90; Lachenschmid, "Christologie und Soteriologie," p. 96.

27. Nevertheless, *Der Christus des Glaubens* served as a paradigm for Kasper's christology. See Kasper, *Jesus the Christ*, pp. 9, 32, 39 n. 36, 270 n. 32.

28. Macquarrie, *Jesus Christ in Modern Thought*, p. 303. Macquarrie's point is supported by the fact that *The Christ of Faith* is cited in J. J. Walsh, "Jesus Christ, II," in *The New Catholic Encyclopedia* 7 (Washington, D.C.: McGraw-Hill, 1967): 918-930, esp. 924, 930.

29. Monika Hellwig, "Re-emergence of the Human, Critical, Public Jesus," *ThS* 50 (1989): 466-80, 468.

30. See Grillmeier, "The Figure of Christ," p. 90.

31. Ibid., p. 82 n. 16.

32. Prior to 1950 festschrifts in honor of Adam were F. Hofmann, ed., *Gesammelte Aufsätze zur Dogmengeschichte* (1936) and an unpublished collection of essays entitled *Karl Adam* (1946).

33. Marcel Reding, ed., *Abhandlung über Theologie und Kirche* (Düsseldorf: Patmos, 1952).

34. Fritz Hofmann, ed., *Vitae et Veritati* (Düsseldorf: Patmos, 1956).

35. Rahner, "Theologie in der Welt," p. 10. See chapter 3, n. 70.

36. Ibid. Rahner reiterated this point near the end of his life when he spoke about the 1920s: "At the start of this period, people like Karl Adam, Peter Lippert, and Erich Przywara had already put a strong stamp on the mentality of German Catholicism"; see Rahner, *I Remember*, p. 38. Rahner referred to *The Spirit of Catholicism* in his essay, "Reflexionen zur Problematik einer Kurzformel des Glaubens," *Schriften zur Theologie* 9 (Einsiedeln: Benziger, 1970): 243.

37. Stelzenberger, "Bibliographie," p. 330.

38. Jakob Laubach, "Karl Adam," in Leonhard Reinisch, ed., *Theologen unserer Zeit* (Munich: C. H. Beck, 1960), pp. 115-36; reprinted in

Theologians of Our Time, trans. C. Henkey (Notre Dame, Ind.: University of Notre Dame Press, 1964), pp. 92-108, 92.

Other discussions of Adam's work include Miguel Angel Fiorito, "Jesuchristo de Karl Adam," *Ciencia y Fe* (1957), pp. 487-98; Werner Harenberg, "Jesus und die Kirchen," *Der Spiegel* 20 (March 28, 1966): 92-116, 100, 102; Rudolf Graber, *Karl Adam (1876-1966)* (Regensburg: Erhardi, 1976). Graber, the late bishop of Regensburg, argues a thesis similar to mine, namely that Adam's work prepared the way for Vatican II and deeply influenced Pope Paul VI. I am grateful to Dr. Paul Mai, Archive Director of the Diocese of Regensburg, for making Graber's pamphlet available to me.

40. Schoof, *Survey of Catholic Theology*, p. 87.

41. See Stelzenberger, "Bibliographie," pp. 333-35. Not only were Adam's books translated into English and reprinted numerous times, but also selections from his books appeared in English anthologies on Catholicism. For instance, as late as 1960, pages from *Christ Our Brother* appeared in Walter Burghardt and William Lynch, eds., *The Idea of Catholicism* (Baltimore: Meridian Books, 1960), pp. 104-105.

42. Adam gained further recognition in 1931 with the publication of *Christ Our Brother* and the appearance of this book's first chapter as "Jesus and Life," *Clergy Review* 1 (1931): 143-50.

43. "Notes and Gleanings," *Fortnightly Review* 39 (October 1932): 235.

44. Adam, "In the Jubilee Year," p. 361. It is likely that George Shuster, the editor of *Commonweal*, was responsible for the translation of the speech and the journal's preface. See chapter 5, n. 49.

45. Paschal Botz has recalled that he brought these articles to the attention of the journal's editor, and Godfrey Diekmann, O.S.B., translated them into English.

46. See Karl Adam "The Sanctification of Marriage," *Orate Fratres* 9 (February-March 1935): 171-76, 218-25; idem, "Dogmatic Bases of the Liturgy," in *Orate Fratres* 11 (October 3, 1937): 481-87, and in *Orate Fratres* 12 (1938): 8-14, 56-59, 97-104, 145-51.

47. Adam, "The Mystery of Christ's Incarnation" (1939); see chapter 2, n. 38.

48. See Karl Adam, "Easter Sermon," *Orate Fratres* 27 (April 1953): 254-56; idem, "Pentecost and Baptism," *Worship* 28 (May 1954): 281-83; idem, "An Act of Faith," *Worship* 31 (1957): 120-25.

49. See R. William Franklin and Robert L. Spaeth, *Virgil Michel* (Collegeville: The Liturgical Press, 1988); also, articles on Michel by R. W. Franklin, Kenneth Himes, and Joseph Chinnici in *Worship* 62 (May 1988).

50. Virgil Michel, *The Liturgy of the Church* (New York: Macmillan, 1937), pp. 53, 56, 80, 213, 216-17.

51. Karl Adam, "To move toward Christian unity," *Commonweal* 54 (1951): 423-26.

52. Schalk, "Karl Adam," p. 19.

53. Karl Adam, "St. John and Christ," *Jubilee* 6 (June 1958): 18-23, 18.

54. The Trappist monk Thomas Merton exclaimed in a letter in 1957: "I love Karl Adam's new book, *The Christ of Faith*"; see T. Merton, *The Road to Joy*, ed. by Robert Daggy (New York: Farrar, Strauss, Giroux, 1989), p. 229.

55. William D. Miller, *Dorothy Day* (San Francisco: Harper and Row, 1982), p. 210.

56. Dorothy Day, *The Long Loneliness* (San Francisco: Harper and Row, 1981), p. 155.

57. Ibid., p. 234.

58. I am drawing extensively on Rose Bowen, "Christology in the Works of Flannery O'Connor," *Horizons* 14 (1987): 7-23.

59. Flannery O'Connor, *The Habit of Being*, ed. Sally Fitzgerald (New York: Farrar, Straus and Giroux, 1979), p. 231.

60. Flannery O'Connor, *The Presence of Grace and Other Book Reviews and Letters, 1958*, compiled by Leo J. Zuber (Athens: University of Georgia Press, 1983), p. 55.

61. Flannery O'Connor, *The Presence of Grace and Other Book Reviews and Letters, 1958*, pp. 51-52. In her review of *The Roots of the Reformation* O'Connor complained that the entire text of the book *One and Holy* should be published in the United States. Soon afterwards, her complaint was remedied.

62. O'Connor, *The Habit of Being*, p. 92.

63. a*SC*, pp. 139-40.

64. O'Connor, *The Habit of Being*, p. 337.

65. a*SC*, p. 31. For the German, see Adam, *Das Wesen des Katholizismus*, p. 41.

66. O'Connor, *The Habit of Being*, p. 308.

67. a*SC*, p. 235.

68. Robert McAfee Brown, *The Spirit of Protestantism* (New York: Oxford University Press, 1961), p. viii. I am indebted to James F. White for this reference.

69. Ibid., p. ix.

70. Ibid., p. 246 n. 3; cf. p. 227 n. 2; p. 228 n. 4.

71. Dulles, *The Catholicity of the Church*, p. 54; cf. p. 120.

72. Avery Dulles, *The Reshaping of Catholicism* (San Francisco: Harper and Row, 1988), p. 64; cf. p. 71.

73. "Abschied auf dem Stadtfriedhof," *Schwäbishes Tagblatt*, April 7, 1966.

74. "In memoriam Prof. Karl Adam," *Schwäbisches Tagblatt*, April 7, 1966.

75. Quoted in Fries, *Wegbereiter und Wege*, p. 26; Kreidler, *Eine Theologie des Lebens*, p. 11.

76. See F. Heiler, "Zum Tod von Karl Adam."

77. See Häring, "In Memory of Karl Adam."

78. Hofmann, "Theologie der Tübinger Schule," p. 262.

79. Ibid., p. 283.

80. Fries, *Wegbereiter und Wege*, p. 25.

81. Ibid., p. 36.

82. "Theological Pioneer: The Achievement of Karl Adam," *Tablet* 210 (April 23, 1966): 473-74.

83. "Karl Adam, R.I.P.," *America* 114 (May 7, 1966): 641. A memorial plaque on the outside wall of St. Ursula Kirche in Pursruck reads: "In memory of the great son of our community, Karl Adam, born in Pursruck on October 22, 1876, ordained to the priesthood in Regensburg on June 10, 1900, died on April 1, 1966, in Tübingen."

84. "Christianity," *Time*, April 1, 1966, p. 42.

85. See Hebblethwaite, "The Need for Reform."

86. a*SC*, p. 32.

7. Catholic Theology and Neoromanticism

1. Bernard Lonergan, *Method in Theology* (New York: Herder and Herder, 1972), p. xi.

2. Karl Rahner, "Ecumenical Theology in the Future," *Theological Investigations* 14, trans. D. Bourke (New York: Seabury, 1976): 254-70, 256.

3. See Claude Geffré et al., eds., *Different Theologies, Common Responsibility* (Concilium 171) (Edinburgh: T. & T. Clark, 1984); Schreiter, *Constructing Local Theologies*.

4. See Kolping, *Katholische Theologie*; O'Meara, *Romantic Idealism and Roman Catholicism*, pp. 138-60.

5. Kasper, "Verständnis der Theologie damals und heute," p. 90.

6. Kasper, *The God of Jesus Christ*, p. ix; Kasper, "Karl Adam," p. 258.

7. Yves M.-J. Congar, "Théologie," in A. Vacant and E. Mangenot, eds., *Dictionnaire de théologie catholique* 15/1 (Paris: Letouzey and Ane, 1946), cols. 341-502. The revised version of this essay in English is *A History of Theology*, trans. and ed. Hunter Guthrie (Garden City, N.Y.: Doubleday, 1968).

8. Congar, *A History of Theology*, p. 184.

9. Ibid.

10. Congar's appraisal has been made in more specific terms by Hans Kreidler; see *Eine Theologie des Lebens*, pp. 34-41; "Karl Adam und Nationalsozialismus," pp. 129-40.

11. Hofmann, "Theologie der Tübinger Schule," p. 282.

12. Kreidler, *Eine Theologie des Lebens*, p. 182.

13. a*SoG*, p. 87.

14. See ibid., p. 93.

15. a*SoG*, p. 109.

16. See ibid., p. 154.

17. a*SoG*, p. 1. Cf. a*COB*, p. 60.

18. Hofmann, "Theologie der Tübinger Schule," pp. 282-83.

19. Kreidler, *Eine Theologie des Lebens*, p. 219.

20. See a*SC*, p. 2.

21. See ibid., p. 14.

22. See ibid., pp. 8-9.

23. Adam, "Jesus Christ and the Spirit of the Age," pp. 145-50.

24. Ibid., p. 36.

25. Karl Barth, *Church Dogmatics* 1/2, trans. G. T. Thompson and H. Knight (Edinburgh: T. & T. Clark, 1956), p. 145. See Kreidler, *Eine Theologie des Lebens*, p. 32 n. 77.

26. Fritz Hofmann, "Geleitwort," in idem, *Gesammelte Aufsätze*, p. 5.

27. Kreidler, *Eine Theologie des Lebens*, p. 32; on Adam's "realism," see p. 119.

28. Pinson, *Modern Germany*, pp. 459-61.

29. Holborn, *A History of Modern Germany*, pp. 399-403.

30. See a*SoG*, pp. 62-75, 88.

31. Fries, *Wegbereiter und Wege*, p. 31.

32. Adam, *The Christ of Faith*, pp. 51-52.

33. Fries, *Wegbereiter und Wege*, p. 31.

34. Adam, "Das Problem der Entmythologisierung und die Auferstehung des Christus," p. 410.

35. Kasper, "Karl Adam," p. 255.

36. Ibid., p. 257.

37. See a*SoG*, pp. 286-300. On Anselm's soteriology, see Kasper, *Jesus the Christ*, pp. 219-221.

38. See Adam, "Jesus Christ and the Spirit of the Age," p. 162. Cf. Kreidler, *Eine Theologie des Lebens*, pp. 138, 206 n. 43.

39. Kreidler, *Eine Theologie des Lebens*, p. 217.

40. Aubert, *Le Probleme de L'Acte de Foi*, p. 537.

41. Kasper, "Karl Adam," p. 253.

42. See a*SC*, p. 10, 179-80; Adam, "Jesus Christ and the Spirit of the Age," p. 153-56.

43. See Kreidler, *Eine Theologie des Lebens*, p. 146. For literature on this axiom, see chapter 5, n. 33.

44. See Karl Rahner, "What Does It Mean to Say: 'God Became Man'?" in idem, *Foundations of Christian Faith*, trans. W. Dych (New York: Seabury, 1978), pp. 212-28. One of the ways in which Rahner safeguards against a misunderstanding of his emphasis upon the incarnation is by expounding a theological anthropology that is more sophisticated than Adam's. Nevertheless, there are risks even in Rahner's approach; see Robert Krieg, "The Crucified in Rahner's Christology," *Irish Theological Quarterly* 50 (1983-1984): 151-67.

45. See Hofmann, "Geleitwort," p. 7; Kreidler, *Eine Theologie des Lebens*, pp. 34-41.

46. Schoof, *Survey of Catholic Theology*, p. 86.

47. Kreidler, *Eine Theologie des Lebens*, p. 39.

48. See ibid., pp. 33-34; idem, "Karl Adam und Nationalsozialismus," passim.

49. See Pinson, *Modern Germany*, p. 461.

50. Scholder, *Die Kirchen und das Dritte Reich* 1:93-109.

51. See Pinson, *Modern Germany*, pp. 485-500; Grunberger, *A Social History of the Third Reich*, pp. 18-25.

52. Kreidler, "Karl Adam und Nationalsozialismus," p. 138.

53. Ibid., p. 139.

54. a*SC*, p. 10.

55. a*SoG*, p. 97.

56. Adam, "Deutsches Volkstum und katholisches Christentums," p. 40.

57. Adam, "Vom gottmenschlichen Erlöser," pp. 22-23.

58. Adam, "Jesus Christ and the Spirit of the Age," p. 134.

59. Ibid., p. 137.

60. Kreidler, "Karl Adam und Nationalsozialismus," pp. 139-40.

61. Dietrich, "Catholic Theologians in Hitler's Reich," p. 21. Cf. idem, *Catholic Citizens in the Third Reich*, pp. 180-214.

62. Adam, "Die katholische Tübinger Schule," p. 392.

63. Kasper, "Karl Adam," p. 258; Kreidler, *Eine Theologie des Lebens*, p. 198.

64. On neoromanticism's influence on Protestant theology, see Ericksen, *Theologians under Hitler*, passim; Theodor Strom, *Theologie im Schatten politischer Romantik* (Munich: Chr. Kaiser, 1970).

65. On christology and culture, see Karl Heinz Öhlig, *Fundamentalchristologie* (Munich: Kösel, 1986).

66. Cf. Schoof, *Survey of Catholic Theology*, p. 86.

67. Cf. Dieckmann, "Besprechung," p. 272.

68. Kasper, "Karl Adam," p. 257.

69. Ibid.

70. See Karl Rahner, "Towards a Fundamental Theological Interpretation of Vatican II," trans. L. O'Donovan, *ThS* 40 (1979): 716–27.

71. a*SC*, p. 2. Cf. idem, *Das Wesen des Katholizismus*, p. 12.

General Bibliography

This list consists of some of the texts that have shaped this book's perspective on the historical context, life, and theology of Karl Adam. A more complete bibliography is given in the notes for each chapter.

Alexander, Edgar. "Church and Society in Germany." In *Church and Society*, edited by J. N. Moody, translated by T. Stolper, 329-581. New York: Arts, 1953.

Aretz, Jürgen et al., eds. *Zeitgeschichte in Lebensbildern.* 6 vols. Mainz: Matthias Grünewald, 1973-84.

Aubert, Roger. "Die Theologie während der ersten Halfte des 20. Jahrhunderts." In *Bilanz der Theologie im 20. Jahrhundert*, vol. 2, edited by H. Vorgrimler, 7-70. Freiburg: Herder, 1969.

———. "Karl Adam." In *Tendenzen der Theologie im 20. Jahrhundert*, edited by H. J. Schultz, 156-62. Stuttgart: Kreuz, 1966.

———. "Les grandes tendances théologiques entre les deux guerres." *Collectana Mechliniensia* 16 (1946): 17-36.

Auer, Alfons. "Karl Adam, 1876-1966." *ThQ* 150 (1970): 131-43.

Barth, Karl. "Roman Catholicism" (1928). In *Theology and the Church*, translated by L. P. Smith, 307-33. New York: Harper and Row, 1962.

Baumgartner, Alois. *Sehnsucht nach Gemeinschaft.* Munich: Ferdinand Schöningh, 1977.

Bluett, Joseph. "The Mystical Body of Christ: 1890-1940." *ThS* 3 (1942): 261-89.

Bouyer, Louis. "Où en est la théologie du Corps mystique." *Revue des Sciences religieuses* 22 (1948): 313-33.

Brine, Crane. "Romanticism." In *EPh* 7: 206-9

Burtchaell, James. "Drey, Möhler and the Catholic School of Tübingen." In *Nineteenth-Century Religious Thought in the West*, vol. 2, edited by N. Smart et al., 111-39. Cambridge: Cambridge University Press, 1985.

Cancik, Hubert, ed. *Religions- und Geistesgeschichte der Weimarer Republik*. Düsseldorf: Patmos, 1982.

Congar, Yves M.-J. *Christ, Our Lady and the Church*. Translated by H. St. John. Westminster: Newman Press, 1957.

――. "Théologie." In *Dictionnaire de théologie catholique*, vol. 15/1, edited by A. Vacant and E. Mangenot, cols. 341–502. Paris: Letouzey and Ane, 1946. English translation: Y. Congar, *A History of Theology*. Translated and edited by H. Guthrie. Garden City, N.Y.: Doubleday, 1968.

――. *Tradition and Traditions*. Translated by M. Naseby and T. Rainborough. London: Burns and Oates, 1966.

Copleston, Frederick. *A History of Philosophy*, vol. 7/1. Garden City, New York: Image Books, 1965.

Coreth, Emerich et al., eds. *Christliche Philosophie im katholischen Denken des 19. und 20. Jahrhunderts*, vol 2. Graz: Styria, 1988.

Craig, Gordon A. *Germany 1866-1945*. New York: Oxford University Press, 1978.

Daly, Gabriel. *Transcendence and Immanence*. Oxford: Clarendon, 1980.

Dietrich, Donald. *Catholic Citizens in the Third Reich*. New Brunswick, N.J.: Transaction Books, 1988.

――. "Catholic Theologians in Hitler's Reich." *Journal of Church and State* 29 (Winter 1987): 19–45.

Dill, Jr., Marshall. *Germany*. Ann Arbor, Mich.: University of Michigan Press, 1970.

Donovan, Daniel. "Church and Theology in the Modernist Crisis." In *Proceedings of the Catholic Theological Society of America* 40 (1985): 145–59.

Dru, Alexander. *The Contribution of German Catholicism*. New York: Hawthorn, 1963.

Dulles, Avery. *Models of the Church*. Garden City, N.Y.: Doubleday, 1974.

――. *Revelation Theology*. New York: Herder and Herder, 1969.

Ehrhard, Albert. *Der Katholizismus und das zwanzigste Jahrhundert im Licht der kirchlichen Entwicklung der Neuzeit*. Stuttgart: Joseph Roth, 1902.

――. "Die neue Lage der katholischen Theologie." *Internationale Wochenschrift für Wissenschaft, Kunst und Technik* 2 (1908): 65–84.

Erdmann, Karl Dietrich. *Deutschland unter der Herrschaft des Nationalsozialismus, 1933-39*. Munich: Deutscher, 1987.

Ericksen, Robert. *Theologians under Hitler*. New Haven, Conn.: Yale University Press, 1985.

Fehr, Wayne. *The Birth of the Catholic Tübingen School.* Chico, Calif.: Scholars Press, 1981.

Franklin, R. William. *Nineteenth-Century Churches.* New York: Garland Publishing, 1987.

———. "The Nineteenth-Century Liturgical Movement." *Worship* 53 (1979): 12–39.

Frei, Hans W. *The Eclipse of Biblical Narrative.* New Haven, Conn.: Yale University Press, 1974.

———. *The Identity of Jesus Christ.* Philadelphia: Fortress, 1975.

———. "Niebuhr's Theological Background." In *Faith and Ethics*, edited by P. Ramsey, 9–64. New York: Harper Torchbooks, 1957.

Fries, Heinrich. *Die katholische Religionsphilosophie der Gegenwart.* Heidelberg: F. H. Kerle, 1949.

———. "Tübinger Schule." In *LThK* 10: 390–92.

———. *Wegbereiter und Wege.* Olten-Freiburg: Walter, 1968.

Fries, Heinrich and Schwaiger, Georg, eds. *Katholische Theologen Deutschlands im 19. Jahrhundert.* 3 vols. Munich: Kösel, 1977.

Fiorenza, Francis Schüssler. "Christology after Vatican II." *Ecumenist* 18 (1980): 81–89.

Fiorenza, Francis Schüssler, and Galvin, John P., eds. *Systematic Theology*, vol. 1. Minneapolis: Fortress Press, 1991.

Fischer, Balthasar. "Vom Beten zu Christus." In *Gottfeiern*, edited by J. Plocer, 94–99. Freiburg: Herder, 1980.

Frings, Manfred. *Max Scheler.* Pittsburgh: Duquesne University Press, 1965.

Gallin, Alice. *German Resistance to Hitler.* Washington, D.C.: Catholic University of America Press, 1961.

———. *Midwives to Nazism.* Macon, Ga.: Mercer University Press, 1986.

Gay, Peter. *The Outsider as Insider.* New York: Harper and Row, 1968.

Geffré, Claude et al., eds. *Different Theologies, Common Responsibility.* Concilium 171. Edinburgh: T. & T. Clark, 1984.

Geiselmann, Josef Rupert. *Die katholische Tübinger Schule.* Freiburg: Herder, 1964.

———. *The Meaning of Tradition.* Translated by W. J. O'Hara. New York: Herder and Herder, 1966.

Gotto, Klaus and Repgen, Konrad, eds. *Die Katholiken und das Dritte Reich.* 3rd rev. ed. Mainz: Matthias Grünewald, 1990.

Grillmeier, Alois. "Zum Christusbild der heutigen katholischen Theologie." In *Fragen der Theologie heute*, edited by J. Feiner et al., 265–99. Einsiedeln: Benziger, 1957. English translation: "The Figure of Christ in Catholic Theology Today." In *Theology Today*, vol. 1, edited by J. Feiner et al., 66–108. Milwaukee: Bruce, 1965.

Grundberger, Richard. *Red Rising in Bavaria*. New York: St. Martin's, 1973.

———. *A Social History of the Third Reich*. London: Weidenfeld and Nicolson, 1971.

Guardini, Romano. *Berichte über mein Leben*. Düsseldorf: Patmos, 1984.

———. *Vom Geist der Liturgie*. Freiburg: Herder, 1918. English translation: *The Church and the Catholic, and the Spirit of the Liturgy*. Translated by A. Lane. New York: Sheed and Ward, 1935.

———. *Vom Sinn der Kirche*. Mainz: Matthias Grünewald, 1922. English translation: *The Church and the Catholic, and the Spirit of the Liturgy*. Translated by A. Lane. New York: Sheed and Ward, 1935.

Hagen, August. "Reformkatholizismus." In *LThK* 8, col. 1085.

———. *Der Reformkatholizismus in der Diözese Rottenburg*. Stuttgart: Schwaben, 1962.

Häring, Bernard. "In Memory of Karl Adam." *Ave Maria* 13 (1966): 6.

Harnack, Adolf. *History of Dogma*. 7 vols. Original German text, 1886–1889. Translated from the 3rd German ed. by N. Buchanan. London: Williams & Norgate, 1894.

———. *What Is Christianity?* Translated by T. Saunders. Original German text, 1900. New York: Harper and Row, 1957.

Harvey, Van. *The Historian and the Believer*. New York: Macmillan, 1966.

Heaney, John. *The Modernist Crisis*. Washington, D.C.: Corpus Books, 1968.

Hebblethwaite, Peter. "The Need for Reform." *Tablet* 241 (August 15, 1987): 863-64.

———. "Understanding German Catholics." *New Blackfriars* 68 (April 1987): 179-91.

Heiler, Friedrich. *Der Katholizismus*. Munich: Ernst Reinhardt, 1923.

———. *Evangelische Katholizität*. Munich: Ernst Reinhardt, 1926.

———. "Zum Tod von Karl Adam." *ThQ* 146 (1966): 257-60

Heiler, Joseph. "Karl Adam." *Die Schildgenossen* 8 (1928): 411-21, 524-35

Hellwig, Monika. "Re-emergence of the Human, Critical, Public Jesus." *ThS* 50 (1989): 466-80.

Helmreich, Ernst. *The German Churches under Hitler*. Detroit: Wayne State University Press, 1979.

Hofmann, Fritz. "Theologie aus dem Geist der Tübinger Schule." *ThQ* 146 (1966): 262-84.

Holborn, Hajo. *A History of Modern Germany*, vol. 3. New York: Alfred A. Knopf, 1969.

Hürten, Heinz. "Bischofamt im 'Dritten Reich.'" *Internationale katholische Zeitschrift* 14 (November 1985): 536-49.

————. *Kurze Geschichte des deutschen Katholizismus 1800-1900.* Mainz: Matthias Grünewald, 1986.

Iserloh, Erwin. *Kirche—Ereignis und Institution*, vol. 1. Münster: Aschendorff, 1985.

Jedin, Hubert, and Repgen, Konrad, eds. *Handbuch der Kirchengeschichte*, vols. 6/1, 6/2, and 7. Freiburg: Herder, 1971-79. In English: Jedin, H., Repgen, K., and Dolan, John, eds. *History of the Church*, vols. 7, 8, 9, and 10. Translated by P. Becker, M. Resch, and A. Biggs. New York: Crossroad, 1981.

Jung, Eva-Maria. "A Modern Approach to Protestants: Una Sancta in Germany Today." *Catholic World* 180 (1955): 411-17.

Jungmann, Josef. *The Place of Christ in Liturgical Prayer.* 2nd rev. ed. Translated by A. Peeler. Staten Island, N.Y.: Alba House, 1965.

Kaiser, Philipp. *Die Gott-menschliche Einigung in Christus als Problem des spekulativen Theologie seit der Scholastik.* Munich: Max Hueber, 1968.

Kasper, Walter. *Jesus the Christ.* Translated by V. Green. New York: Paulist, 1976.

————. "Karl Adam." *ThQ* 156 (1976): 251-58.

————. *Theology and Church.* Translated by M. Kohl. New York: Crossroad, 1989.

————. "Verständnis der Theologie Damals und Heute." In *Theologie im Wandel*, vol. 1, edited by J. Ratzinger and J. Neumann, 91-115. Munich: Erich Wewel, 1967.

Kelsey, David. *The Uses of Scripture in Recent Theology.* Philadelphia: Fortress, 1975.

Klinger, Elmar. "Tübingen School." In *Sacramentum Mundi*, vol. 6, edited by Karl Rahner et al., 318-20. New York: Herder, 1970.

Kolping, Adolf. *Katholische Theologie.* Bremen: Carl Schüneman, 1965.

Kraus, Andreas. *Geschichte Bayerns.* Munich: C. H. Beck, 1983.

Kreidler, Hans. *Eine Theologie des Lebens.* Mainz: Matthis Grünewald, 1988.

————. "Karl Adam und Nationalsozialismus." In *Rottenburger Jahrbuch für Kirchengeschichte*, vol. 3, edited by the Geschichtsverein der Diözese Rottenburg-Stuttgart, 129-40. Sigmaringen: Jan Thorbecke, 1983.

Krieg, Robert. "The Crucified in Rahner's Christology." *Irish Theological Quarterly* 50 (1983-1984): 151-67.

————. "Is Jesus the Focus of Küng's Christology?" *Heythrop Journal* 22 (1981): 243-60.

————. "Karl Adam's Christology." *Heythrop Journal* 25 (1984): 456-74.

————. "Narrative as a Linguistic Rule." *International Journal for the Philosophy of Religion* 8 (1977): 190-205.

————. *Story-Shaped Christology*. New York: Paulist, 1988.

————. "Zur Aktualität der Christologie Karl Adam." Translated into German by J. Meyer zu Schlochtern. *ThQ* 166 (1986): 92-107.

Kulka, Otto Dov, and Mendes-Flohr, Paul, eds. *Judaism and Christianity under the Impact of National Socialism*. Jerusalem: The Historical Society of Israel and The Zalman Shazar Center for Jewish History, 1987.

Lachenschmid, Robert. "Christologie und Soteriologie." In *Bilanz der Theologie im 20. Jahrhundert*, vol. 3, edited by H. Vorgrimler and R. Vander Gucht, 82-120. Freiburg: Herder, 1970.

La Piana, George. "Recent Tendencies in Roman Catholic Theology." *Harvard Theological Review* 25 (1922): 233-92.

Laubach, Jakob. "Karl Adam." In *Theologians of Our Time*, edited by L. Reinisch, 92-108. Notre Dame, Ind.: University of Notre Dame Press, 1964.

Lewy, Guenther. *The Catholic Church and Nazi Germany*. New York: McGraw Hill, 1964.

Lindbeck, George. "The Bible as Realistic Narrative." In *Consensus in Theology?* edited by L. Swidler, 81-85. Philadelphia: Westminster, 1980.

Loome, Thomas. *Liberal Catholicism, Reform Catholicism, Modernism*. Mainz: Matthias Grünewald, 1979.

Maas-Ewerd, Theodor. *Die Krise der liturgischen Bewegung in Deutschland und Österreich*. Regensburg: Friedrich Pustet, 1981.

McCool, Gerald. *Catholic Theology in the Nineteenth Century*. New York: Seabury, 1977.

————. *From Unity to Pluralism*. New York: Fordham University Press, 1989.

McGrath, Alister. *The Making of German Christology*. New York: Basil Blackwell, 1986.

Macquarrie, John. *Jesus Christ in Modern Thought*. Philadelphia: Trinity Press International, 1990.

Madges, William. *The Core of the Christian Faith*. New York: Peter Lang, 1990.

Mann, Thomas. "Gladius Dei." In *Gesammelte Werke* 8, 197-215. Oldenburg: S. Fischer, 1960.

————. *The Magic Mountain*. Translated by H. T. Lowe-Porter. New York: Vintage, 1969.

Matheson, Peter. *The Third Reich and the Christian Churches*. Grand Rapids, Mich.: William B. Eerdmans, 1981.

Misner, Paul. *Social Catholicism in Europe*. New York: Crossroads, 1991.

Möhler, Johann Adam. *Die Einheit in der Kirche*. Tübingen: Heinrich Laupp, 1825.

———. *Symbolik*. 5th edition. Mainz: Florian Kupferberg, 1838. English translation: *Symbolism*. Translated by J. B. Robertson. London: Gibbings, 1894.

Müller, Josef. *Der Reformkatholizismus*. Würzburg: Echter, 1898.

Neuner, Peter. *Religion zwischen Kirche und Mystik*. Frankfurt am Main: Josef Knecht, 1977.

Öhlig, Karl Heinz. *Fundamental-christologie*. Munich: Kösel, 1986.

O'Meara, Thomas F. *Church and Culture*. Notre Dame, Ind.: University of Notre Dame Press, 1991.

———. "Revelation and History: Schelling, Möhler and Congar." *Irish Theological Quarterly* 53 (1987): 17-35.

———. *Romantic Idealism and Roman Catholicism*. Notre Dame, Ind.: University of Notre Dame Press, 1982.

Perrin, Norman. *Rediscovering the Teaching of Jesus*. New York: Harper and Row, 1976.

Pesch, Christian. *Compendium theologiae dogmaticae*. Rev. ed., vol. 3. Freiburg: Herder, 1921.

Pfammatter, Josef. "Katholische Jesusforschung im deutschen Sprachraum." In *Theologische Berichte*, vol. 7, edited by J. Pfammatter, 101-148. Zurich: Benziger, 1978.

Pinson, Koppel S. *Modern Germany*. New York: Macmillan, 1954.

Przywara, Erich. *Katholische Krise*. Edited by B. Gertz. Düsseldorf: Patmos, 1967.

———. "Le mouvement théologique et religieux en Allemagne." *Nouvelle Revue Théologique* 56 (1929): 565-75.

———. *Ringen der Gegenwart*. 2 vols. Augsburg: B. Filser, 1929.

Rahner, Karl. "Chalkedon—Ende oder Anfang?" In *Das Konzil von Chalkedon*, vol. 3, edited by A. Grillmeier and H. Bacht, 3-49. Würzburg: Echter, 1954. English translation: "Current Problems in Christology." In *Theological Investigations*, vol. 1, translated by C. Ernst, 149-200. Baltimore: Helicon, 1961.

———. "Ecumenical Theology in the Future." In *Theological Investigations*, vol. 14, translated by D. Bourke, 254-70. New York: Seabury, 1976.

———. "The Eternal Significance of the Humanity of Jesus for Our Relationship with God" (1953). In *Theological Investigations*, vol 2, translated by C. Ernst, 35-46. Baltimore: Helicon, 1967.

———. *I Remember*. Translated by H. Egan. New York: Crossroad, 1985.

———. "Theologie in der Welt." *Frankfurter Allgemeine Zeitung* (1956).

———. "Towards a Fundamental Theological Interpretation of Vatican II." Translated by L. O'Donovan. *ThS* 40 (1979): 716-27.

———. "What Does It Mean to Say: 'God Became Man'?" In *Foundations of Christian Faith*, translated by W. Dych, 212-28. New York: Seabury, 1978.

Rauscher, Anton, ed. *Religiös-kulturelle Bewegungen im deutschen Katholizismus seit 1800*. Paderborn: Ferdinand Schöningh, 1986.

Reinhardt, Klaus. *Der dogmatische Schriftgebrauch*. Munich: Ferdinand Schöningh, 1970.

Reinhardt, Rudolf. "Die katholische-theologische Fakultät Tübingen im 19. Jahrhundert." In *Kirche und Theologie im 19. Jahrhundert*, edited by G. Schwaiger, 55-87. Göttingen: Vandenhock and Ruprecht, 1975.

———. *Tübinger Theologen und ihre Theologie*. Tübingen: J. C. B. Mohr [Paul Siebeck], 1977.

Schäffler, Richard. *Die Wechselbeziehungen zwischen Philosophie und katholischer Theologie*. Darmstadt: Wissenschaftliche Buchgesellschaft, 1980.

Schalk, Adolf. "Karl Adam." *Jubilee* 4 (June 1956): 16-21.

Schanz, Paul. "Die katholische Tübinger Schule." *ThQ* 80 (1898): 1-49.

Scheler, Max. *Formalism in Ethics and Non-Formal Ethics of Values*. Translated by M. Frings and R. Funk. Evanston, Ill.: Northwestern University Press, 1973.

———. "Soziologische Neuorientierung und die Aufgaben der deutschen Katholiken nach dem Krieg" (1915/1916). In *Gesammelte Werke*, vol. 4, edited by M. Frings, 373-472. Bern: A. Franck, 1982.

———. "Vorbilder und Führer" (1921). In *Gesammelte Werke*, vol. 10, edited by M. Scheler, 257-88. Bern: A. Francke, 1957.

Schillebeeckx, Edward. *God Is New Each Moment*. Translated by D. Smith. New York: Seabury, 1983.

Schmitt, Richard. "Phenomenology." In *EPh* 6: 135-51.

Schnadelbach, Herbert. *Philosophy in Germany, 1831-1933*. Cambridge: Cambridge University Press, 1984.

Schnitzer, Joseph. *Der katholische Modernismus*. Berlin: Protestantische Schriftenvertrieb, 1912.

Scholder, Klaus. *Die Kirchen und das Dritte Reich*. Vols. 1 and 2. Frankfurt: Ullstein, 1977-1988. English translation: *The Churches and the Third Reich*. Vols. 1 and 2. Translated by J. Bowden. Philadelphia: Fortress Press, 1987.

Schoof, T. Mark. *A Survey of Catholic Theology, 1800-1970*. New York: Paulist, 1970.

Schreiter, Robert. *Constructing Local Theologies*. Maryknoll, N.Y.: Orbis, 1985.

Schweitzer, Albert. *The Quest of the Historical Jesus*. Translated by W. Montgomery. New York: Macmillan, 1968.

Seckler, Max. *Theologie vor Gericht*. Tübingen: J. C. B. Mohr [Paul Siebeck], 1972.

Söhngen, Gottlieb. "Neuscholastik." In *LThK* 7 (1962): cols. 923-26.

Spael, Wilhelm. *Das katholische Deutschland im 20. Jahrhundert.* Würzburg: Echter, 1964.

Spiegelberg, Herbert. *The Phenomenological Movement.* 3rd rev. ed. The Hague: Martin Nijhoff, 1982.

Stelzenberger, Johannes. "Bibliographie Karl Adam." *ThQ* 137 (1958): 330-47.

Strom, Theodor. *Theologie im Schatten politischer Romantik.* Munich: Chr. Kaiser, 1970.

Thiel, John. "Karl Adam and the Council." *Month* 17 (November 1984): 378-81.

Trippen, Norbert. *Theologie und Lehramt im Konflikt.* Freiburg: Herder, 1977.

Troeltsch, Ernst. *The Absoluteness of Christianity and the History of Religions.* The original German text, 1902. Translated by D. Reid. Richmond, Virginia: John Know Press, 1971.

———. *Der Historismus und seine Probleme.* In *Gesammelte Schriften,* vol. 3. Tübingen: J. C. B. Mohr, 1922.

———. "Historical and Dogmatic Method in Theology" (1898). In *Religion in History,* translated by J. L. Adams and W. F. Bense, pp. 11-32. Minneapolis: Fortress Press, 1991.

———. "Historiography." In *Encyclopedia of Religion and Ethics,* edited by J. Hastings, 716-23. New York: Charles Scribners Sons, 1955.

Tuchman, Barbara. *The Guns of August.* New York: Macmillan, 1962.

Vidler, Alec. *The Modernist Movement in the Roman Church.* Cambridge: Cambridge University Press, 1934.

Welch, Claude. *Protestant Thought in the Nineteenth Century.* Vol. 2. New Haven, Conn.: Yale University Press, 1985.

Wellek, René. "Romanticism Re-examined." In *Concepts of Criticism,* edited by S. G. Nichols, 199-221. New Haven, Conn.: Yale University Press.

Wust, Peter. "Die Rückkehr des deutschen Katholizismus aus dem Exil." In *Die Rückkehr aus dem Exil,* edited by K. Hoeber, 16-35. Düsseldorf: L. Schwann, 1926.

Zahn, Gordon. *German Catholics and Hitler's Wars.* Original Edition, 1963. Reprint. Notre Dame, Ind.: University of Notre Dame Press, 1988.

Zeender, John. "The Genesis of the German Concordat of 1933." In *Studies in Catholic History,* edited by N. Minnich et al., 617-65. Wilmington, Del.: Michael Glazier, 1985.

Zorn, Wolfgang. *Bayerns Geschichte im 20. Jahrhundert.* Munich: C. H. Beck, 1986

Publications by Karl Adam

This bibliography cites only the texts that are mentioned in this book. For the complete bibliography, see Johannes Stelzenberger, "Bibliographie Karl Adam," *ThQ* 137 (1958): 330-37

Der Kirchenbegriff Tertullians. Paderborn: Ferdinand Schöningh, 1907.

Die Eucharistielehre des heiligen Augustin. Paderborn: Ferdinand Schöningh, 1908.

"Notizen zur Echtheitsfrage der Augustin zugesprochen Schrift 'De unite ecclesia.'" *ThQ* 91 (1909): 86-115.

"Der Antimodernisteneid und die theologischen Fakultäten." *Katholische Kirchenzeitung für Deutschland* 1 (1910): 83-85.

Das sogenannte Bussedikt des Papstes Kallistus. Munich: Kirchenhistorischen Seminar, 1917.

Die kirchliche Sündervergebung nach dem heilgen Augustin. Paderborn: Ferdinand Schöningh, 1917.

Die geheime Kirchenbusse nach dem heiligen Augustin. Kempton: Kösel, 1921.

"Glaube und Glaubenswissenschaft im Katholizismus." *ThQ* 101 (1920): 131-55. Reprinted as "Theologischer Glaube und Theologie." In K. Adam, *Glaube und Glaubenswissenschaft im Katholizismus*, 2nd, rev. ed. 17-43. Rottenburg: Bader, 1923.

Das Wesen des Katholizismus. Augsburg: L. Schwann, 1924. English translation: *The Spirit of Catholicism*. Translated by J. McCann. New York: Macmillan, 1929.

"Durch Christus, unsern Herrn." *Seele* 8 (1926): 321-29.

Christus unser Bruder. Regensburg: Joseph Happel, 1926. Enlarged: *Christus unser Bruder*. 2nd, rev. ed. Regensburg: Joseph Happel, 1930. English translation: *Christ Our Brother*. Translated by J. McCann. New York: Macmillan, 1931.

231

"Die Theologie der Krisis." *Hochland* 23/2 (1926): 271–86. Reprinted in *Gesammelte Aufsätze zur Dogmengeschichte*, edited by F. Hofmann, 319–37. Augsburg: Haas & Cie, 1936.

"Die katholische Tübinger Schule." *Hochland* 24/2 (1926–1927): 581–601. Reprinted in *Gesammelte Aufsätze zur Dogmengeschichte*, edited by F. Hofmann, 389–412. Augsburg: Haas & Cie, 1936.

Christus und der Geist des Abendlandes. Munich: Josef Kösel & Friedrich Pustet, 1928. English translation: *Christ and the Western Mind*. Translated by E. Bullough. New York: Macmillan, 1930.

Die geistige Entwicklung des heiligen Augustinus. Augsburg: Haas and Grabheer, 1931. English translation: *St. Augustine: The Odyssey of His Soul*. Translated by J. McCann. New York: Macmillan, 1932.

"Le Christ dans l'Eglise." *Revue Apologetique* 52 (1931): 257–72.

Jesus Christus. Augsburg: Haas & Grabheer, 1933. English translation: *The Son of God*. Translated by P. Hereford. New York: Sheed and Ward, 1934.

"Deutsches Volkstum und katholisches Christentum." *ThQ* 114 (1933): 40–63.

"Vom gottmenschlichen Erlöser." In *Glaubenstage und Glaubenswallfährten*, 111–45. Paderborn: Bonafacius, 1934. Reprinted as "Christus gestern und heute, Christus allezeit," in *Katholik Sonntagszeitung*, Mainz (February 25, 1934), 9–11. Abridged, English translation: "In the Jubilee Year," *Commonweal* 19 (August 10, 1934): 361–63.

"The Sanctification of Marriage." *Orate Fratres* 9 (1935): 171–76, 218–25.

Jesus Christus und der Geist unserer Zeit. Augsburg: Haas & Grabheer, 1935. English translation: "Jesus Christ and the Spirit of the Age." In *Germany's New Religion*, edited by W. Hauer, K. Heim, and K. Adam, translated by T. S. K. Scott-Craig and R. E. Davies, 117–68. New York: Abingdon, 1937.

Gesammelte Aufsätze zur Dogmengeschichte. Edited by F. Hofmann. Augsburg: Haas & Cie, 1936.

"Dogmatic Bases of the Liturgy." *Orate Fratres* 11 (1937): 481–87, and *Orate Fratres* 12 (1938): 8–14, 56–59, 97–104, 145–51.

"Das Geheimnis der Inkarnation und seines mystischen Leibes. Vom Ärgernis zum sieghaften Glauben." In *Die Eine Kirche*. Paderborn: Bonafacius, 1939. English translation: "The Mystery of Christ's Incarnation and of His Mystical Body." *Orate Fratres* 13 (1939): 337–44, 392–99, 433–40.

"Jesu menschliches Wesen im Licht der unchristlichen Verkündigung." *Wissenschaft und Weisheit* 6 (1939): 111–20.

"Jesus, der Christus, und wir Deutsche, I & II." *Wissenschaft und Weisheit* 10 (1943): 73–103.

"Jesus, der Christus, und wir Deutsche, III." *Wissenschaft und Weisheit* 11 (1944): 10-23.

"Das Problem des Geschichtlichen im Leben der Kirche." *ThQ* 128 (1948): 257-300.

Una Sancta in katholischer Sicht. Düsseldorf: Patmos, 1948. English translation: *One and Holy*. Translated by C. Hastings. New York: Sheed and Ward, 1951.

"To move toward Christian unity." *Commonweal* 54 (1951): 423-26.

"Das Problem der Entmythologisierung und die Auferstehung des Christus." *ThQ* 132 (1952): 385-410.

"Easter Sermon." *Orate Fratres* 27 (1953): 254-56.

Der Christus des Glaubens. Düsseldorf: Patmos, 1954. English translation: *The Christ of Faith*. Translated by J. Crick. New York: Pantheon, 1954.

"Pentecost and Baptism." *Worship* 28 (1954): 281-83.

"An Act of Faith." *Worship* 31 (1957): 120-25.

"St. John and Christ." *Jubilee* 6 (1958): 18-23.

Index

235